THE EASTERN QUESTION AND THE VOICES OF REASON:
AUSTRIA–HUNGARY, RUSSIA, AND THE BALKAN STATES 1875–1908

JELENA MILOJKOVIĆ-DJURIĆ

EAST EUROPEAN MONOGRAPHS, BOULDER
DISTRIBUTED BY COLUMBIA UNIVERSITY PRESS, NEW YORK

2002

EAST EUROPEAN MONOGRAPHS, NO. DXCII

Library of Congress Control Number 2002101940
ISBN 0–88033–490–8

Printed in the United States of America

Contents

Contents

Preface

My inquiry of the Eastern Question seeks to discern the interdependence of political and cultural issues underlying the long-standing relations between Austria-Hungary, Russia and the Balkan States.

Austria-Hungary received the mandate of the Berlin Congress of 1878 to occupy Bosnia-Hercegovina and improve the livelihood of the population by helping to introduce much needed agrarian- and educational reforms.

To this end, the archival holdings of the Provincial Government in Sarajevo and of the *Haus-, Hof- und Staatsarchiv* in Vienna suggest a historical narratives of pointed epistemological significance. These documents provide a unique insight into decisions and directives influencing the shaping and fruition of some cultural activities as well as the curtailing or denial of others. Selected documents pertained to the issues of education as well as to the monitoring of cultural organizations such as reading halls, church school communities, choral and musical groups, theatrical and musical performances. In particular, the censorship criteria of dailies and periodicals testified to the vigilance of the authorities to control the public discourse.

The juxtaposition of everyday public discourse, literary renderings and political circumstances during the 1875-1878 uprising in Bosnia-Hercegovina, and the subsequent Austro-Hungarian occupation, provide new points of view of these historic events. The first four chapters examine the assessments of the Eastern Question by outstanding politicians, writers and scholars. The next three chapters study the archival sources in the context of cultural history.

About the chronology, the first pages of this book were written at the time when the recent civil war in Bosnia-Hercegovina was replicating the Eastern Question in its current phase. The lessons that history may impart seemed to have been lost in the numerous hastily suggested assessments of the situation in the Balkans.

Thus, I turned to the study of the situation in Bosnia-Hercegovina 1878-1908 in order to elucidate the inherent complexities of this region as well as the perils of foreign interventions. In the aftermath of the Berlin Congress, the Austro-Hungarian occupation of Bosnia-Hercegovina did not fulfill the given mandate but intensified the economic, social and ethnic divisiveness.

I would like to acknowledge the valuable assistance obtained during the writing of this book. Most of all, I am grateful for the interest in my work expressed by Professors Dimitrije Djordjević, Milorad Ekmečić, Stephan Fischer-Galati, and Alex Dragnich. I appreciate the input of Dimitrije E. Stefanovic, Institute for Serbian Language, Serbian Academy of Sciences and Arts, who shared his recollections about his grandfather, Petar Rimski. Rimski was an esteemed teacher and theologian at the Serbian School in Saint André. My colleagues, Professors Don Dyer, John Treadway, Bogdan Rakic and Benjamin Stolz continue in many ways to encourage and support my research.

The seminars at the Center for Humanities Research, Texas A&M University, provided a much needed impetus for my work. At the early stages of my research for this book, in October of 1997, I presented a paper dealing with Tolstoy's and Dostoievsky's responses to the Eastern Question during the 1875 uprising in Bosnia-Hercegovina. I am grateful to James Rosenheim, Director of the Center for Humanities Research, and Julia Blackwelder, Head of the Department of History, Texas A&M University, for their interest in my work and valuable support.

I am thankful to Professors Michael Katz and Joan Neuberger, respectively, for two grants, received in 1997 and 1999, from the Center for Russian, East European and Euro-Asian Studies at the University of Texas. I also received a research grant from The Russian and East European Center, University of Illinois, to attend the 1999 Summer Research Laboratory on Russian and Eastern Europe. This grant enabled me to conduct research of some valuable holdings in the University Library.

Some of the ideas explored in this book were initially examined in articles published by the journals *Balkanistica*, *Serbian Studies*,

East European Quarterly, and *Zbornik SANU za Bosnu i Hercegovinu*. I appreciate the invitation of Professor Ekmečić to participate with a paper at the 1998 International Conference *Europe and the Eastern Question 1878-1923*,, at the Serbian Academy of Arts and Science. In 1999, I moderated a Round Table Discussion on the Balkan Crisis at the Annual Meeting of Southwest Association of Slavic Studies, Texas A&M University, and benefited from the ensuing discussion and the valuable observations of Professor Ron Hatchett. Professor Ewa Thompson invited me to present a lecture in November of 2000 at the Center for the Study of Cultures, Rice University. My lecture *The Habsburg policies during the Austro-Hungarian Occupation of Bosnia-Hercegovina* elucidated several chapters of my present book.

My daughter Mara Djurić Hill read all the chapters of this book and offered comments from the perspective of a trained contextual anthropologist.

INTRODUCTION

In the aftermath of the Berlin Peace Treaty, the Austro-Hungarian Empire sought to assure the world community that the occupation of Bosnia-Hercegovina would introduce economic reforms and much needed educational and cultural advancements. In spite of all initial resistance, the people of Bosnia-Hercegovina accepted the decision of the Great Powers hoping that the occupation would accomplish needed improvements. There was a shared hope among the population of the provinces that the Ottoman feudalism would be abolished introducing a just solution for the agrarian question. Most of all, the recognition of the independence of Serbia and Montenegro as well as confirmation of Romania's independence, which had been already proclaimed, presented positive achievements of the Berlin Congress.[1]

The Austro-Hungarian occupation of Bosnia-Hercegovina proved to be a take-over of all the domains of public life. New ordinances were passed imposing strict control over the population, monitoring of the exploitation of natural resources, and tax revenues. The population soon realized that the Austro-Hungarian authorities did not plan to solve the agrarian question. Yet, in Bosnia-Hercegovina, the large majority, 90 percent of the population, depended on agriculture. The feudal bondage of the tenants continued, and the Turkish taxation system was retained.[2]

In addition, new taxes were introduced, burdening the tenants to a disproportional extent. Moreover, the young men, both

---

1 Dimitrije Djordjević, "The Berlin Congress of 1878 and the Origins of World War I," *Serbian Studies*, Vol. 12, No.1, 1998, p. 7.

2 Milorad Ekmečić, "Istorijski značaj ustanka u Bosni i Hercegovini," *Radovi iz istorije Bosne i Hercegovine*, Belgrade, BIGZ, 1997, p. 206.

Christian and Muslim, were obliged to serve in the army which presented a real difficulty for the agrarian households by depriving many families of their primary labor force.

The policies of the Provincial Government were directed most of all towards the consolidation of Austro-Hungarian domination of Bosnia-Hercegovina. The Balkan peninsula, including Bosnia-Hercegovina, was designated as the desired and important "economic zone" of the Monarchy. The leading Austrian economist Singer acknowledged that the Balkan Peninsula was of major economic and strategic significance for the Habsburg Monarchy. In his book *Unsere Orientinteresse,* Singer stated that the whole area was in reality "our European India." [3]

The uprising in 1882 presented a powerful protest of the occupied population against the new administration. The subsequent placement of Benjamin von Kállay at the helm of the Austro-Hungarian Joint Finance Ministry, brought hope for betterment. Furthermore, Kállay was an astute historian and writer of the well received *History of Serbs* , in addition to his considerable political career. Soon enough, Kállay decided to postpone the agrarian reforms and continue with the feudal bondage of the tenants. He had reached the conclusion that the wealthy, mostly Muslim, landowners represented the foundation of the society. In order to win their support, the old and antiquated taxation system was retained. Thus, the Provincial Government decided to rely on the support of the rich landowners to the detriment and growing resentment of the vast majority of the population.[4]

Furthermore, new obligations were introduced increasing the burden on the peasants to a great extent. Communal fields and forests were appropriated by the state and the right of grazing stock and harvesting lumber was curtailed. This brought an added stress to the agriculture. The rampant exploitation of the natural resources and of the domestic labor force fulfilled various concessions granted predominantly to Austrian and German investors. The investment of foreign capital was encouraged in

---

[3] Quoted after Milorad Ekmečić, *Stvaranje Jugoslavije 1794-1918,* Belgrade, Prosveta, 1989, p. 9. Singer's book *Unsere Orientintersse* was published in 1878 in Vienna.

[4] Ekmečić, *Stvaranje Jugoslavije 1790-1918* , p. 83 and p. 95.

order to harness the riches of the land by promoting the principles of a colonial capitalistic economy.

The improvements of the road system and narrow track railroads enabled an easier access to markets encouraging economic development.[5] Additional measures were introduced in order to generate growth of revenues. The government decided to increase the allotted time for the mandatory labor *(kuluk)* by ten percent. All eligible peasants from the age of 16 to 60 had to work, when called, on the construction of roads. The new roads were the pride of the Austro-Hungarian authorities, although the funding was derived from local revenues. Furthermore, the new roads were constructed by the Bosnian peasants providing virtually millions in free wages yet the government took solely the credit for all these accomplishments.[6]

All these measures did produce a noticeable economic growth in particular during Kállay's early tenure. During the 1890s, the industrial production reached fifteen percent per year and several state sponsored industrial enterprises were founded. However, these enterprises demanded higher tax revenues, aggravating mostly the Serb and Croat tenants.[7] In the ensuing period, the industrial production progressively decreased due, in part, to the backwardness of an impaired and predominantly agrarian economy. Large-scale enterprises, primarily sawmills and iron ore mines, could not sustain the interest of the Austrian or Hungarian investors. Around the turn of the century the industrial production experienced a steady decline and dropped off to barely three percent for the period of 1906-1913.[8]

These conditions continued to plague the economy of Bosnia Hercegovina. In the aftermath of the Annexation in 1908, Dušan Vasiljević, a prominent public figure, criticized the resulting situation

---

[5] Ekmečić, *Stvaranje Jugoslavije, 1790-1918*, , p. 83 and p. 95.

[6] Ekmečić, *Stvaranje Jugoslavije, 1790-1918*, p. 83 and p. 95.

[7] John R. Lampe, *Yugoslavia as History*, Cambridge University Press, Cambridge and New York, 1996, pp. 66-67.

[8] Lampe, *Yugoslavia as History*, p. 80.

and compared the state of economy to a senseless pursuit of riches at the expense of the population of Bosnia-Hercegovina:

> On one hand expensive and mismanaged economic experiments, and on the other advertising commercials in the style of Barnum spectacles with free dinners and free railroad tickets for foreign travelers and for journalists, horse races and shooting of the doves with large prizes for sportsmen and professionals. In the meantime, the agrarian question was not solved. Yet, this was the vital question for the country where the large majority—90 percent of its population—depended on agriculture since it presented their livelihood. Speaking for the Austro-Hungarian government, Minister Burian repeatedly stated that the agrarian question as such does not exist in Bosnia-Hercegovina. [9]

Most of the arable land had remained in the possession of wealthy landholders, mostly Muslims. The land was cultivated by the peasants and share croppers who were as a rule Orthodox Christians, and by a smaller number of Croatian and Muslim tenants.

The new regulations instituted by the Provincial Government required registration of land ownership. Previously, the Ottoman laws did not acknowledge the ownership of the landlords outright and allowed for an uninterrupted cultivation of the land by the tenants—*kmets* in perpetuity. The ownership registration enforced landlords' rightful claim of the land changing the established customary ways. Eventual disputes about land ownership were adjudicated by the government and became a matter of unending contests between the *agas* (chieftains) and *kmets*, effectively between the Muslims and Christians. [10]

The occupation resulted in a relatively small number of educated individuals and a large pool of poorly educated and even illiterate rural population. According to the official evaluation of a special Austrian delegation, headed by J.M. Bärenreiter, only 14 percent of

---

[9] Dušan Vasiljević, *O Bosni i Hercegovini,* Belgrade, Ljub. M. Davidović, 1909, pp. 19-20.

[10] Vasiljević *O Bosni i Hercegovini,* pp. 19-23.

eligible school children attended elementary schools during the 1905/1906 school year. Thus, more than 85 percent of all youths in Bosnia-Hercegovina grew up without any education as a result of the policies imposed by the Provincial Government during the 28 years of occupation. In spite of such a deplorable educational record, the mentioned report expressed support for the proposed annexation of both provinces. [11]

Orthodox Serbs chose through their own efforts to maintain 112 private schools which were sponsored by their local church communities. These communities supported the schools expenditures and teachers salaries. Nonetheless, the Serbs had to pay 10 percent surcharge for the overall support of churches and parochial schools in Bosnia-Hercegovina. This surcharge was known "crkveno-prosvjetni prirez." [12]

The Provincial Government in Bosnia-Hercegovina was in the hands of bureaucrats who came predominantly from Austria, Germany, as well as from Hungary, Poland, and Bohemia. These bureaucrats did not speak the Serbo-Croatian language or had only some vague knowledge of it. Thus, the poor language skills were apparent in legal documents and presented an additional obstacle for proper understanding of official records. The writer Petar Kočić feared that the innate clarity of the native language was obscured in official bulletins and various communications addressing the population at large. Such poor and distorted writing presented a dangerous precedent:[13]

Kočić ascertained that the intellectual enslavement in Bosnia-Hercegovina was introduced with numerous appointments of a host of foreign educators, judges, and legal clerks assigned to the newly created educational and administrative posts. The majority of

---

[11] J.M. Bärenreiter, *Bosnische Eindrücke*, Vienna, 1908, p. 14. Quoted after Jovan Cvijić, *Aneksija Bosne i Hercegovine i Srpski Problem*, Belgrade, Državna štamparija, 1908, p. 36.

[12] Vasiljević, *O Bosni i Hercegovini*, p. 25.

[13] Petar Kočić, "Jezik u zakonskim tekstovima," *Sabrana Djela*, 1967, III, pp. 67-71. Quoted after Miodrag M. Vulin, Petar Kočić,*Pisac i delo* , Sarajevo, Svjetlost, 1990, p. 380.

bureaucrats, serving in Bosnia-Hercegovina, performed their duties with indifference and solely for the sake of a perfunctory career advancement. Their professional accomplishments were superficial and the population was sadly aware of the indifference of the petty bureaucrats when dealing with the public.

It is noteworthy that Benjamin von Kállay, the powerful Finance Minister in charge of Bosnia-Hercegovina, was also cognizant of the inadequate performance of Austrian bureaucrats. Kállay deplored the lack of initiative in execution of work-related assignments by officers in charge. Very often, the official reports from Bosnia-Hercegovina did not show any effort to present the situation in the provinces with an independent point of view. The officers compiling these reports hastened to comply with the directives drafted by the offices in Vienna and did not introduce modifications or refinements of suggested goals.

Some modest reforms in the civil service resulted in increased salaries and were carried out in 1906, just two years prior to the annexation of Bosnia-Hercegovina. These reforms were conducted in a hasty manner without adequate analysis of the economic situation and the real needs of the people. Moreover, the judicial reforms were funded by raised court taxes. The taxation reforms of industrial enterprises and investment companies were not implemented. Many of these enterprises paid only minimal taxes in the amount of four percent from their realized profits, and many were even declared free from taxation. [14]

Most of all, the creation of an invented "Bosnian consciousness" was promoted under the pretext of preventing a rift between the Serbs, Croats and the Muslims. In reality, the Provincial Government did not treat all citizens in an impartial way. The authorities feared a possible assimilation *(Einverleibung)* of Muslims by the Serbs since many Muslims were cognizant of their Slavic descent.[15] Soon enough, the rich class of landowners, who were as a rule Muslims, enjoyed a privileged position. The members of the Christian Orthodox denomination were not given the same

---

[14] Vasiljević, *O Bosni i Hercegovini*, p. 26.

[15] Valeria Heuberger, Heinz Ilming, *Bosnien-Hercegovina 1878-1918, Alte Ansichten vom gelungenen Zusammenleben*, Vienna, Christian Brandstätter, 1994, p. 23.

consideration and were put at a disadvantage. Thus, the existing differences became more pronounced and even magnified.

Prior to the Austro-Hungarian occupation the reformed Turkish administration strove to introduce the European spirit in Bosnia-Hercegovina by encouraging the building of public edifices in the European architectural style of this period. Yet, the supposedly enlightened Provincial Government in Sarajevo proceeded to cultivate urban planing reminiscent of the earlier days of the Turkish Empire. Subsequently, a number of imposing public buildings were erected in a pseudo-Islamic style providing the city space with an anachronistic, picturesque and colonial atmosphere. The only exception presented few buildings in the neoclassical style, most notably the new railroad station, designed by the Viennese architect Josip Vandas .[16]

The Austrian journalists and writers of numerous travelogues and related writings promoted exotic images of Bosnia and Hercegovina as if locked in a state of arrested development. In this way, the unusual shapes of dwellings, and religious edifices supported Austria-Hungarian claims to dominance. The displayed picturesque ambiance, in remote or abandoned regions of Bosnia-Hercegovina, demonstrated an apparent need for modernity.[17]

Furthermore, the Provincial Government tried to introduce a "Bosnian language," and a "Bosnian culture," leading to eventual creation of a "Bosnian nation". On June 6, 1879, a new ordinance was posited ordering the hiring of new elementary teachers to teach the contrived Bosnian Land language *(bosansko zemaljski jezik)* and a beginning course of the German language.[18]

---

16 Milorad Ekmečić, *Stvaranje Jugoslavije 1790-1918*, Prosveta, Belgrade 1989, p. 100.

17 Heuberger, Ilming, *Bosnien-Herzegovina 1878-1918, Alte Ansichten vom gelungenen Zusammenleben.* This book includes a collection of postcards and title pages of travelogues depicting Bosnia as a backward but beautiful and often desolate place.

18 Šćepan Grdjić, "Prosvetna borba," Pero Slijepčević, Ed., *Napori Bosne i Hercegovine*, Sarajevo 1929, p. 114. Compare also, Valeria Heuberger,

Because of the shortage of teachers willing to teach an invented language, the authorities recruited non commissioned petty officers *(Unterofizieren—podčasnici)* who obviously lacked needed credentials and experience for teaching. Nonetheless, the occupied territory was responsible for the teachers salaries, as well as for the upkeep of old facilities or the building of new schools, including the operating costs and the heating and lighting.[19]

These policies aimed to weaken the historic ties that existed between the Serbian and Croatian population and their respective cultural centers in Belgrade or Zagreb. Interestingly enough, these efforts produced the opposite effect by strengthening the national consciousness of both Croats and Serbs.

Political activities of any kind were strictly forbidden. A number of ordinances were posted establishing rules and regulations in regard to the civic and cultural life in the newly occupied provinces. In January 1879, an ordinance was issued stipulating that all meetings were forbidden unless the authorities have issued a permit: "Assemblies and meetings of any kind are forbidden until a permit is secured from the political or military authorities. A representative of the government must attend such meetings."[20]

The imposed restrictions of the authorities curtailing the freedom of speech and peaceful assembly belied the official assurances about projected improvements in the field of educational and cultural endeavors. These restrictions testified most of all to the determination of authorities to preserve their presence in the occupied provinces at all cost.[21]

Hans Ilming, *Bosnien-Herzegovina 1878-1918, Alte Ansichten vom gelungenen Zusammenleben*, p. 22.

19 Grdjić, "Prosvetna borba," p. 114. Compare also, Heuberger, Ilming, *Bosnien-Herzegovina 1878-1918, Alte Ansichten vom gelungenen Zusammenleben*, p. 22.

20 Vasiljević, *O Bosni i Hercegovini*, p. 13.

21 Risto Besarović, Editor, *Kultura i Umjetnost u Bosni i Hercegovini pod Austrougraskom Upravom, Gradja za proučavanje političkih, kulturnih i socijalnio-ekonomskih pitanja iz prošlosti Bosne i Hercegovine,* XIX i XX vijek, Sarajevo, Arhiv BiH, 1968, p. 8.

As a rule, prominent members of the communities strove to comply with the imposed requirements while trying to enhance the education and general well being of the population. Notably the members of the young and educated generations were the most outspoken and radical proponents of needed reforms in governmental policies and, most of all, in education. In the course of the 1890s the distress of the populace at large seemed to inspire a sense of mission among the concerned native elite in pursuit of education and civil liberties. This attitude was criticized by the ranking bureaucrats including the Finance Minister Benjamin von Kállay. The officials were puzzled by the absence of collaboration with the regime among the wealthiest citizens of Bosnia-Hercegovina. The well-to-do classes usually preferred a conservative outlook and supported the government. Kállay thought that such a demeanor would have been useful for the few prosperous Christian citizens aiming to uphold their wealth and privileged station in life. Notwithstanding Kállay's expectations, the affluent Serbian Orthodox citizens were renown for their liberal orientation.[22]

The cultural and social life of the population was mainly centered around educational societies, reading halls and chorale groups. Dušan Kecmanović summed up the role of these societies in view of strict censoring practices imposed on the population at large: "All social and educational life of the Serbs in townships throughout

---

22 Kállay wrote: "Während anderswo die finanziel gut situierten Bürger eines Staates schon des Vorteiles halber den ihnen eine Anlehnung an die Staatsgewalt bietet zu den conservativen Stützen der Regierung zählen bietet sich hier zu Lande das Bild dass unter den Orthodoxen gerade die reichsten Häuser in radikaler und staatsfeindlicher Gesinnung hervortreten." Quoted after, Tomislav Kraljačić, *Kalajev rezim u Bosni i Hercegovini 1882-1903,* Sarajevo, Veselin Masleša, 1987, p. 218.

Bosnia-Hercegovina was centered around the small world of singers societies and reading halls."[23]

It has been suggested that the study of the Eastern Question should not be limited to diplomatic proceedings, partition proposals, and state treaties, but should devote more attention to culture, education, religion, and altruistic endeavors.[24] In this regard, the archival holdings of the former Provincial Government *(Landesregierung)* in Sarajevo and of the *Haus-, -Hof und Staatsarchiv* in Vienna have acquired crucial epistemological significance. These sources helped to examine the historical narrative by focusing on the modes of implementations of sociopolitical measures influencing to a great extent cultural policies of the Provincial Government.[25]

These documents pertained to the issues of education and school curricula as well as to the monitoring of cultural organizations such as libraries and reading rooms, choral- and musical societies, theatrical and operatic performances. Some of the entreaties dealt with disputes over Austrian censorship of dailies and journals. The so called "preventive censoring" stipulated that the galley proofs *(Bürstenauszug)* of every issue should be first examined by the authorities in charge of censorship. Any criticism of the Provincial Government and its policies was severely punished by imprisonment and/or monetary fines. It was not only the writer of the article who

---

23 Kecmanović's article was published in the daily *Srpska riječ*, Sarajevo 21 June, 1905, No. 87, p. 2: "Naša pjevačka društva i knjižnice ...su preuzele ulogu svih kulturnih ustanova drugih naroda."

24 Theophilus C. Prousis, *Russian Society and the Greek Revolution*, Northern Illinois University Press, DeKalb, 1994, p. VIII.

25 Risto Besarović, *Kultura i Umjetnost u Bosni i Hercegovini pod Austrougraskom Upravom, Gradja za proučavanje* političkih, *kulturnih i socijalnio-ekonomskih pitanja iz prošlosti Bosne i Hercegovine, XIX i XX vijek*. The archival documents collected in this book are preserved in the Archives of Bosnia-Hercegovina in Sarajevo, Haus-, Hof- und Staatsarchiv in Vienna, Archive of the Serbian Academy of Arts and Sciences in Belgrade and the Archive of the City of Sarajevo.

was punished: the editor of the paper, and even the local seller of the censured publication was liable as well.[26]

The harshness of the censoring policies testified to the vigilance of those in power to control the public opinion declining any possibility of a free discourse. The projected good offices of the Empire should not be tarnished in front of the enlightened Europe; even a benevolent critique should be eradicated at any cost.

Most importantly, these archival sources proffered a unique insight into imposed directives influencing the shaping of cultural policies during the occupation and subsequent annexation of Bosnia-Hercegovina. Some documents brought to light unexpected testimonies that personified the voices of a legion searching for an elusive equality and respect of human dignity.

26 Djordje Pejanović, *Štampa Bosne i Hercegovine 1850-1941*, Sarajevo, Svjetlost, 1949, pp. 12-13.

Chapter 1

THE UPRISING IN BOSNIA-HERCEGOVINA 1875-1878

In early July of 1875, the outbreak of a peasant revolt in Hercegovina once again opened the Eastern Question. The revolt spread quickly throughout the neighboring region of Bosnia instigating the Great Power's conflict over the situation in the Balkans. The uprising started in Gabela in southern Hercegovina and quickly spread to Nevesinje; by early August, the fighting engulfed the neighboring region of Bosnia. There was a growing discontent of the Christian South Slav tenantries against the misrule of Muslim landholders. The issues were primarily economic and social; the insurgents called for the protection of the population, their civil, and proprietary rights. Moreover, these events instigated a resurgence of Panslav aspirations generating a renewed interest in the fate of the Southern Slavs under Turkish occupation, and the unsolved Eastern Question. The uprising initiated a three-year crisis involving once again the Great Powers conflict over Balkan affairs.[1]

---

[1] David MacKenzie, *The Serbs and the Russian Panslavism, 1856-1878,* Ithaca, N. Y., Cornell University Press, p. 30. Branimir Janković,*The Balkans in International Relations*, New York, St. Martin Press, 1988, p. 8. Compare also, Arthur J. Evans, *Through Bosnia and the Herzegovina on Foot during the Insurrection, August and September 1875.* Reprint edition, New York, Arno Press, 1971, p. 336. Evans left a unique image of Bosnia and Hercegovina, during the insurrection in August and September of 1875. Evans, a well known archaeologist, pointed out is that the insurrection was in its origin agrarian rather than political: "it was largely an affair of tenant-right."

In response to the uprising in Hercegovina and Bosnia, an International Relief Committee was formed in Paris in August of 1875. The Committee elected unanimously the Serbian Metropolitan Mihail Jovanović for the position of its president. The primary concern of the Relief Committee was to help the numerous refugees from the embattled regions. Metropolitan Mihail accepted the nomination and asked the Croatian bishop Josip Strosmayer to share the duties of presidency on an equal footing with him.[2] Metropolitan Mihail, an ardent supporter of Panslav mutuality and collaboration, was counting on Russian support for the refugees. Educated in Russia, he received his higher theological and philosophical education at the Kiev Ecclesiastic Academy. Subsequently, after his return to Serbia, he continued to enjoy close ties with Russia's intellectual elite and even the Tsar's court.[3]

During this time, the Slavic Benevolent Societies exerted great influence upon the Russian society at large due to their numerous charitable efforts on behalf of the South Slavs. The prominence of the Slavic Benevolent Societies in Russia rose to an all time high.[4] The Slavic Benevolent Societies continued to offer help by actively involving themselves in Balkan affairs. Their concerted actions resulted in the sending to Serbia of about three thousand volunteers headed by general Mikhail Grigor'evich Cherniaev, the well known hero of the Asian conquest. Cherniaev was also renown as a man of letters and former editor of *Russkii mir.* As a proponent of Slavic solidarity, Cherniaev went to Serbia without the official permission

---

[2] *Zarubezhnye Slaviane i Rossiia, Dokumenti i arhiva M. F. Raevskogo 40-80 XIX veka,* Moscow, Akademiia Nauk SSSR,1989, p. 150.

[3] Ivan S. Aksakov, *Slavianskii Vopros , 1860-1886* , Moscow 1886, p. 359; compare also Živan Živanović, Politička *istorija Srbije u drugoj polovini devetnaestoga veka,* Belgrade 1924, p. 32; also Slobodan Jovanović, *Vlada Milana* Obrenovića. Belgrade 1934, Vol. II, pp. 416-417.

[4] V. A. D'iakov, *Slavianskii vopros,* Moscow, Nauka, 1993, p. 129.

of the Russian government. Moreover, the Serbian authorities had not extended an official invitation for his participation.[5]

In Russia, the political circles headed by minister Gorchakov, with the support of Alexander II, tried repeatedly to promote negotiations and avoid any military intervention in the Balkans. Alexander II directed his principal attention toward long overdue domestic reforms in accordance with the established state policy of *recueuillement*. Thus, in foreign affairs, the tsar aspired to safeguard previous treaties such as the Three Emperor's Alliance aiming to preserve the balance of Great Powers in Europe.

The noted journal *Vestnik Evropy* published an article by Aleksander Nikolaevich Pypin, a prominent figure of the current cultural scene. Pypin stated that in Russia the spirit of solidarity encouraged a remarkable development. A veritable democratic movement had reached such proportions that even foreign observers noted a positive self reliance and a general upsurge in public life not observed since the war of the 1812.[6] There was a genuine grass-roots feeling of solidarity for the plight of the Southern Slav people. The Serbian-Turkish war caused great concern among the Russian people in all walks of life.[7]

Even some Russian political emigrants felt compassion with the insurgents in Bosnia-Hercegovina. In the summer of 1875, the revolutionary Sergei Mikhailovich Kravchinskii was in France as a fugitive from the tsarist regime. He learned that in Hercegovina the Orthodox Serbs had risen against the Turks. He decided quickly to take the side of the insurgents and together with Mikhail P. Sazhin, another Russian refugee, left Paris. Kravchinskii thought that the participation of Russian revolutionaries in a Slavic struggle for

---

5 David MacKenzie, *The Serbs and Russian Pan-Slavism*, Ithaca, New York, Cornell, 1967, p. 30.

6 *Vestnik Evropy*, 1876, Kn. 10, p. 80. Quoted after Pisarev, "Traditsii druzhby ... ," *Sovetskaia kul'tura 70 let razvitiia*, p. 259.

7 N. K. Mikhailovskii, *Zapiski Profana*, 1897; cited after A. Pisarev, "Traditsii druzhbi ... ," *Sovetskaia kul'tura 70 let razvitiia*, p. 259.

independence would help not only the Balkan people, but the Russians themselves. They would get the experience of an armed uprising for their struggle with the Monarchy.

While in Hercegovina, Kravchinskii became acquainted with the Italian followers of Garibaldi who came as volunteers to Hercegovina. He became particularly close to the well-known Italian revolutionary Enrico Malatesta.

Kravchinskii was, at first, in a very optimistic frame of mind and he wrote to his friends that it was worth coming to the embattled Hercegovina. He soon realized that the uprising had no revolutionary goals since it was mostly caused by the near starvation of the population due to the dire economic situation in the country:

> The uprising is purely popular, peasant in origin. There are no obvious social goals in it, but there is no deceit either ... The uprising is not only growing, but becoming more organized. Sympathy is all-encompassing.

As the time wore on, Kravchinskii understood that the uprising was not permeated with revolutionary aspirations, it was mostly concerned with the betterment of living conditions. Kravchinskii himself was unprepared for this fight and its goals were never quite clear to him. He wrote that: "... there is not even a hint of socialism here. The struggle is purely political: liberation from the Turks. What this will lead to, no one knows." [8]

A young writer from Russia, Gleb Ivanovich Uspenskii, left a poignant eye-witness report of the Serbian-Turkish war. Uspenskii was obviously moved by the events in the Balkans and felt compelled to travel himself to the embattled territory. His testimonies about the unfolding of historic events were factual and descriptive, with many characteristic and well-chosen details. These writings, in the form of letters, were in essence realistic sketches depicting Russian

---

[8] N. Pirumova, B. Itenberg, V. Antonov, Eds., *Russia and the West: 19th Century*, Moscow, Progress Publishers, 1990, p. 254.

volunteers at the moment of their arrival in Serbia. His letters also described his views about the social and cultural situation in Serbia and its population. The direct recounting of daily events preserved the immediacy of his observations.

Uspenskii described the demeanor of Russian volunteers who "came to fight the Turk," and to help a small, brotherly Slavic nation. Uspenskii presented well-chosen human stories of a number of well meaning yet obviously impoverished Russians who fought in the Serbian uprising against the Turkish forces. With a keen eye of an observant reporter, he described in his *Letters* the faces and voices lost in the crowd of this improvised "party of volunteers."[9]

Fedor Mikhailovich Dostoevsky wrote about the Serbian and Bulgarian uprising and the subsequent Russo-Turkish war in a number of articles published during 1876 and 1877 in his *Diary of a Writer*. Dostoevsky described the repercussion of these events on the Russian society as a whole. He also analyzed the responses of the Western Powers in regard to the uprisings in the Balkans. Most of all, he felt that all of Russia experienced a strong commitment to the cause of the Southern Slavs. When uprisings flared up in the Balkans, the news of this event reverberated in the consciousness of the Russian society at large. People in all walks of life were ready to offer their assistance in many ways, and be it only with money.[10]

Dostoevsky feared that in Europe no one would believe in Russian genuine wish to help. Each time the Eastern Question arose, Europe's ignorance and misunderstanding of Russia reoccurred and nothing was solved. At the time, it seemed that the Europeans were

---

[9] G. I. Uspenskii, *Pis'ma iz Serbii, Novye vremena, novye zaboty*, Polnoe sobranie sochinenii, Vol. 4, Moscow, Akademiia Nauk SSSR, 1949, p. 367. Compare, Jelena Milojković-Djurić, *Panslavism and National Identity in Russia and in the Balkans*, East European Monoraphs, 1994, pp. 105-111.

[10] Dostoevsky, *A Writer's Diary*, Evanstone, Northwestern University, 1993, pp. 607-9.

questioning themselves about the Russians and their resolve to save the Southern Slavs.[11]

Dostoevsky discussed the sometimes conflicting reports published abroad in regard to the Russian involvement in the Balkans. Even in parts of the Slavic intelligentsia and their highest leaders there existed a certain mistrust of Russian motives. Dostoevsky discerned this attitude among the educated Serbs and Czechs alike. In Serbia, among the prominent leaders, there were some to whom it seemed that Russia was scheming to conquer them.[12]

Dostoevsky discerned that a part of the Russian intelligentsia was also beset by many misunderstandings, while discussing the situation in the Balkans. Various doubts about the feasibility of such an involvement, heard in conversations, were reflected in a number of literary works. [13] At the outset of the war even the Russian press had misgivings about the prospects of Russian military involvement. Some writers questioned the ability of Russia to lead the oppressed Bulgarians in a successful fight against the Turks. An article in the prestigious *Vestnik Evropy* stated:

> We cannot give to the Bulgarians anything more than our military power: as liberators we should give them full freedom, but we cannot give them something we do not have ourselves.[14]

The journalists warned that once the Russian soldiers crossed the Bulgarian border they would have to feed not only their own army but also the "starving Bulgarians." Contrary to such expectations, the Bulgarians seemed to be well off: they raised their

---

Dostoevsky, *A Writer's Diary,* p. 615 and p. 663.

12 Dostoevsky, *A Writer's Diary,* p. 623.

13 *Vestnyk Evropy,* Volume II, 1878; quoted after Pelagić, *Istorija,* p. 116.

14 Dostoevsky, *A Writer's Diary,* pp. 1194-1195.

own food and ate well, perhaps even better than any prosperous peasant in Russia.

The Russians arriving in Bulgaria, before the battle for Plevna, were stunned and angered. Many Russians made the difficult decisions to leave their own homeland and offer help to the needy Bulgarian population. They became indignant over the unexpected set of circumstances and most of all by Bulgarian prosperity. Voices were raised and the correspondents with the army were the first to comment on the situation. These reports were followed closely by the Russian press, particularly in the Petersburg press. Dostoevsky felt that these were passionate, convinced voices full of most righteous indignation. A significant number of soldiers were also angered by this situation: their long and potentially dangerous journey was, at the best, unnecessary.

Moreover, the Russians thought that the Bulgarians "looked askance" when greeting them since they considered them as "new masters." Dostoevsky argued that due to historic circumstances the Bulgarians could not believe that these "new masters" were in reality benevolent brothers ready to help. The Bulgarians lived as slaves for four centuries and they still feared that the "old masters" might return.

The Russians expected to find misery and poverty and instead they found prosperity. Thus, their mission seemed pointless. Although they were offered bread and salt upon their arrival by the welcoming people's delegations, it seemed as if the Bulgarians were not pleased to see them. The Russians were roused from the far away shores of the Gulf of Finland and all the rivers of Russia in order to help. They were ready to shed their blood for the oppressed and maligned. They did not expect to encounter a polite distrust and misgiving about their assumed roles of liberators.

Dostoevsky tried to explain this adverse reaction of the newly arriving Russians as a peculiar condition of human nature. Most of all, this indignation was caused by the realization that the role of Russians, as protectors, seemed to have no foundation in the immediate reality. They could not help but to feel angry and betrayed in their expectations. While the Russians were ready to help the oppressed Bulgarian people, they were not ready to encounter plenitude: it seemed as if the Bulgarians lived "in the bosom of Christ."[15]

Worst of all, the Bulgarian fears were realized: the Turks returned and recaptured these regions once more. The villages were plundered, reduced to ashes and "wiped from the face of the earth." The petty houses, the well-tended fields, the gardens and the livestock were destroyed. The Bulgarian population suffered tremendous losses.[16]

Dostoevsky finished his report with an assessment of the uncertain existence of the Bulgarian population deprived of essential human rights. The idyllic images of peaceful village life were only a false facade of fleeting prosperity. Time and again these villages were plundered and burned.

"And so, when those who had become indignant over Bulgarian prosperity lived to see the sorrowful end of the matter, they could not but realize that Bulgarian life was in essence only a stage decoration; that all these houses and gardens, and the wives, children, and little boys and girls in these houses - all of it, in essence belongs to the Turk and will be taken by him whenever he wishes. And he does take it; he takes it also in times of peace and in times when it is flourishing . . . and if, in spite of it all, the country continued to flourish, it was only because the Turk did not want to destroy utterly such a fertile meadow, thinking to draw from it in the future."[17]

Finally, Dostoevsky concluded all those who had become incensed over Bulgarian prosperity lived to see this brutal end. Dostoevsky understood well that the final settlement of the Eastern

---

15 Dostoevsky, *A Writer's Diary*, p. 1196.

16 Dostoevsky, *A Writer's Diary*, pp. 1197-1198.

17 Dostoevsky, *A Writer's Diary*, pp. 1064-1065.

Question would be difficult to achieve. He was aware of the complexity of the whole issue, but nevertheless believed that Russia's intervention would provide a platform for a new beginning. Therefore, he interpreted the Russian military action as a confirmation of faith in Russia's capacity to undertake a formidable task:

> The fact is, in the spring our great war was launched for a great feat which, sooner or later, despite all the temporary setbacks that delay settlement of the issue, will nonetheless be brought to its conclusion, even though its complete and desired conclusion may not be reached in the present war. This feat is so great and the aim of the war so improbable from Europe's point of view that Europe is bound to be indignant over our cunning ... Believe me, Europe is not frightened so much by the supposed growth of Russia's power as by the very fact of Russia's capacity to undertake such tasks and have such aims. Note that particularly. Undertaking something not for one's own direct benefit seems so bizarre to Europe, so at odds with international practice, that Europe takes Russia's action ... as something immoral, dangerous to her, and supposedly a threat to her great civilization. [18]

Dostoevsky discerned the fear from Russia's presence in the European sphere of interests and he pointed out several misconceptions about Russia's role in this context. Most of all, there existed the fear for a possibility of a Russian clash with Europe. In addition, the naturalness of the Slavic brotherhood was emerging more distinctly from beneath everything that had prevented it for ages. On the home front, the liberation of the peasants in 1861 presented yet another measure of Russia's spiritual strength. Yet, Dostoevsky noted with distress that Europe was far from understanding Russia.

---

[18] Dostoevsky, *A Writer's Diary*, pp. 1066-1067.

In Russia, Dostoevsky observed, Europe was highly respected by all factions of the intelligentsia. The Slavophiles revered Europe as the land of miracles with all its great nations. The admiration of Europe was a characteristic trait of Slavophiles, who had deep appreciation for the European cultural heritage. After all, their education was based on the wisdom of European enlightenment. These learned Slavophiles had a noble vision of a "new word," of a unified humankind, and were dubbed by Dostoevsky as "dreamers":

> Gentlemen, never did you, as Europeans and Westernizers love Europe so much as we, Slavophile-dreamers who, as far as you are concerned, are her mortal enemies! ... And in our dread of conflict with Europe in the current war we fear most of all that Europe will not understand us, and as before, as always, will meet us with arrogance, contempt and her sword, as if we were wild barbarians, unworthy of speaking in her presence. ... Evidently we still have so little of anything that might be intelligible to her and earn us her respect. Our fundamental, main idea, our emerging "new word" she will not understand for a long, long time yet. [19]

Dostoevsky bemoaned the fact that even the Russian who felt themselves as Europeans had a low esteem for Russia and the Russians. He named this segment of Russian intelligentsia as "Russian Europeans." These earnest individuals worshipped Europe and thought that the simple Russian people could never aspire for a place of honor. The Russians were incapable of serving the whole of humanity:

> For heaven's sake, how could we aspire for such a thing ... our ugly mugs in a place of honor. Rendering a service "to the whole of humanity." We are not cut for that sort of work; we are too

---

19 Dostoevsky, *A Writer's Diary*, p. 1188.

> repulsive ourselves to think of "liberating humanity." And what illiberal notions all these are: "Russia liberating enslaved peoples—what an illiberal notion!" [20]

Dostoevsky then aimed to clarify his own position. He declared himself to be a Slavophile although he did not believe himself to be a "complete Slavophile." His evaluation of Slavophilism pointed to the fact that this doctrine remained to be impalpable and interpreted in a variety of ways. Thus, Slavophilism continued to be vague as it was the case in the past even during the height of the discussions between the Westerners and Slavophiles.

Dostoevsky felt that ambiguities about Slavophilism persisted during the 1870s: this doctrine was still indefinite. For some Slavophilism still meant only *kvas and radishes* , as it did long time ago for Belinskii, to take an example. For others Slavophilism meant striving for the liberation and union of all Slavs under Russian leadership, although this union might not be strictly political. For the third group, the Slavophile doctrine meant a spiritual union of all Slavs within a global context of unanimity and goodwill. Furthermore, such a coalition aspired for a new universal alliance led by Russian people. Dostoevsky believed that the Russian people possessed mighty powers for the future solution of many fateful misapprehensions of western European civilization. Dostoevsky counted himself as a member of the latter group.

Dostoevsky's comprehension of Slavophilsm contained clearly the essence of the Panslavic doctrine, as advanced at first, by the Slovak poet Jan Kollar and subsequently in Russia by the historian Mikhail Petrovich Pogodin.[21] Early on, many Slavic scholars supported the evolving framework of Panslavic cultural

---

Dostoevsky, *A Writer's Diary,* p. 1063. Compare: Jelena Milojković-Djurić, *Panslavism and National Identity in Russia and in the Balkans 1830-1880: Images of the Self and Others,* East European Monographs, Boulder and New York, Columbia University Press, 1994, p. 119.

21 Milojković-Djurić, *Panslavism and National Identity in Russia and in the Balkans 1830-1880*, East European Monographs, pp. 1-2 , 81-83.

collaboration and reciprocity *(vzaimnost')*. However, they asserted equally the importance of preserving the national language, literature as well as cultural and political independence.[22]

In his *Writer's Diary*, Dostoevsky continued to emphasize the importance of Russia's humanitarian help devoid of any imperialistic notions. The Russian volunteers who came to fight the Turks did not come in support of expansionist policies. The volunteers did not fight for the crown heads or for a Panslav political unification. Dostoevsky thought that Russian foreign policy was at times misplaced and unjustified. He reiterated that Europe was inclined to believe in Russia's avidity to bring the Slavs under her rule as soon as possible. Therefore, he believed that the most complete turn around in Russia's political life would come only when Europe would acknowledge that Russia had no desire to bring anything under her realm.

Russia's aim should be to live by superior and selfless ideas in order to serve humanity and not to serve her own interests. Then a new era would begin, both for Russia and for Europe. The conviction of Russia's disinterest, should it come, will help change the whole situation in Europe. Dostoevsky believed strongly that Russia would be served best if acting selflessly in pursuit of the well-being of all of the humankind.[23]

Dostoevsky trusted that the comprehension of a new world order would ultimately result in an universal alliance of all nations around the world. It is not by suppressing the national personalities of other nations that Russia should strive to achieve prosperity. On the contrary, the well-being should be achieved only in the freest and most independent development of all other nations, and in fraternal unity with them, enhancing the other, learning from them and teaching them. Only such a communion of nations of the world would provide the foundation for a lasting peace in a global context.

Dostoevsky wanted to explain to the intelligentsia at large, as well as to the political decision makers, that Russia would be served

---

23 Ibid.

best by acting selflessly in pursuit of the well-being of all of the humankind.

It is noteworthy that Vasa Pelagić, a Bosnian Serb, shared some of the concerns expressed by Dostoevsky. Pelagić, a theologian and historian, left a very valuable analysis of the situation in Bosnia-Hercegovina and causes of the uprising in 1875. He also examined, in retrospect, the pronouncements of Russian writers concerning the situation in the Balkans as well as the Russian humanitarian assistance.[24] In the aftermath of the Serbian-Turkish and Russian-Turkish wars, followed by the signing of the San Stefano and Berlin Peace Treaties of 1878, Pelagić felt that these historic events should be scrutinized in order to provoke the rethinking of the future plans and important priorities. To this end, Pelagić penned the first history of the uprising entitled, *Istorija Bosansko-ercegovačke bune u svezi sa srpsko i rusko-turskim ratom (The History of the Bosnian-Hercegovinian Uprising in Connection with the Serbian- and Russian-Turkish War).*[25] The characteristic subtitle, *Studija za narod i drzavnike (A Study for the People and Statesmen),* pointed to his wish to provide an analysis of the past events that would be useful both to the people and their leaders in avoiding similar conflicts in the future. The first edition of his book appeared in 1879, one year after the signing of the Treaty of Berlin.

In his youth, Pelagić was a Russian protégé, and a recipient of a scholarship from the Moscow Slavic Benevolent Committee. He received this scholarship thanks to the recommendation of the Serbian Metropolitan Mihail Jovanović and the city council in Brčko. The scholarship enabled him to spend two years in Russia as a graduate student at the Historical and Philological College of the Moscow University. After his return to Bosnia in 1865, Pelagić remained in correspondence with two outstanding members of the Slavic Benevolent Committee, M. P. Pogodin and I. S. Aksakov.

---

[25] Hornjanski Press, Budapest, 1879. The second edition appeared in 1880. The references in this book pertain to the 1880 edition.

Pelagić presented in much detail his account of the Eastern Question during the period 1875-1878. He discerned the worsening of the economic situation as the main cause of the dissension leading to the uprising. He also evaluated the responses of the great powers to the evolving changes of the situation in the Balkans. Pelagić preserved with great acuity the images of the social, political and economic relations in Bosnia-Hercegovina during the turbulent decade of the 1870s. As a disciple of Auguste Comte and John Stuart Mill, Pelagić endeavored to depict the social and economic conditions influencing the everyday life of the Christian and Moslem population in Bosnia-Hercegovina. Thus, he gave a human face to the uprising by showing how the struggle of the Great Powers played in the local political and cultural context.

Pelagić questioned the ability of Russia to lead the South Slavs in a successful fight against the Turks. He also analyzed the Russian assessment of the situation in the Balkans and the internal problems facing Russian society at large. Pelagić reiterated the opinions of some Russian writers casting doubts about the feasibility of liberation. Thus, he quoted an article published in the prestigious *Vestnik Evropy,* that questioned the role of Russians as liberators: "We cannot give to the Bulgarians anything more than our military power: as liberators we should give them full freedom, but we cannot give them something we do not have ourselves." [26]

Pelagić agreed with the opinions of some Russian thinkers who doubted the true nature of the policies addressing the Christians under Turkish occupation. The Imperial court assumed a righteous pose while aiming to exploit the sympathies of the South Slav people and enable the Russian annexation of the South Slavic lands at an opportune moment in the future. Obviously, Pelagić was influenced in his evaluation of the current situation by the writings of Dostoevsky and Saltikov-Shchedrin, among others.[27]

---

26 *Vestnik Evrope* , Volume II, 1878, quoted after Pelagić, *Istorija* ... , p. 116.

27 Dostoevsky, *A Writers' Diary,* p. 615. Compare also, Mikhail Evgrafovich Schedrin, *Polnoe sobranie sochineniia,* Moscow, 1939, Vol. 19, p. 80.

Pelagić believed that the Bosnians and Hercegovinians were fighting mostly for the betterment of their livelihood, for their human rights and freedom from tyranny. They did not fight for the great Slavic empire, or for a Panslav unification. Panslavism was an elusive dream of the educated few, at best. Pelagić thought that a Bosnian peasant reasoned in a different way, since he was concerned principally about the hardship and difficulties of everyday living. Pelagić stated bluntly:

> The Bosnian and Hercegovinian ... are fighting to be free of tyranny ... for their material well-being and for their rights and freedom. The Bosnian peasant would not be willing to give even his chickens for the realization of Panslavism not to speak of some greater sacrifices.[28]

Pelagić stressed the economic factor as the leading cause of the outbreak of dissent. Most of all, Pelagić emphasized the necessity of profound economic reforms both in Turkey and in the Balkan Principalities as a precondition for the desired changes leading towards prosperity. He dismissed the influence of Panslavism as a guiding ideology of the peasants' unrest. The lofty goals of cultural collaboration and solidarity remained to be a dream of the educated classes. Most importantly, Pelagić realized that Panslavism as a doctrine was developed unevenly among the social groupings in Bosnia-Hercegovina. The intellectuals and the educated classes were captured by national consciousness and supported Panslav postulates of cultural reciprocity. As to the popular masses—workers, servants, and peasants—Pelagić thought that they were the least to be affected by notions of Panslavism.[29]

---

[28] Pelagić, *Istorija Bosansko-Ercegovačke Bune*, Budapest, Hornjanski, 1880, p. 77.

[29] Miroslav Hroch observed in his book on national revival in Europe that the peasantry on the whole was relatively unwilling to accept national consciousness. M. Hroch, *Social Preconditions of National Revival in Europe*, Cambridge, Cambridge University Press, 1985, p. 180. Eric

Pelagić showed that in June 1876, at the outset of the Serbian war for liberation from the Turks, the native population thought that a war for a just cause would be quickly resolved. In fact, even the efforts of distinguished adherents of Panslavism abroad could not generate needed support for the beleaguered population of Bosnia-Hercegovina. Pelagić described the help proffered by other Slavic nations as a symbolic token that could not provide real relief in a complicated and prolonged armed conflict. Moreover, Pelagić commented on the reactions of the political circles in the Habsburg Empire, France and England pertaining to the uprising in Bosnia-Hercegovina. Pelagić commented in particular on the efforts of Hungarian statesman Andrássy to bring calm to the embattled region. In December of 1875 Andrássy issued a program of reforms providing for land and tax reforms as well as religious equality. The program was approved by Bismarck and accepted by the Porte. Pelagić thought that it was unfortunate that the insurgents rejected Andrássy's proposal.[30]

As the suffering of the population in Bosnia-Hercegovina increased, Serbia and Montenegro went to war against Turkey by the end of July 1876. Serbia was counting on help from enlightened European countries. In reality, the appearance of Serbia and Montenegro on the battlefield, aided by the Russian volunteers and their generals, seemed to endanger the established political order in Europe. The fear of the spreading of the ideology of Panslavism was on the minds of many European politicians, so too was the possibility of Slavic expansion at the expense of others. Such a change was against the interests of some countries in Europe, while the presence

---

Hobsbawm expressed a similar view while analyzing the advent of nationalism in 19th century Europe. Compare E. Hobsbawm, *Nations and Nationalism since 1780, Program, Myth, Reality,* Cambridge, 1990, p. 12.

30 Pelagić, *Istorija Bosansko-Ercegovačke Bune,,* pp. 70-71. Compare also, Barbara Yelavich, *A Century of Russian foreign Policy 1814-1914,* Philadelphia and New York, Lippincott, 1964, p. 177.

of Turkey was an accepted fact. The Russian imperialistic policies in Asia brought an added danger to the existing balance of powers.

In the height of the Eastern crisis from the fall of 1876 to the spring of 1877, the Russian government repeatedly attempted to secure the conclusion of peace treaties for Serbia and Montenegro and the enactment of long overdue reforms in Hercegovina, Bosnia and Bulgaria. Although these negotiations did not succeed, there continued to be a strong difference of opinions on the questions of military intervention.[31] The Emperor and his ministerial council acknowledged that a war at that time could be ruinous for Russia's financial position. However, the response of the Russian intelligentsia, and the response of the wide masses of people throughout Russia, influenced the reexamination of the official position. During a long discussion with his ministers, the Tsar felt that there "are moments when one must forget all but the defense of his honor." On April 24, 1877, Alexander II issued the declaration of the Russo-Turkish war.[32]

The Russo-Turkish war ended with a Russian victory and the signing of the Treaty of San Stefano in March of 1878. The Treaty caused dissatisfaction of the English and Austrian governments. Notwithstanding, the San-Stefano Peace Treaty could have provided for the political and administrative autonomy of Bosnia-Hercegovina.[33] Dušan Vasiljević, a well known member of the Serbian intellectual elite in Bosnia, wrote in retrospect that the autonomy of Bosnia-Hercegovina, as stipulated in the San Stefano Treaty, could have enabled a peaceful and favorable development of this region. Vasiljević was aware that the San Stefano Treaty was not acceptable to all parties involved, Serbia and Montenegro in

---

31 Barbara Jelavich, *Russia's Balkan Entanglement 1806-1891*, Cambridge, Cambridge University Press, 1991, pp. 170-172.

32 Jelavich, *Russia's Balkan Entanglement 1806-1891*, p. 172.

33 Milorad Ekmečić, "Istorijski značaj ustanka u Bosni i Hercegovini," *Radovi iz istorije Bosne i Hercegovine*, Belgrade, BIGZ, 1997, p. 249.

particular. Most importantly, the Great Powers objected that the enlargement of Great Bulgaria could facilitate Russia's expansion to the Black Sea and Balkans.[34]

After separate negotiations in London and Vienna, England demanded a revision of the Treaty of San Stefano. The settlement of the Eastern Question was eventually reached at the Congress of Berlin and the signing of the Treaty of Berlin in July of 1878. The Congress of Berlin agreed to confer a mandate to Austria-Hungary for occupation and administration of Bosnia-Hercegovina in order to ensure protection of its population.

Pelagić, among many others, criticized the Treaty of Berlin as a betrayal of vital interests of Southern Slavs. The Treaty of Berlin included concessions granted by Russia causing great harm to the Balkan peoples and the shared hope for a commonwealth of Slav nations. The Serbian poet Jovan Jovanović-Zmaj wrote an appropriate commentary for this allegedly shameful policy of the Russian government. The last verse repeated the doubts about the true nature of Russian policy towards Serbia. Jovanović-Zmaj ended each verse by calling on Ivan Sergeevich Aksakov to explain this debacle.

And it was finished in an unjust manner
And signed with a golden feather
And celebrated with a lofty feast.
And the Serbian disaster was proclaimed as peace.
Furthermore, Aksakov would explain![35]

Aksakov did criticize openly the Treaty of Berlin in his speech at the meeting of the Moscow Slavic Benevolent Committee in June of

---

34 Dušan Vasiljević, *O Bosni i Hercegovini*. Lecture presented to the Slavic Benevolent Society in St. Petersburg on April 12, 1909. Belgrade, Štamparija Davidović, 1909, pp. 10-12.

35 Quoted after Pelagić, *Istorija* ... p. 113. Translation into English J. Milojković-Djurić.

1878. He denounced Russian diplomats and compared them to nihilists who were devoid of all historical consciousness and national feelings.[36] In response to these outspoken critical pronouncements, Aksakov was exiled to the country estate of his father-in-law, the poet Fedor Ivanovich Tiutchev, and stayed there in exile for three months.

During the uprising in Bosnia-Hercegovina the Panslav leaders did not succeed to mobilize sufficient support and to offer substantial help to the beleaguered population. Most importantly Panslavism as a doctrine was developed unevenly among the social groupings. The intellectuals and the educated class were first captured by national consciousness and notions of Panslavism. The peasants and workers were the last to be affected by it. Moreover, the regional diversities and economic inequalities both in Russia and in the Balkans have been notably neglected.[37]

Although the populace both in Russia or in the Balkans did not fully comprehend the Panslav ideology, the manifest idea of a broader Slavic consciousness was clearly present. The Russian volunteers repeatedly stated that they came to help a brotherly nation, although they did not know much about the people they wanted to protect. Dostoevsky understood the gravity of the situation in the Balkans, and he praised the voluntary help of Russian people supporting the cause of the embattled South-Slavs. This generous help was exemplary in view of the difficulties facing many of them in their own homeland. Observing from a vantage point, Dostoevsky envisaged the solution of long-standing problems in a new world order promoting collaboration among the nations devoid of self-serving interests and expansionist policies.

The testimonies of writers and historians, who wrote about Bosnia-Hercegovina, Russia, and Serbia during the 1870s, furnished

---

36 Andrzej Walicki, *The Slavophile Controversy*, Oxford, Clarendon Press, 1975, p. 503. Also, Pelagić, *Istorija ...* p. 103.

37 Miroslav Hroch, *Social Preconditions of National Revival in Europe*, p. 180.

a number of valuable reports offering a broader implication of the Eastern Question. Pelagić, as the first historian of the uprising in Bosnia-Hercegovina, saw the role of history as a deterrent of violent transgressions and an invaluable teacher for the time to come. Moreover, Pelagić pleaded for the effacement of narrow nationalistic or Panslav perceptions acknowledging the importance of peaceful coexistence and world-wide cooperation. Although primarily concerned with the impoverished populace in the Balkans, Pelagić was addressing the human lot in general. Clearly, Dostoevsky's eloquent supplication for an unmitigated dialogue of all nations influenced Pelagić's own appeal for cessation of deplorable confrontations ensuring peace and prosperity for the humankind as a whole.

Chapter 2

TOLSTOY'S AND DOSTOEVSKY'S RESPONSES TO THE EASTERN QUESTION 1875-1877: IMAGES OF THE SELF AND OTHER

When Dostoevsky began publishing *A Writer's Diary* in January of 1876, he intended to record his assessments of outstanding current events. He aspired to provide a personal account of what was seen, heard and read each month: all twelve issues would form a whole, a book "written by a single pen," preeminently dealing with actual happenings. Since he wanted to write a diary, in the literal sense of the word, he decided not to include literary criticism. Soon enough Dostoevsky realized that he could not impose on himself some artificial obligation and conceal possibly his strongest impressions because they pertained to Russian literature. The publication of Tolstoy's *Anna Karenina* was the case in point. Tolstoy's new novel, on which Dostoevsky refrained from commenting, became much more than a literary work.[1]

Dostoevsky acknowledged the perfection of Anna Karenina as a work of art. The novel acquired additional significance since the publication of its last installment coincided with the declaration of Russo-Turkish war in April of 1877. Both impressions, the novel and the declaration of war, connected in Dostoevsky's mind and he found their point of contact striking. Dostoevsky stressed that the novelist was an enormous talent, a remarkable mind, and a man highly respected by the intelligentsia. Tolstoy's views regarding the current

---

1 Fyodor Dostoevsky, *A Writer's Diary*, Translated by Kenneth Lantz, Evanstone, Northwestern University Press, 1993, July and August 1877, p. 1063.

Russian reality and the Eastern Question presented a matter holding interest to all Russians.[2]

Tolstoy's understanding of the Eastern Question followed, by and large, the Russian state policy of recueillement. The Emperor, Alexander II, directed his principal attention toward long overdue internal reforms. In foreign affairs, the official circles attempted to preserve peace and negotiate an acceptable solution to the Eastern crisis. However, Tolstoy's views on the Balkan crises, expressed in the final chapter of *Anna Karenina*, were criticized by a number of eminent writers and caused a literary uproar of a sort. Dostoevsky opposed also Tolstoy's views and favored a decisive intervention on behalf of the oppressed population in the Balkans under Turkish rule. Moreover, he praised the Russian people for understanding the Eastern Question in no other way than the liberation of the Orthodox Southern Slavs.

Dostoevsky recalled that shortly after the outbreak of the war in April of 1877, he met one of his favorite fellow writers. His friend did not look like a man of strong enthusiasm yet he at once began discussing *Anna Karenina* with passionate insistence. Although Dostoevsky shared his friend's admiration for Tolstoy's work, he was struck by the perceptive insight and firm praise of the novel. As it happened, Dostoevsky just finished reading part seven of the novel and he recalled the following views of his interlocutor:

> It's something unprecedented, a first. Are there any of our writers who could rival it? Could anyone imagine anything like it in Europe? Is there any work in all their literature over the past years, and even much earlier, that could stand next to it? [3]

Dostoevsky compared *Anna Karenina* to a powerful fiction. He also compared it with a "poema," thus suggesting similarities with another literary work that he admired Gogol's masterpiece *The Dead Souls*.[4] Dostoevsky wrote elsewhere in his Diary that he read often Gogol's work. He could not remember how many times he talked about *The Dead Souls* and read the work with his young

---

[2] Dostoevsky, A Writer's Diary, p. 1063.

[3] Dostoevsky, *A Writer's Diary*, p. 1067.

[4] Dostoevsky, *A Writer's Diary*, p. 840.

friends. In those days of his youth, on a Petersburg "white night," as bright as a day, two or three friends would get together and start reading Gogol very often all through the night.[5]

However, everything changed in Dostoevsky's mind with the appearance of the eighth part of Tolstoy's novel. Dostoevsky noted that the concluding part of *Anna Karenina* was not published in *The Russian Messenger* although the novel had been appearing in this journal since its very first installment. The final chapter was published separately and Dostoevsky bought the booklet with the concluding chapter. After reading it, he found it by no means "innocent," and he even described it as "unfortunate."[6] Although he had a distinct distaste for making criticism of contemporary literary figures and their works, he decided that he would certainly write about it in the forthcoming issue of his Diary.

Dostoevsky's criticism and repudiation of the author of the novel was not a solitary occurrence. As Dostoevsky noted, the editors of the journal *The Russian Messenger* rejected the publication of the final part of *Anna Karenina*. The informed literary circles knew that the eighth part was rejected because of its disagreement with the journal's policy and the convictions of the editors. The differences occurred specifically in regard to Tolstoy's view on the Eastern Question and the Russo-Turkish war of 1877.

In 1875 and 1876 continued Turkish oppression led to revolts in Hercegovina, Bosnia and Bulgaria. The difficult fate of the South Slavs under Turkish occupation became known to the whole of Europe. An International Relief Committee was formed in Paris, headed by the Serbian Metropolitan Mihail Jovanović and aided by the Croatian Bishop Josip Strosmayer as its vice-president. The Committee aimed to alleviate the hardship of refugees from these regions and was assisted by many charitable organizations. The Committee was also supported by the Slavic Benevolent Society with its outstanding members Ivan Aksakov and countess Antonina Bliudova.[7]

---

[5] Dostoevsky, *A Writer's Diary*, p. 840.

[6] Dostoevsky, *A Writer's Diary*, p. 1072.

[7] *Jugosloveni i Rusija,* Dokumenti iz arhiva M.F. Rajevskog 40-80 godine XIX veka, Belgrade, Istorijski institut i Akademiia Nauk SSSR, 1989, p. 150.

A number of writers and journalists testified to a grass-root feeling of solidarity for the suffering South Slavs. Thus, the noted journalist and contributor to *Otachestvennyie zapiski,* N.K. Mikhailovskii wrote:

> The casack from Don, the muzhik from Samar, the orderly at the Andreevski green market who enlisted as a volunteer ... the old woman ... the young girl who took the shirt off her back for the Slavs—all these unknown people did not operate with the concept of the 'greatness' of their nation or with the 'interests of their nation.'[8]

The journal *Vestnik Evropy* published an article by A.N. Pypin, a well known figure in the Russian cultural life. Pypin stated that the spirit of solidarity with the South Slavs encouraged a remarkable development. A veritable democratic movement had reached such proportions that even foreign observers noted a positive self reliance and invigorated public life not observed since the war of 1812.[9]

The Russian church and the church's representatives collected assistance for the refugees. Contributions flowed into specific points: editorial offices of magazines, branches of the Slavic Committees. Dostoevsky posited that Russian volunteers began to step forward:

> ... the flow of contributions increased, and the whole of Russia rose up to make them. Over the last year there were not all that many volunteers—a few thousand—but certainly the whole of Russia was with them on their way to Serbia, and the people in particular—the real people, not the idle trash, as the angry

---

8 N.K. Mikhailovskii, *Zapiski Profana,* 1897; cited after A. Pisarev, "Traditsii druzhbi narodov kak iavlenie kul'tury: Osvoboditel'naia bor'ba balkanskikh narodov protiv osmanskogo iga i rossiiskaia intelligentsiia," *Sovetskaia Kul'tura, 70 let Razvitiia,* Moscow, Akademiia Nauk, 1987, p. 259.

9 Liudmila I. Rovniakova, *Bor'ba iuzhnikh slavian za svobodu i russkaia periodicheskaia pechat; 50-70- gody XIX veka,* Leningrad, Akademia Nauk SSSR 1986, p. 227. Compare also Jelena Milojković-Djurić, *Panslavism and National Identity in Russia and in the Balkans 1830-1880: Images of the Self and Others,* Boulder and New York, East European Monographs, Columbia University Press, 1994, pp. 96-123.

> Levin particularly insists; he regards the volunteers as idle trash as well. But this is not so; this affair did not happen in some out-of-the way corner, it was known to everyone—the whole of Russia, that is—decided that this cause was a good one. The people displayed so much that was noble … that it will unquestionably remain one of the finest pages in their history.[10]

All these events were of utmost interest for the Russian society. Dostoevsky noted that in the final part of Tolstoy's novel, one of the protagonists, the mentioned "angry" Levin, mused about the responses of the Russian society to the unresolved Eastern Question and the uprising in the Balkans. In reality, Levin was not a real person but a vehicle for author's views. Levin was merely the invention of the novelist and the voice of the author himself. Therefore, his deliberations merited special attention:

> Thus, when we discuss the non-existent Levin, we shall be discussing the actual view of one of our most remarkable contemporary Russians on current Russian reality. And this is already a serious topic for discussion … This view of so remarkable a Russian writer, and on a matter holding such interest to all Russians as does the general national movement of all Russian people over the last two years regarding the Eastern Question, is expressed precisely and decisively in this same eight and final part of his work, the part rejected by the editors of The Russian Messenger because the author's convictions did not coincide with their own and that appeared only recently as a separate booklet.[11]

Dostoevsky then summarized his understanding of the essence of Tolstoy's views as expressed by Levin. First of all, the Russian people by no means shared the aims of the so called national movement in support of the South Slavs. Secondly, Tolstoy thought that much about this issue was fabricated by journalists. Thirdly, the volunteers who went to fight the Turks in Serbia were either desperate and drunken people or simply fools. The fourth point

---

[10] Dostoevsky, *A Writer's Diary*, p. 1083–1084.

[11] Dostoevsky, *A Writer's Diary*, p. 1061

presented the argument that the so-called upsurge of Russian national feeling was fabricated by well-known people and supported by hired journalists "contrary to our most fundamental principles." Tolstoy obviously equated the mentioned 'fundamental principles' with the official concept of Russian foreign policy avoiding military involvement in the Balkans. Furthermore, he was denying the fact that the concern for the Slavs became a widespread phenomenon of solidarity with the oppressed population in the Balkans. Finally, all the barbarities and unprecedented tortures inflicted upon the Slavs cannot arouse in Russians any direct feeling of compassion. Such direct feeling for the oppression of the Slavs did not and could not exist. The last point was expressed finally and categorically:

> So it is that the 'pure in heart' Levin has set off to dissociate himself ... from the overwhelming majority of Russians. ... However, I will also note that even though many insist—and even I see clearly (as I said above)—that the author uses Levin to express many of his own views and convictions, putting them into Levin's mouth. ... I still refuse to confuse the author himself with the figure of Levin as his creator depicted him. As I say this, I find myself in a painful quandary, because even though very much of what the author expresses through Levin evidently concerns only Levin himself as an artistically depicted character, I still did not expect this from such an author! [12]

As a writer, Dostoevsky was aware of the incidence of an unexpected aptitude in a fictional character of a novel in the process of its creation. In his Notebooks for several of his major novels, he often examined various possibilities in shaping a character's relative independence influencing the outcome of the novel itself. The actual process of writing a novel did not provide a predetermined design or structure. In his Notebooks, Dostoevsky used to sketch many courses of action, thus allowing the hero to be free to choose among possible directions of his life's odysseys.[13] Yet, Dostoevsky obviously drew a line in commenting Levin's deliberation concerning the Eastern

---

[12] Dostoevsky, *A Writer's Diary*, p. 1062

[13] Gary Saul Morson, "Strange Synchronies and Surplus Possibilities: Bakhtin on Time," *Slavic Review*, Vol. 52, No. 3, 1993, p. 486.

Question while declaring Levin's and Tolstoy's outlook as unfortunate and unexpected.

Dostoevsky then analyzed Levin's response to the atrocities committed by the Turks after a Bulgarian city had been plundered. In the aftermath of the pilferage in this town, two hundred corpses were found in a church. Levin's reaction to this desperate situation was expressed blatantly by his refusal to acknowledge this tragedy. After reading the report about mass killings in a Bulgarian church, Levin reasoned that this was not his immediate concern touching his own life:

> Kitty is in fine spirits and had a good appetite today; we have given the boy a bath and he has begun to recognize me; what do I care what goes over there in another hemisphere? There is no immediate feeling for the oppression of the Slavs and there cannot be any, because I don't feel anything.[14]

At this point in time, Levin was most of all absorbed in providing for the well being of his own family delighting in trivial details of their domestic life. Yet, in the context of the discussed situation in the Balkans, Levin's concerns acquired unwillingly a callous, selfish and unethical connotation. Obviously, Tolstoy did not think that juxtaposing the sufferings of a distant nation with Levin's immersion in his private world would produce sharp criticism and cause a literary uproar of a sort.

Tolstoy probably thought that Levin's reasoning would project a rational approach of a young head of a family dealing with immediate obligations on his country estate. Levin appreciated the good health of his wife Kitty, her fine spirits and good appetite. He rejoiced thinking about their little son who had begun to recognize his father. Why should he care about human beings so far away from his home?[15]

Dostoevsky voiced his disbelief that a father who had a young son himself would brush away so easily the sufferings of others while rejoicing in life's little pleasures without any feeling of guilt. His demeanor was devoid of any compassion for other peoples'

---

14 Dostoevsky, *A Writer's Diary*, p. 1099.

15 Dostoevsky, *A Writer's Diary*, p. 1036.

sufferings. He talked about a good appetite of his wife, the bathing of his little son, while thousands of people faced hunger and destitution. Such an attitude was unjustifiable: Levin's lack of sensitivity and ethical comportment could not be accepted as a norm of honorable behavior.

Dostoevsky even accused Tolstoy of shortsightedness and an inability to see events in proper perspective. Tolstoy saw clearly only what was standing right before his eyes, and could not fathom what was standing beside him left or right:

> The author of *Anna Karenina*, despite his immense artistic talent, has one of those Russian intellects that sees clearly only that which is standing right before his eyes, and so it keeps pushing away at the same point. Such intellects don't have the ability, apparently, to turn to the right or to the left so as to make out what is standing beside them: to do that they have to turn the whole body. And then, perhaps, they'll start to talk about just the opposite thing, since on any occasion they are always absolutely sincere. Such a turnabout may never happen at all, but it may happen within a month, and then the respected author will begin shouting with the very same passion that we have to send volunteers and make lint for bandages, and he'll be saying all the things we are saying[16]

In fact, Tolstoy captured well the fascination of the Russian intelligentsia with the Eastern Question. Thus, in the last chapter of *Anna Karenina*, Tolstoy described the lively discussion of the guests who came from Moscow to visit Levin's country estate. Upon their arrival they were seated under the trees by the apiary and served honey and fresh cucumbers. The first topic centered around Russia's role in the Balkans:

> . . .and the guests at once start on the honey and the Eastern Question. All this happens last year . . . you can remember Cherniaev, the volunteers, collecting donations. A heated

16 Dostoevsky, *A Writer's Diary*, p. 1037.

conversation quickly develops because everyone has an irrepressible urge to get to the major topic of the day.[17]

Obviously Tolstoy agreed that the Eastern Question was indeed the major topic of the day: the events on the Balkans were followed with great interest by the Russian society at large. Moreover, during the conversation by the apiary, one of the guests, the old Prince, expressed a political theory that was not new but already repeated many times before:

. . .even before the Bulgarian atrocities I simply couldn't understand why all Russians developed such a sudden affection for their Slavic brethren, while I did not feel any love at all . . .I see that there are others beside me who are interested only in Russian and not their Slavic brethren."[18]

Dostoevsky commented on the false profundity of such a statement implying that the interest of the Russian society should address only Russia. Moreover, he was puzzled by such a narrow conception of Russian interests as the Prince purported to be the case. Dostoevsky was even more puzzled by the conversation that took place somewhat earlier. The old Prince asked for an explanation as where all these Russian volunteers are going, and whom are they going to fight. He did not know who had declared the war: "But who has declared war on the Turks? Ivan Ivanovich Ragozov and Countess Lidia Ivanovna along with Mme Stahl?" [19]

Dostoevsky thought that the posed hypothetical question contained a malignant overtone and an exaggeration implying that someone in Russia, behind the back of the government, had declared the war on the Turks. In fact, nobody declared war: the Russian people only wanted to help and alleviate the sufferings of those close to them. Commenting on the conclusion of *Anna Karenina*, Dostoevsky posed the question:

---

[17] Dostoevsky, *A Writer's Diary*, p. 1080.

[18] Dostoevsky, *A Writer's Diary*, p.1080.

[19] Dostoevsky, *A writer's Diary*, p.1078.

> Is this how Levin ends his epic? Is he the one the author wants to set forth as an example of a righteous and honorable man? People like the author of *Anna Karenina* are the teachers, while we are merely their pupils. So what is it, then, that they are teaching us.[20]

In reality, Tolstoy supported the official policy of *recueuillement* while engaged in the writing of *Anna Karenina.* Tolstoy understood well the need for the continuation of major reforms introduced in the 1860s. Moreover, Alexander II attempted to avoid involvement in foreign policy issues that might cause dangerous consequences for Russia. Alexander II directed his principal attention toward domestic affairs and internal improvements while avoiding military interventions in the Balkans.

Levin's attitude concerning his private microcosm, reflected a similar mode of reasoning. Most of all, he aspired to improve his country estate and the life of the people around him. He was not concerned with what was happening "in another hemisphere" in the far away Balkans.

However, the response of the Russian intelligentsia, the activities of the Slavic Benevolent Committees, and the response of the wide masses of people throughout Russia influenced the reexamination of the official position. The prominent personalities spoke often on behalf of the South Slavs such as I.S. Turgenev, M.E. Saltykov Schedrin, I.S. Aksakov, F.I. Tiutchev, G.I. Uspenski, V.I. Nemirovich Danchenko. Peter Chaikovsky was also a supporter of Slav solidarity and his composition, *March Slav*, was often performed at festive events. Chaikovsky used in this composition Serbian folk music idioms as well as the Russian hymn pointing metaphorically to the cultural ties of these two Slavic people. Although Alexander II aspired to maintain peace and safeguard the Three Emperor's Alliance, he still had to acknowledge the strong support for the South Slavs in Russia as well as abroad.

In England, the distinguished English statesman Lord William Evart Gladstone stood out as the most influential personality on behalf of the South Slavs. His famous speeches in the Parliament aroused a kind of spirited idealism and sincere wish to help.

---

20 Dostoevsky, *A Writer's Diary*, p. 1099.

Moreover, the English clergy headed by the Metropolitan and Archbishop A.C. Cantuar and the Canon of St. Paul's Cathedral H.P. Liddon voiced from their pulpits their support for the Christian South Slavs.[21]

Among many others expressing concern, the poet Oscar Wilde wrote the following note addressed to Gladstone in May of 1877:

> Your noble and impassioned protests, both written and spoken, against the massacres of the Christians in Bulgaria have so roused my heart that I venture to send you a sonnet which I have written on the subject ... [22]

Wilde was not the only poet to express his disdain. In March of 1877, Alfred Tennyson wrote his celebrated sonnet Montenegro to focus attention on the Balkan wars for liberation. Tennyson's association with Lord Gladstone heightened his concern for the distant Montenegrins. The sonnet illustrated Tennyson's interpretation of the implications caused by the historic conflict of Turkey and Montenegro. Tennyson was elevated to the much esteemed position of the court poet, "poeta laureatus." His poetic eloquence resounded in a number of political poems relating to issues that he witnessed. His sonnet Montenegro was published in May of the same year in the review *The Nineteenth Century*. Tennyson considered this sonnet as one of his finest, placing it first among his other poems. In the same issue, Gladstone published his lengthy historical treatise about Montenegro as a commentary on Tennyson's sonnet *The Nineteenth Century.* [23]

All these voices raised on behalf of the South Slav cause had a considerable impact on the decision making policies of an enlightened monarch. Alexander II and his minister Gorchakov attempted to avoid involvement in foreign policy issues that might cause dangerous consequences. In addition, Alexander II aimed to preserve the Three Emperors' Alliance of Russia, Austria and

---

21 R.T. Shanon, *Gladstone and the Bulgarian Agitation 1876*, Connecticut, Archon, 1975, p. 187.

22 Quoted after R.T. Shanon, *Gladstone and the Bulgarian Agitation 1876*, p. 187.

23 *The Nineteenth Century*, Vol. I, No. III, May 1877, p. 359 and pp. 360-379.

Germany, instituted in 1872, mainly to protect the established balance of power in Europe. Thus, from the fall of 1876 to the spring of 1877 repeated attempts were made to secure the conclusion of peace treaties for Serbia and Montenegro and the enactment of reforms in Hercegovina, Bosnia and Bulgaria.[24]

Although these negotiations did not succeed, there continued to be a strong difference of opinions on the question of war. The Tsar acknowledged that a war at that time was not in the national interest and would be ruinous in view of Russian financial position. Nevertheless, the final decision to declare the war appeared to be imminent. During a discussion with his ministers, the Tsar felt that there "are moments that when one must forget all but the defense of his honor." Thus, on April 24, 1877 after the declaration of the Russo-Turkish War Alexander II issued a proclamation:

> Our faithful and beloved subjects know the lively interest which we have always devoted to the destinies of the oppressed Christian population in Turkey. Our desire to ameliorate and guarantee their condition has been shared by the whole of the Russian nation, which shows itself ready to-day to make fresh sacrifices to relieve the condition of the Christians in the Balkan Peninsula. ... During two years we have made incessant efforts to induce the Porte to adopt such reforms that would protect the Christians of Bosnia, Hercegovina, and Bulgaria from the arbitrary rule of the local authorities. The execution of these reforms followed, as a direct obligation, from the anterior engagements solemnly contracted by the Porte in the sight of all Europe. Our efforts, although supported by the joint diplomatic representations of the other Governments, have not attained the desired end.[25]

After the declaration of the war, Dostoevsky described in his Diary of April 1877 the reaction of the people in the streets of Saint Petersburg that he witnessed. Moreover, everyone throughout

---

24 Barbara Jelavich, *Russia's Balkan Entanglements 1806-1891,* Cambridge, Cambridge University Press, 1991, p. 155 and p. 171.

25 Edward Hertslet, *Map of Europe by Treaty,* IV, London, Buttersworths 1875-1891, pp. 2298-2299. Quoted after Jelavich, *Russia's Balkan Entanglements 1806-1891,* p. 172.

Russia sensed that something decisive had begun and that the long drawn resolution of an issue from the past would somehow be brought to an end. The people rushed to the churches and prayed:

> When they read the Tsar's manifesto the people crossed themselves and everyone congratulated each other on the war. We have seen this with our own eyes and heard it, and all this is happening even here in Petersburg. And once more the same activities have begun and the same facts come to light as last year: peasants in rural districts are donating money, as their means allow, and sending carts; and suddenly these thousands of people exclaim as one, donations and carts are little enough; we will all go off to fight![26]

There was an instinctive premonition of a new beginning. Yet, Dostoevsky noted that skepticism among some wise men continued. These "wise" men, members of the intelligentsia questioned Russia's readiness, morally and materially, to take such a decisive step. They argued that Russia should seek a prolonged peace in order to overcome internal disorganization and only then help the embattled South Slavs. Dostoevsky thought that such narrow spiritual horizons promoted social decay and isolation. He questioned whether a narrow-minded attitude would help the transformation of Russians "from beasts and blockheads into real people." [27]

Dostoevsky stressed that the Russian intelligentsia should no longer remain isolated from its people. He trusted that everyone would eventually turn away from these skeptics and invest their hopes in the Tsar and his people. Throughout Russia, people in all walks of life offered help in a generous and selfless way. Dostoevsky believed that the Russian people knew their political, social, and moral mission, although enserfed until recently and often disparaged by the same "wise men," members of the intelligentsia. [28]

Dostoevsky concluded that the Russo-Turkish war would not only help "our brothers Slavs" who have been suffering from the Turks. The war would help broaden the narrow domestic horizons

---

[26] Dostoevsky, *A Writer's Diary*, p. 930.

[27] Dostoevsky, *A Writer's Diary*, p. 930.

[28] Dostoevsky, *A Writer's Diary*, pp. 894-900.

and help solve the internal disorganization and stagnation. Most importantly, the war should help to bridge the alienation of the intelligentsia from its people. Dostoevsky trusted that the solution of the Eastern Question would heal many internal rifts and bring salvation to Russia as well.[29]

Tsar's decision was praised in England by Lord Gladstone. A politician of considerable stature, Gladstone acknowledged the Russian declaration of war as a noble and visionary act. He expressed his forthright admiration for Russia's intervention in the liberation of Southern Slavs. Dostoevsky promptly published Gladstone's response in his Diary of July and August of 1977:

> Whatever one might say about certain other chapters of Russian history, by the liberation of many millions of enslaved peoples from a cruel and humiliating yoke, Russia renders humanity one of the most splendid services history can recall, a service which shall never be erased from the grateful memory of a nation. [30]

As Dostoevsky predicted, Tolstoy eventually revised his position, "and started saying all the things we are saying," casting his support for the South Slavs. According to the testimony of his wife Sofia Andreevna, Tolstoy decided to join the Russian volunteers:

> All the Russia is there, and I should go myself. It took a great deal of persuasion to convince him that he could accomplish more with his writings at home than with his travel to the far away Balkans. [31]

It is noteworthy, that some thirty years later, at the crucial moment of the Austrian annexation of Bosnia-Hercegovina, Tolstoy stood once again firmly behind the Serbian cause. He decided to cast his voice and authority against the Austrian annexation of Bosnia

---

29 Dostoevsky, *A Writer's Diary*, p. 930.

30 Dostoevsky, *A Writer's Diary*, p. 1188.

31 A. Pisarev, "Traditisii druzhby narodov kak iavlenie kul'tury: Osvoboditel'naia bor'ba balkanskikh narodov protiv osmanskogo iga i rossiiskaia intelligentsiia." *Sovetskaia kul'tura 70 let razvitiia,* Ed. B.B. Piotrovskii, Moscow, Nauka 1987, p. 98.

and Hercegovina. Approaching the end of his life, he wrote one of his last finished and published books, *On the Austrian Annexation of Bosnia-Hercegovina.* Tolstoy presented his views and discussed once again the Eastern Question in a historic perspective. The book was published in Berlin in 1908.[32]

Dostoevsky observed correctly that although Russia was aiming to liberate the Slavs from Turkish oppression, the liberation alone would not solve all the inherent difficulties: it was only the beginning of a long process. Most importantly, Russia should not use this event to promote any self-serving or nationalistic goals:

> We shall be first to declare to the world that it is not by suppressing the national personalities of other tribes that we strive to achieve our own well-being; on the contrary we see that well-being only in the freest and most independent development of all other nations and in fraternal unity with them, each enhancing the other, learning from them and teaching them ... having achieved universal unity through the communion of nations of the world ...[33]

Dostoevsky knew that these words were not new but old, yet he believed that the faith in Slavdom would not wither away. The path leading to the new world order was already chartered: Russia had entered an unprecedented war for the sake of the weak and oppressed, to give them liberty, not to take it away. Russia had drawn her sword against the Turks. Dostoevsky interpreted the Russian declaration of war as a confirmation of Slavophile's faith in Russia's capacity to undertake the settlement of the Eastern Question:

> What's the purpose of all this? Why should Russia take on such a task? The purpose of it is to live a higher life, a superior life; to illuminate the world with a great, selfless, and pure idea ... If nations do not live by superior, selfless ideas and by the superior

---

[32] The book was entitled: *O prisoedinenii Bosnii i Ertsegoviny k Avstrii.* Quoted after I.I. Anisimov et al., *Tolstoi i zarubezhnyi mir*, Moscow, Akademiia nauk SSSR, 1965, pp. 302, 494, 502.

[33] Dostoevsky, *A Writer's Diary*, p. 936-937.

> aims of serving humanity, but only to serve their own "interests," than these nations will certainly perish; they will lose feeling, grow impotent, and die. But there are no aims higher than those which Russia sets for herself in selflessly serving the Slavs and not demanding their gratitude ...[34]

In the final analysis, Alexander II also chose the high road upholding Russia's honor and commitment to the South Slavs. The diplomatic negotiations with Turkey have not achieved the desired results since the Porte refused to ameliorate the condition of the Christian population in the Balkans. Alexander II tried to avoid the military confrontation: he knew that he had to wage the war alone although the proposition of reforms was negotiated in concert with the European powers. He knew of the possible high human and economic costs, yet he felt that he had to defend Russia's long standing commitment to the South Slav cause protecting their human rights. His concern was shared by the Russian people who showed readiness to make new sacrifices. Alexander aspired to safeguard Russia's honorable position and assert Russia's moral, political and military strength.

Both Tolstoy and his splendid colloquist Dostoevsky offered in their complementary testimonies an exceptional insight in the inherent complexities of the political reality in the Balkans and Russia. Dostoevsky repeated that only Russia's selfless help manifesting benevolent disinterestedness can bring the true resolution of old conflicts.

Thus, the analyses of the Eastern Question expostulated by great writers remain to be invaluable for all those willing to learn. Dostoevsky referred to Tolstoy as to the distinguished teacher of all the Russians since the great writers should be the teachers of a nation. Dostoevsky himself remained to be the Teacher: he understood the universality of the human quest, a quality that he admired in Pushkin and professed to be, at the best, a Russian trait. Dostoevsky's own evaluation of the complexities of the historic, social, and political realities in the Balkans and in Russia remained valuable even at the close of the twentieth century.

---

34 Dostoevsky, *A Writer's Diary*, p. 1204.

Chapter 3

BENJAMIN VON KALLAY'S REASSESSMENT OF THE EASTERN QUESTION: CONCEPTS FOR A SOLUTION

Benjamin von Kállay's professional entanglement with Serbia's foreign policies attested to his long-standing interest in the Eastern Question and related issues. Kállay's early political career was influenced by his study of nationalities and, in particular, in the issues regarding the Serbian minority in Hungary. In 1865, Kállay decided to run for a seat in the Parliament as a representative of the Serbian minority in the district of Saint-André (Szent-Endre). He was only 26 years old when he campaigned among the voters in this Serbian community for their support. This campaign marked the beginning of Kállay's long and distinguished political career. Although Kállay did not win the election, his campaign brought him to the attention of the influential statesman Gyula Andrássy.

Following the Compromise Agreement, the Austro-Hungarian government decided to appoint a new consul to the Serbian court.[1] In March of 1868, with Andrássy's recommendation, Kállay was appointed to the post of the general consul and special diplomatic agent to the court of the Serbian Prince Mihailo Obrenović. This was Kállay's first diplomatic mission and he approached his task

---

1 Ludwig von Thallóczy, "Einleitung, Lebensbild und Persönlichkeit Benjamin von Kállays," *Geschichte des Serbischen Aufstandes 1804-1810,* p. IX.

with great determination, aiming to distinguish himself in his mission, and to justify the confidence shown to him. [2]

In his formative years as a student, Kállay was inspired by the ideas of the Hungarian uprising of 1848-1849 that resulted in the short lived independence from Austrian rule. A number of Hungarian revolutionary leaders, such as Laszlo Teleki and Lajos Kossuth, aspired for a close collaboration with neighboring Balkan states. These political leaders projected Hungary's future in a broadly conceived union of Balkan states envisioning the possibility of a Hungarian-Serbian-Romanian federation.[3]

After the defeat of the Hungarian revolution, a number of Hungarian politicians strove to cultivate good relations with the representatives of the respective minorities in Hungary. Prior to the Compromise Agreement, the prominent personalities like Gyula Andrássy, Jozsef Eötvös, Kalman Tisza, Pal Nyary, Benjamin Kállay, and others, had attended Serbian public events in Budapest and in the Serbian enclave of Saint-André (Szent-Endre). Notably, the celebration of St. Sava's Day was observed by acknowledging the continuity of Serbian literacy and cultural heritage.[4]

Such an event was recorded on the pages of a Serbian newspaper published in St. André. In August 1865, Kállay came to St. André to attend the graduation ceremony. Earlier, he had promised to the magistrate in St. André the sum of three ducats yearly as a prize for the students who had excelled in studies of Serbian language and catechism. Kállay obviously remembered the benefits from his own bilingual educational background. There was a sizable and prosperous Serbian minority centered around Saint André. The

---

[2] Thalóczy, Einleitung, *Geschichte des serbischen Aufstandes 1807-1810*, p. IX. Compare also Andrija Radenić , Ed., *Dnevnik Benjamina Kalaja 1868-1875*, Belgrade, Novi-Sad, Istorijski institut za istoriju Vojvodine, 1976, pp. 8-9.

[3] Compare, Milorad Ekmečić , "Garašanin, Čartoriski i Madjari 1848-1849," *Srpsko-madjarski odnosi i saradnja 1848-1867*, Odeljenje jezika i knjizevnosti, SANU, Belgrade, 1987.

[4] Radenić , *Dnevnik Benjamina Kalaja*, pp. XII-XV.

reception, that had been arranged for Kállay, became a public event with many guests in attendance. The students greeted Kállay while holding a Serbian flag, and Kállay responded "in a powerful and well spoken Serbian language." [5]

During this convocation Kállay's article entitled "Glas iz Ugarske" (A Voice from Hungary) was read from the pulpit. His article was recently published and obviously well received as an important contribution to the ongoing discussion concerning nationality issues. The reading was interrupted several times with tumultuous approval. Kállay then took the floor and concluded: "Gentlemen, I would like this nice union to encompass all of our peoples. Let God grant to the Serbs and Hungarians from today to be true and sincere to each other like real blood brothers." These friendly visitations promoting goodwill diminished after the Compromise. Already in January of 1867, a newspaper article stated that only the St. André representative Ach, and the landowner Kállay attended the Saint Sava celebration in Pest while other personalities, who usually attended these festivities, were absent.[6]

Kállay arrived in Belgrade on April 19, 1868. Already the next day, Kállay was summoned to present his credentials to Prince Mihailo Obrenović. Kállay left a vivid description in his diary of his first visit to the Serbian court. At the appointed time, the Prince had kindly dispatched his aide with a carriage for the Austrian diplomats. Kállay arrived at the court accompanied by the former Austrian consul, August von Lenk, who was his predecessor. Kállay and Lenk

---

[5] Kállay's visit was discussed in retrospect by Dimitrije E. Stefanović in his rendition of the biography of Petar Rimski supplied with extensive bibliography, "Autobiografija Petra Rimskog 1800-1874," *Sveske Matice srpske*, Gradja i prilozi za kulturu I drustvenu istoriju, Novi Sad, 1986, p. 12. Petar Rimski was the organizer of this festivity. Rimski was a minister and well respected religious instructor in the Serbian school in St. André. Compare also, Dr. Mih. Gavrilović , "Kalaj o prvom srpskom ustanku od 1807-1810," *Srpska riječ* No. 277, 18/31. December,1910, Sarajevo, 1910. Quoted after Tomislav Kraljačić , *Kalajev rezim u Bosni i Hercegovini*, Sarajevo, Veselin Masleša, 1987, p. 47.

[6] Ibid.

were escorted to the yellow salon where Kállay presented his accreditation to Prince Mihailo. Lenk formally introduced Kállay to the Prince as his successor. Kállay than gave a speech explaining that his appointment to the position of a diplomatic agent, in addition to consular duties, presented a new proof of sympathies towards the Prince and Serbian people. Afterwards, Kállay noted in his diary that his speech was too short, and that he managed to say only half of what he intended to convey. He attributed his somewhat abrupt talk to his inexperience in similar matters. He obviously felt overwhelmed by the novelty of the diplomatic pomp and circumstance.[7]

According to Kállay's entry in his diary, Prince Mihailo responded in fluent French language expressing his pleasure in endorsing Kállay's appointment. Kállay knew that it was customary to praise the new appointee, but hoped to deserve much higher praise after accomplishing his mission in Serbia and taking his final leave. Kállay evidently intended to devote himself wholeheartedly to the improvement of reciprocal relations between Austria-Hungary and Serbia.

Kállay was uniquely qualified for this position. He spoke Serbian well since he had devoted great attention to the study of Serbian history and culture. Kállay's interest for Serbian history was in part due to the fact that his mother Amalie née Blaskovic de Ebetska, was of Serbian descent. Her noble ancestors left Serbia after the onslaught of the Turkish invasion and settled in Hungary. The subsequent Turkish occupation caused great demographic shifts and two major migrations of the predominantly wealthy population from the southern regions of Serbia. The descendants of these families preserved, by and large, the legacy of their forebears; they erected churches and schools in the new settlements forming Serbian enclaves in Hungarian territory. In time, the members of the Serbian upper social class became gradually integrated into the new society and often distinguished themselves serving their new homeland

7 Radenić , *Dnevnik Benjamina Kalaja*, p. 5.

well. Yet many of them continued to support the educational, professional, and literary endeavors of Serbs in Hungary by forming humanitarian foundations such as the famous Tekelianum, the endowment created by the philanthropist Sava Tekelija.

Kállay's father came from one of the oldest families in Hungary with land grants in the region of Great Kaloa which were in their possession from the early thirteenth century. The Kállay family's high social prestige was well established, although their land holdings were encumbered with debts and many mortgages. His father, Stephan Kállay, had served for 30 years as a high governmental officer and administrator of the Maramaros district. Stephan Kállay was not a participant of the 1848 revolution, he died in 1845 when his son was only five years old.[8]

Amalie von Kállay took over the care for Kállay's education and directed his interest to Slavic studies, and in particular to Serbian history. She spoke Serbian and it is very likely that her son heard some of her reminiscences relating to the country of her ancestors. She engaged two excellent teachers in the persons of Josef Benedek de Csik-Tusnad and Mihalj Tančić (Tancsics). Tančić was well known as a populist tribune and revolutionary publicist. He was also of Serbian extraction.[9]

While her son occupied the position of the Austro-Hungarian consul in Belgrade, Amalie von Kállay visited him often, and sometime accompanied by her daughters. She was accepted by the highest social circles and exchanged visits with the Serbian social elite including the venerated matriarch of the ruling dynasty

---

[8] Thallóczy, Einleitung, *Die Geschichte des Serbischen Aufstandes 1807-1810*, Vienna 1910, p. XII.

[9] Gyorgy Spira, *The Nationality Issue in the Hungary of 1848-1849*, Budapest, Kiado, 1992, pp. 86-87. Josef Benedek, who also taught the young Kállay, was of Slovak extraction.

Tomanija Obrenović. She followed political and cultural life both in Hungary and in Serbia to the end of her life.[10]

Prior to Kállay's departure to take up the new post in Belgrade, the Austro-Hungarian minister for foreign affairs, Friedrich Ferdinand von Beust, instructed him about the desired political goals and diplomatic policies of the Monarchy.[11] These policies were outlined in confidential papers dated 5 April 1868. Beust recognized the potency of the spirit of nationalism spreading among the South Slavs. The Serbian state, acting as a moving force, could proceed to unite the South Slavs and establish close ties with other Slavic nations. Beust was opposed to the formation of a strong Slavic state in the Balkans. Moreover, Beust stressed that the Serbian aspirations in regards to Bosnia-Hercegovina could not be supported by Austria-Hungary. Under no circumstances should Serbia be allowed to take over these provinces, even if Serbia would elect to continue paying tribute to the Porte.

Clearly, Beust had in mind the Italian struggle for unification and the resulting Austrian losses of Italian provinces Lombardy and Venetia. Beust reasoned that a strong Slavic state would present another threat to the integrity of the whole of Monarchy. Kállay was advised to refute the existence of any Austro-Hungarian annexation plans in regard to Bosnia-Hercegovina. Most of all Serbia should be warned not to start an aggressive action against Turkey under Russian influence. Kállay was to explain that Turkey, although not as strong as before, was still in command of an impressive military force.[12]

Shortly after his arrival in Belgrade, Kállay summed up his evaluation of the situation in Serbia in one of his first reports addressed to Beust. Kállay aimed to present a broad picture by

---

[10] Ludwig von Thallóczy, *Benjamin Kállay, Gedenkrede*, Budapest 1909, pp. 6-7;

[11] Radenić , *Dnevnik Benjamina Kalaja*, p. XXI.

[12] Haus-, Hof- und Staatsarchiv; PA, Serbien, XXXVII K.17. Quoted after Radenić , *Dnevnik Benjamina Kalaja*, p. XXI.

discussing the conditions in Serbia and also in the Serbian provinces under Turkish rule. All in all, he thought that the South Slav provinces under Turkish domination were weak, and accordingly presented no inherent danger to the Monarchy. Moreover, Kállay realized that the Serbian people strongly supported the aim for national independence and therefore needed help. If they could rely on the good offices of Austria-Hungary in pursuing the Serbian struggle for independence, as well as for their political and material growth, then "not one Serb would think about Russia anymore." Such a Serbia would be, in Kállay's opinion, "the strongest barrier against the Russian aspirations and Panrussianess." [13]

As a new member of the diplomatic corps, Kállay was introduced to Milivoje Blaznavac, the eminent statesman and minister of warfare. Kállay soon became well acquainted with Blaznavac and shared long talks while attending various functions, social outings and riverside entertainment. Kállay recorded in his diary a conversation with Blaznavac on 26 June 1868, including his own commentaries. Kállay obviously felt that the conversation was important as it revealed similar outlooks in regard to the fate of Balkan states and the Eastern question.[14]

Blaznavac considered it as necessary, for the time being, to uphold the integrity of the Turkish Empire as a buffer against Russian imperialistic aspirations in the Balkans. Blaznavac thought that the rule over Bosnia-Hercegovina should eventually pass to the Serbian government, with the provision that Serbia would continue to pay tribute to the Porte. Blaznavac was ready to eliminate the customs barriers provided the friendly collaboration between Hungary and Serbia continued. Blaznavac believed that the South Slavs, Hungarians, Greeks, and Romanians were called upon to organize a strong alliance. The formal organization of this alliance

---

[13] Kállay to Friedrich Ferdinand von Beust , 22 June 1868. DAB, PA, XXXVIII, Haus, Hof und Staatsarchiv. Quoted after Kraljačić , *Kalajev režim u Bosni I Hercegovini 1882-1903,* Sarajevo, Veselin Masleša, 1987, p. 50.

[14] Radenić , *Dnevnik Bejamina Kalaja 1868-1875,* p. 44.

could not be determined right away but it could be formed either as a large Danubian republic or a confederation of smaller states. It was his opinion that only such an alliance could safeguard their future and could create greatness for each state individually and for all of them together. After the meeting, Kállay recorded his conversation with Blaznavac in his *Diary* in an entry dated June 26, 1868.[15]

Kállay shared the same opinion. He readily remembered that since his student days at the Budapest University he had entertained the idea of an imagined confederation of Balkan nations. He envisaged a Danubian confederation of independent nations as an ideal solution for all Balkan states. He was also cognizant of the importance of a just resolution of minority issues and in particular of the Serbian question within the multinational Hungarian state.

> My old ideas. All that Milivoje said occupied my thoughts for a long time. The Great Danubian confederation was present in my views, a confederation based on democratic principles uniting different but approximately equal in size people, each fearing that a foreign power would encroach on their respective nationality and individuality. United in a friendly union all of them can safeguard their individuality and protect each other from foreign influences. It would be an unusual quirk of destiny if I could assist in the realization of these ideas. I was carried away by these ideas already as a youth, alone in my lonely little room. Milivoj promised to talk to me in greater detail, but only with me, and without any intermediary when things calm down. I do not have any reason to suspect Milivoj's sincerity, especially since he disclosed his plan about Bosnia. All this seemed plausible including his (Blaznavac's) own personal ambition; I should trust him in this respect. He very likely concealed that, in his vision of the future, he gave the main role to Serbia, as I also did not reveal that I gave the same place to Hungary. I could not

---

15 Radenić ,*Dnevnik Benjamina Kalaja 1868-1875*, pp. 44-46.

resist to tell him that if he would succeed in this plan, he would be one of the greatest men of the more recent times.[16]

Furthermore, Blaznavac expressed his assurance that he would strive to establish an alliance between Hungary and Serbia. This alliance would protect both Hungary and Serbia from Russian or Turkish influences, as well as from Austrian intrusions. Blaznavac thought that a Hungarian-Serbian rapprochement would be beneficial in many ways. Thus, Blaznavac would even encourage the Serbian population in Hungary to improve relations with Hungarian administration. It seemed as if Blaznavac assumed that Kállay was foremost a Hungarian politician concerned mainly for the future of Hungary, and that these concerns took precedence over Kállay's allegiance to the Austrian Monarchy.

While serving as the Austro-Hungarian diplomat in Belgrade, Kállay was intermittently reprimanded for his continuous support of the notion of a Danubian confederation. Thus, an article in the paper *Neue Freie Presse,* published in Vienna, stated that Kállay was not helping to sustain and consolidate diplomatic ties with Serbia. Kállay had been cast in the diplomatic career from an obscure milieu of a gentry's estate. Overall, the main culprits for the worsening of relation with Serbia were the Hungarian political leaders who "imagined in their arrogance that the East is their domain." Kállay's mission as the Austro-Hungarian consul was supposed to strengthen the influence of the Dual Monarchy. Still, the unknown writer of the report stated bluntly that Kállay did not succeed in promoting his diplomatic mission since he was most of all a staunch supporter of Hungarian aspirations for a Balkan commonwealth.[17]

---

16 *Dnevnik Benjamina Kalaja 1868-1875,* pp. 44-45. This conversation took place shortly after the demise of Prince Mihailo. Hence, Blaznavac reference to the unsettled situation and assurance that he would elaborate more about future plans "when things calm down."

17 *Neue Freie Presse,* 18 August 1872, No 2867. Quoted after Radenić , *Dnevnik Benjamina Kalaja,* pp. 116, 438, 450.

In August of 1868, Kállay decided to visit Andrássy in his country home Terebesh were Andrássy was vacationing. Kállay obviously felt a need to visit his former mentor and report about the situation in Serbia. He also discussed the essence of his numerous talks with Blaznavac. Kállay pointed out that the South Slavs, and Serbs in particular, were not exceedingly attached to Russia. If any sentiment of loyalty existed it was because Russia had helped them in the past. Kállay reasoned that if Hungary would help, the Serbs would develop favorable relations with Hungary especially with the present regime headed by the Regency.[18]

Kállay discussed the feasibility of handing parts of Bosnia over to Serbia. Andrássy was in favor and agreed with Kállay about the advantages of such a plan. Kállay believed that the Serbian government showed sympathies for Hungary and trusted that only Andrássy could arrange for a rapprochement with Serbia.

Andrássy was pleased with Kállay's assessment and he authorized Kállay to convey to the Serbian government his support for their plans about Bosnia. According to Kállay's notes entered in his diary, Andrássy suggested that the Serbs should write a memorandum explaining the validity of their idea and the manner of its execution. Andrássy demanded that the memorandum would provide for the continuous integrity of Turkey. In addition, Kállay urged for a swift agreement about the postal convention with Serbia. He also transmitted the wish of the Serbian government for a trading treaty.[19]

In December of 1870, Kállay visited the eminent Serbian politician and ruling regent Jovan Ristić . Kállay mentioned that the members of the diplomatic corps were discussing the problems facing Bosnia-Hercegovina. In particular, the French consul Engelhardt thought that the time had come, and "something should be done about Bosnia." The Russian consul in Belgrade, Nikolai Pavlovich Shishkin, stated that Russia was willing to help with this question.

---

[18] Radenić ,*Dnevnik Bejamina Kalaja 1868-1875*, pp. 77-78.

[19] Radenić ,*Dnevnik Bejamina Kalaja 1868-1875*, p. 78.

Kállay then informed Ristić that "the ideas that we have discussed were generally speaking acceptable. The Emperor was informed and he had approved; the treaty should be signed by the minister of foreign affairs." [20]

Kállay suggested that "since the war was not imminent we could come to a basic understanding that could be useful for the eventual conclusion of the treaty." Ristić took a piece of paper and noted the following tentative agreement:

1. In the case that Serbia would come to a conflict with the Porte, Serbia would be responsible to provide this information to Austria-Hungary. During this confrontation, Austria-Hungary would remain neutral and even urge others not to intervene.

2. In the case of a war between Austria and Russia, Serbia should remain neutral. In return Austria-Hungary promised to secure for Serbia the provinces of Bosnia-Hercegovina and Old Serbia after the end of war, under the same conditions under which Serbia was presently bound to Turkey. The borders would be determined later. As soon as Serbia took possession of the mentioned provinces, the regions from Vrbas and Neretva would be annexed to Austria. Ristić also added a provision that if Serbia should capture Bosnia-Hercegovina and Old Serbia with military force, the hegemony of Turkey should cease and Serbia should be declared independent. Kállay declared that he could not respond right away since this version of the agreement was new to him and different from previous negotiations. He wanted to talk to Blaznavac and afterwards confer about the matter. [21]

Kállay thought often about the situation in Bosnia and recorded in his diary his innermost thoughts concerning the Eastern Question. He repeatedly broached the possible solution, and reasoned that if

---

[20] Radenić ,*Dnevnik Bejamina Kalaja 1868-1875,* pp. 348-349. The entry was dated 27 December, 1870. Shishkin (1830-1912) was consul in Belgrade from 1863 to 1875.

[21] Radenić , *Dnevnik Benjamina Kalaja,* pp. 348- 349. This entry was dated 27 December 1870.

Bosnia-Hercegovina would be given to Serbia two important political goals would be reached. Firstly, the separation of Serbia from Russia, and in turn Serbia would establish firm ties with the Monarchy. Secondly, this move would help the creation of a perpetual division between the Serbs and Croats. Bosnia would became the "apple of discord" between the competing Serbian and Croatian parties thus preventing internal consolidation. On a sinister note, Kállay presumed that this intervention would end the Serbo-Croat collaboration towards establishing an unified Yugoslav platform and the existing rapprochement would necessarily end. The possible contention arising among the Serbs and Croats would paralyze the energies from both parties and ensure the hegemony of the Germans and Hungarians in the Habsburg Monarchy.

For such great political gains, Kállay was ready to give to the Serbs "Bosnia or a larger part of the regions." Moreover, he thought, the realization of these plans would have unforeseen beneficial consequences for the Monarchy, and in particular for Hungary.[22]

While serving in Belgrade, Kállay used every opportunity to learn more about Serbia and Serbian people traveling to many towns and villages. Kállay noted that he started his first travel, in autumn of 1868, visiting East-Serbia. It was a fortuitous coincidence that Kállay could join F. Ph. Kanitz who already had extensive knowledge of Serbia. Kanitz planned to spend two weeks touring the Krajina region in East Serbia in order to continue his previous research. Kállay used this opportunity to join Kanitz whose latest book, *Serbien, Historisch-ethnographische Reisestudien 1859-1868,* and a travelogue: *Reise in Sudserbien und Nordbulgarien im Jahre 1864* were just published.[23]

---

22 Radenić , *Dnevnik Benjamina Kalaja,* pp. 116, 450 and 436.

23 F. Ph. Kanitz, *Serbien, Historisch-ethnographische Reisestudien aus dem Jahren1859-1868,* Leipzig 1868. Also, *Reise in Sudserbien und Nordbulgarien im Jahre 1864* , Denkschrift der kaiserlichen Akademie der Wissenschaften, Vienna 1868.

During the travel through East Serbia in Kanitz's company, Kállay discovered that the churches and monasteries were not kept in good repair. Moreover, Kállay noticed that many churches and monasteries were destroyed or greatly damaged. Even the repair of some of the destroyed churches required a permission from the Muslim overlords which was hard to receive. The ones which remained in fairly good conditions were situated in hard to reach and secluded places, such as river gorges or rocky precipices. These sights were chosen to discourage an easy plunder of the premises. Only very few churches still existed more or less intact and were open for worship. Kállay was surprised by the scarcity of churches: approximately every tenth village had a church, and people had to travel sometimes a considerable distance for religious celebrations, weddings, baptisms and in particular the yearly meetings *sabor*. Many churches did not have a belfry even in more important towns like Negotin, Zaječar, and Radujevac. The Turks did not allow a highly visible display of crosses or the sound of the church bells. Therefore, people used to carve the sign of a cross on tree trunks serving as markers *(zapis)* for the processional route on special religious holidays.[24]

Kállay's visitations of the remote monasteries and churches had not been easy since these edifices were situated often in the mountainous areas and hard to reach places. Kállay observed correctly that the monasteries safeguarding old manuscripts, frescoes and icons were important "supporters and guardians of nationality."[25]

Kállay left a unique travelogue embedded in his writing about historic events of the past. On his extensive tours he visited often remote sights yet he never complained about any shortcomings or difficulties in traveling the distant country roads. Nor did he mention possible discomfort of lodgings in modest inns by the roadside. Once he slept in the courtyard of an inn under the sky's

---

24 Kállay, *Geschichte der Serben*, pp. 200 -201.

25 Kállay, *Geschichte der Serben*, p. 204.

canopy since all rooms had been taken. He chose to remember only the beauty of the countryside and historic edifices that he obviously admired. His travels through Serbia seemed to present a pilgrimage to the country of his maternal forbears, and he walked in their footsteps retracing their life's odysseys.

His interest in Serbian landmarks and history guided him in his numerous trips that he found even more beguiling than previously imagined. Furthermore, he himself wrote that he spent many years studying Serbian and Russian languages, history and literature, and therefore had already a heightened sense of appreciation when visiting some of the places he tried to envisage earlier in his thoughts.

He traveled often throughout Serbia and neighboring regions under Ottoman rule in order to gain more knowledge about the people and their livelihood. He admired the natural beauty of the lush green countryside as well as the impressive landmarks of the historic past. He collected various artifacts produced in the country and amassed an extensive collection of folk art which he eventually bestowed to the Museum in Budapest.[26]

In addition to his official duties of a general consul, Kállay diligently pursued research for his book dealing with the history of Serbs. He conducted extensive archival research examining a great number of sources. He had the opportunity to examine some original documents *de viso* in various libraries and archives in Belgrade. The eminent historian Stojan Novaković who served as the Librarian of the Serbian Learned Society, noted Kállay's daily presence in the reading hall of the Society's Library.

Novaković held Kállay in high esteem as a hard working and informed historian. He also appreciated Kállay's diplomatic efforts as a young consul espousing Serbophile notions. Novaković praised Kállay's first book titled *Geschichte der Serben (History of Serbs)* as a book written by a scholar with an open mind. It was a book penned

---

26 *Vidov dan,* No 97, 1875, Quoted after A. Radenić , *Dnevnik Benjamina Kalaja*, p. XXXIV.

by a historian who was a "free thinker." [27] Novaković had a different opinion about the second book written by Kállay *Geschichte des serbischen Aufstandes 1807-1810.* He thought that Kállay adopted another attitude in the presentation of researched data pertaining to the history of the Serbian uprising. Novaković compared Kállay's changed approach to that of a statesman "carefully formulating his evaluations."[28]

In the Foreword to his *History of Serbs,* Kállay noted that he "copied about 600 documents from the University Library in Belgrade that were, to a large extent, not yet published." Kállay mentioned also several reference works that he used for writing his book: Ranke's book on the Serbian revolution *Die Serbische Revolution (The Serbian Revolution),* Nil Popov the relations between Serbia and Russia *Serbia i Rossia (Serbia and Russia),* Matija Nenadović 's *Memoari (Memoirs).* His knowledge of languages and his long-standing pursuit of Slavic studies enabled him to examine the necessary literature and primary sources, and to better comprehend the innermost life of the Serbs, their way of reasoning, customs and habits,*"die richtigere Auffassung des inneren Lebens der Serben, ihrer Denkweise, Sitten und Gebräuche."* [29]

In the Foreword to his *History of Serbs* , Kállay stated that his main intention was to write objectively the historical truth as much as he could discern it. He stressed that he did not want to write "even one line guided by sympathy or antipathy." Instead, he hoped to evaluate impartially the available data: *"Mein Hauptstreben war: getreu der historischen Wahrheit, insofern ich nämlich diese aufdecken vermochte."* [30]

---

[27] Stojan Novaković , "Vaskrs drave srpske i njegovi istorici," Offprint *from Godiišnjica Nikole Cupica,* Vol. 30, Belgrade, Državna štamparija, 1910, pp. 5-6.

[28] Novaković , "Vaskrs države srpske i njegovi istorici,"p. 6.

[29] Kállay, *Geschichte der Serben,* pp. V -VIII.

[30] Kállay, *Geschichte der Serben,* p. VIII.

Kállay felt that his residence in Serbia helped him in the understanding of Serbian people, their ethical and moral codes. It was fortuitous that he could examine valuable sources and documents that would have been difficult or even impossible otherwise. He traveled extensively through Serbia visiting famous historic sites and monasteries showing a keen interest for the people, their religious and secular customs.

He was enchanted by the natural beauty of Serbia and even described the countryside that impressed him:

> There is no other land in Europe that is so blessed by nature as Serbia. The fertile soil stretches not only in the plains of Mačva or throughout the wide Morava valley, but extends also to the mountain sides almost to the very top. Moreover, there are forests with enormous trees; meadows and fields watered by numerous rivers and streams. Mountain chains are rich with ore and coal deposits and already the Romans established profitable mining operations. The hillsides are covered with vineyards, and almost in every district there are mineral water wells. Finally the Morava valley, stretching from the north to the south all the way to Danube, offers the shortest connecting thoroughfare of the occidental trading route—these are all the advantages that if managed right could transform Serbia into one of the richest lands. Nature endowed propitiously this rather small country with natural treasures as well as with beauty. Rolling hills, smiling valleys, rocky precipices and long stretches of mountains interchange in a picturesque way …. With the exception of a few rocky stretches, the meadows and fields everywhere retain the vibrant green hues until late autumn gracing this land with unexpected and beautiful sights.[31]

Kállay than briefly described some of the places he repeatedly visited while residing in Serbia. He mentioned the fertile plains of

---

31 Kállay, *Geschichte der Serben*, pp. 182-183.

Mačva extending to the cliffs overlooking the Drina river. On one of this rocky heights, he visited the fortress Sokol. He traveled along the rivers Ibar and Morava. He also visited the cities of Karanovac and Krusevac. He climbed the Kopaonik mountain in order to have a glimpse of the faraway Kosovo battle field.

Kállay then continued to guide his readers through the regions and townships he frequented and knew well. His lively style of writing testified to his keen appreciation of the inherent beauty of the places on his itinerary. He described a number of places in great detail, such as the Roman archeological sites and mosaics in the vicinity of Gamzigrad in East Serbia. He also admired the steep sides of the near by mountain Rtanj rising some five thousand feet above the plains. He noted the fragrance of the lush herb and grasses on the foothills surrounding Rtanj perfuming the clean mountain air.[32]

Kállay did not only visit interesting places, he also liked to meet the people and attend some of the local festivities. He noted that he visited several times the yearly gatherings known as *sabor* commemorating a patron saint of a monastery. Kállay pointed out that the monasteries had enjoyed a special place as religious edifices as well as places of learning and enlightenment. The clergy was highly regarded as spritual advisors and learned teachers. He described *sabor* as a unique festivity that provided an opportunity for people to meet and discuss matters of mutual interest. In particular, young people seemed to enjoy each others company. They would dance in a round the traditional *kolo* accompanied by the tunes played on a recorder*(frula)* or a bagpipe *(gajde)*. Some heads of households conducted business deals and others had some personal goals to accomplish. Kállay praised the good food and the roasted meat on a spit but he singled out the thick sour broth *(kisela čorba)* and proclaimed it to be an ubiquitous national dish.[33]

---

32 Kállay, *Geschichte der Serben*, p. 183. This area is famous for its rare herbs with medicinal value that are presently harvested and managed by a number of pharmaceutical companies in Sokobanja and Zaječar.

33 Kállay, *Geschichte der Serben*, pp. 205-206.

Kállay was admired by many for his knowledge of Serbia and his efforts on Serbia's behalf. Nevertheless, as a diplomatic agent representing both Austria and Hungary in the Serbian capital, he often bore the brunt of rebukes in view of new policies of reprisals instituted by the Hungarian administration in Voivodina after the Compromise Agreement. The writer Jovan Jovanović -Zmaj, who was a well-known physician, wrote a number of satirical verses illustrating the discontent of the Serbian population. The cited verses were popular in the early 1870s:

Kalaj viče:
Milane! Zdravo gospodaru!
Primi opet madjarsko prijateljstvo staro.
Milan opet Kalaju: Zašt' robuje Laza?
Il' u slavu moje vlade? Il madjarske pravde."

(Kállay is shouting: Milan! Greetings to the Chief. Please accept again the old Hungarian friendship.

Milan is replying to Kállay. Why is Laza in prison? Is this in celebration of my rule? Or because of Hungarian justice.)[34]

Jovanović -Zmaj bemoaned the gradual suspension of civil liberties and worsening of general living conditions of the population in Voivodina following the Compromise Agreement. Oppressive measures were introduced by curtailing the freedom of assembly and free speech and by censoring journals, books and various other publications. The authorities vigorously monitored the whereabouts of prominent personalities and intensified the harassment and jailing of political leaders and well known writers with large followings. The latter was the fate of the outspoken and illustrious writer Laza Kostić who was mentioned in the quoted verses.

In 1875, Kállay asked to be relieved of his duty as a general consul in Serbia. Kállay wished to take a more active role in the political life of the Dual Monarchy. He was soon after seated as a representative in the Hungarian Parliament in Budapest. He also

34 Žiža, No. 30-31, 28. IX 1872. Quoted after Radenić , *Dnevnik Benjamina Kalaja*, p. XXXIII.

wanted to conclude the writing of his book which was devoted to the history of Serbian people. Kállay's *History of Serbs* was first published in Budapest in 1877. The German translation of his book, *Geschichte der Serben,* was published only one year later in Leipzig in 1878.[35] The timing of these publications was fortuitous since Kállay's *History of Serbs* appeared at the time when the Eastern question became central to the Austro-Hungarian political debate.[36]

Subsequently, Kállay's *History of Serbs* was translated into Serbian by Gavrilo Vitković , a cultural historian, who supplied an introduction praising Kállay's work. Kállay's *Istorija Srpskog naroda* was published in Belgrade in 1882. Kállay wrote a preface for the Serbian translation of his book stating that he wrote the *History of Serbs* guided by his great interest in the subject and by the desire to present objectively the historic events. Nonetheless, objectivity did not preclude his sincere appreciation for the history of Serbian people having in view his long residence in Serbia:

> It is only natural that I undertook the writing of the history of the Serbs with the feeling of special interest and real affinity. This history is important even from the general point of view, and more so than what one would consider it at first. In the Medieval Ages, the Serbian state did not exist only in the East, but had its place in Europe together with the best known and most powerful nations.[37]

---

[35] Benjamin von Kállay, *Geschichte der Serben.* Aus dem Ungarischen J.B. Schwicker, Budapest, Wien und Leipzig, Verlag W. Lauffer, 1878.

[36] Thalloczy, Einleitung, *Die Geschichte des serbischen Aufstandes 1807-1810,* pp. III-XXXIX.

[37] Venjamin Kalaji, *Istorija Srpskog Naroda,* preveo Gavrilo Vitković , Beograd, Državna štamparija, 1882, pp. X-XI. "Naravno je dakle, da sam, proživevši u Srbiji toliko godina, preduzeo ne samo sa interesom već i sa pravom simpatijom, da napišem istoriju srpskog naroda. Ova je istorija medju tim značajna već i sa opšteg pogleda. U srednjem veku srpska država ne samo na istoku, no može se reci i u ostaloj Evropi, umela je da izvojuje sebi mesto u redu najznatnijih i najsilnijih država."

While taking part in various sessions of the Hungarian Parliament, Kállay had repeated opportunities to address the members of the Parliament. Kállay succinctly summed up his political outlook in his speech delivered on 26 July 1877. According to Lajos Thaloczi, historian and long time personal friend, this speech presented the high point of Kállay's political career in the Parliament.

At the time, public consensus supported a strong Turkophile policy. This policy gained acceptance due to the fear of Russian influence in Balkan affairs. Turkey's presence in the Balkans was tolerated as a protective buffer against Russian expansion. Therefore, the Hungarian Parliament accepted the Turkophile policy with an overwhelming majority.

In his speech Kállay aimed to explicate the Hungarian position in relation to the surrounding Slavic countries. He also gave an overview of Panslav and Panrussian ideologies. Kállay became aware of the tense situation in the Parliament while he was delivering his speech. He was interrupted several times with loud shouting "Listen to the Moskowite" ("Hört den Moskowiter!) and even declared a Slavophile[38] According to Thalloczy, who witnessed the speech in the Parliament, Kállay continued calmly to proceed with his presentation.

Kállay argued that Turkey could eventually achieve a progressive development provided favorable conditions prevailed. He warned that one should not have a high opinion of the Turkish constitutionality. He would not delude himself or others about the fact that the Turkish state was on the way to disintegration. Turkey still possessed a considerable military might. However, even a successful intervention could accelerate the Turkish downfall with all its consequences of inner turmoil. Kállay stressed that he would not wish to see the dissolution of the Turkish Empire, but could not

---

[38]Thallóczy, Einleitung, p. XXV.

foresee the purported integrity of the Turkish state against existing odds.[39]

Kállay elucidated convincingly the situation in Turkey as well as in the neighboring Slav countries, pointing to the benefits of good relations. He pleaded for a just understanding of historic goals of Southern Slavs. He pointed out that the Slavs had asked time and again for Austrian help against Turkish oppression but were not given due consideration.[40]

In 1882, another uprising in Hercegovina manifested a powerful protest against the Austro-Hungarian administration. The uprising spread to Bosnia causing considerable concern throughout the Dual Monarchy. Public opinion expressed apprehension about the failure of the occupation in spite large expenditures for the military intervention. A number of members of the Parliament voiced their opposition to any further interference in Hercegovina, and suppression of the uprising. Conversely, some members of the ruling party feared that such an attitude would eventually result in the abandonment of both provinces. Although the uprising was eventually subdued, the situation in the provinces was not peaceful and orderly. A stream of refugees from Hercegovina, Muslim and Orthodox, had fled to the neighboring lands.

Benjamin von Kállay was called once again to serve the Austro-Hungarian government. On June 5 1882, Kállay was named to the position of the Joint Minister of Finance in charge of the occupied provinces of Bosnia-Hercegovina. Kállay was charged to restore peace and reestablish the authority of the Monarchy. Moreover, Kállay was expected to procure plans for a long lasting rule of the Austro-Hungarian government leading to the incorporation of Bosnia-Hercegovina into the Dual Monarchy.

---

[39]Thallóczy, Einleitung, p. XXV.

[40]Thallóczy pointed out that Kállay's views were not only the result of solidarity with the position of Julius Andrássy. Kállay expressed similar views already in 1875 in an article publisehd in the journal *Budapest Szemle* while he was still residing in Belgrade. p. XXV.

The longtime friend and colleague of Kállay, L. Thalloczy, thought that such far reaching and overly ambitious plans would inevitably fail to be realized in the relative short span of any politician's life. Yet, Kállay proceeded to solve some of the pressing problems on the road to consolidation.[41] As the highest officer in charge of the occupied provinces, Kállay observed most of all the interests of the Dual Monarchy. Kállay decided that the agrarian reforms in Bosnia-Hercegovina should be postponed in order to protect the position of the Muslim landowners counting on their support. Kállay argued that the wealthy landowners provided needed stability in the state building process in both provinces. Nevertheless, the needs and aspirations of the vast majority of impoverished rural population had not been considered. Furthermore, the rising state-sponsored industrialization drive was financed by additional taxation of the rural communities, supplemented by foreign, mostly German, investments. All these measures produced a stagnation of the largely agrarian economy already afflicted by low productivity. The consequences of uneven economic growth, and unresolved land reforms, remained at the center of a difficult social and economic situation.

Kállay repeatedly aimed to provide an overriding and lofty philosophy for his rule. As a historian, he felt that he had a better insight into the historical development that shaped the underlying make-up of the people in the Balkans and in particular in Bosnia as the region that came under his long lasting jurisdiction. He was aware of the efforts of his predecessor in fostering a new Bosnian entity and codifying an invented language named at first *Landessprache - zemaljski jezik* (Land language) and later *Bosnisch-bosanski.* He expanded these premises by explaining that Bosnia had a historic specificity of its own. Most importantly, Bosnia was permeated with the spirit of the ancient East more so than with Medieval anachronisms or with the ideas of the Western world. Therefore, according to Kállay, new institutions and innovations

---

[41]Thallóczy, Einleitung, p. XXIX..

should be carefully introduced taking into account the existing circumstances:

> As soon as I stepped at the helm of the government of these provinces I knew that I had to act decisively if I wanted to accomplish something worthwhile. That meant to awaken the spirit of the West, the strong feeling of statehood without harming the peculiarities of the single-minded, yet not to let the petty and divisive particularities to continue to take root. The sorry state of the south-eastern part of Bosnia could demonstrate where this spirit of particularity was leading. So long that I am at the helm of these lands, I shall strive to instill in the Bosnian people the spirit of statehood, and moreover of a great and powerful statehood. So long that I adhere to the gist of our obligations that we have taken in respect to these lands, I will continue with my efforts to create something good not only for Bosnians but also for the Monarchy . [42]

At the outset of his tenure, Kállay did act decisively following the established policy of the Monarchy boasting military power. This policy did not provide for integration and interaction of the population necessary for binding the new domains of the Habsburg Empire to one another. Kállay relied on the large military contingency in order to assure peaceful conditions in Bosnia-Hercegovina.

Bosnia and Hercegovina were surrounded by largely nationally homogenous states of Serbia, Montenegro and Croatia which would have liked to incorporate adjacent territories inhabited by their co-nationals. Kállay was aware of these aspirations and promptly ordered the building of a *cordon militaire* consisting of a dense network of watchtowers to be swiftly completed by the end of 1882. Each watchtower had at minimum 40 to 50 men in attendance. These

[42] Quoted afterThallóczy, Einleitung, pp. XXXV-XXXVI.

measures were taken "so that the danger of a new uprising would be removed."

Kállay took great precautions in establishing a strict watch on the Serbian and Montenegrin borders. There were 35 watchtowers in operation. In 1885, Kállay reported that the *cordon militaire* was working well according to the plan. In addition to an excessive cost to the government, the *cordon militaire* almost brought to a halt any contacts between the populations of these neighboring lands.[43]

While it was earlier purported that the cordon was established to pacify the border and establish order, the real goal was the creation of a permanent rift between the population of Montenegro and Hercegovina. In a note to the Ministry of War, Kállay stated that the Hercegovinian population should be guarded from the political agitation generated in Montenegro. The *cordon militaire* should "prevent a continuous contact between the populations and induce the weakening of the mutual feelings of closeness among related tribes by blood and religion. The existing ties with the neighboring population of Montenegro should be severed and directed to develop a complete and conscious devotion to our state."[44] Obviously, the military forces were adamant in keeping the borders under tight control. All these manipulations of the Austro-Hungarian authorities were known in Montenegro, and the Hercegovinian border became known as the proverbial "Chinese Wall."[45]

Moreover, the Austro-Hungarian government entertained the idea of creating another barrier between Montenegro and Hercegovina with settlements of foreign colonists along the border of these two provinces. Already in the early 1870s, Kállay took part in the ongoing colonization debate and expressed his support for the erection of an 'ethnic wall.' Kállay voiced his concern over the

---

43 Archive of Bosnia and Hercegovina, Joint Ministry of Finance, BH, Pr. No. 98/1885; quoted after Kraljačić , *Kalajev režim u Bosni i Hercegovini (1882-1903)*, pp. 100-101.

44 Quoted after Tomislav Kraljačić, *Kalajev* režim *u Bosni i Hercegovini (1882-1903)*, pp. 101-102. The date of the mentioned report was 1889.

45 Kraljačić, *Kalajev* režim *u Bosni i Hercegovini (1882-1903)*, p. 106.

influence of the Serbian national movement spreading into Hungary. He suggested: "Furthermore, I consider it as necessary, that the Hungarians should be settled along Danube in order to separate our Serbs from the one on the other side".[46] In the given context, Kállay's reference "to our Serbs" meant the Serbs living under Hungarian rule.

A similar idea was entertained by Baron Nikolich, the former Joint Finance Minister, concerning the border regions of Hercegovina facing Montenegro. Nikolich wrote to Kállay: "It would be most effective for us, if we could settle the Tirolians as colonists in Hercegovina, close to the Montenegro border. The Tirolians would provide a very good protection against Montenegro. I believe that this idea should be thoroughly checked." By the end of 1882, a detailed plan was furnished, but turned out to be very costly due to relocation costs. In the final analyses, the plan was not accepted mostly due to the fear of discrediting the Austro-Hungarian Provincial Government in the face of foreign observers.[47]

In 1883, a new colonization proposal was put forth suggesting the relocation of Catholic Albanians in order to thwart any purported aspirations of Montenegro towards Hercegovina.[48] Although all these plans were not realized, the fact that such notions were entertained showed how much effort was directed towards accomplishing a complete isolation of Bosnia-Hercegovina from the population in Montenegro.

In the course of the 1880s, Kállay reconsidered the colonization plan and decided to proceed with its gradual implementation. In order to close off the border between Bosnia and Serbia, a colony was founded in the region of Bijeljina and named in honor of the Emperor, Franz Josefsfeld. Soon enough, sixty-one families from the Torontal region in Southern Hungary were settled in this colony.

---

46 Radenić, *Dnevnik Bejamnina Kalaja*, p. 518. This discussion took place in 1873.

47 Kraljačić, *Kalajev rezim u Bosni i Hercegovini (1882-1903)*, pp. 106-107.

48 Kraljačić, *Kalajev rezim u Bosni i Hercegovini (1882-1903)*, pp. 107-108.

The colonists were German Protestants. New colonists arrived in a steady stream, and the number of families was doubled by 1886..[49]

After the abdication of King Milan, the colonization of the border regions had increased even more. In 1891, new German colonies had been founded on the banks of river Drina, in Dugo Polje, and Branjevo. These colonies were strategically positioned to monitor the Serbian border from Koviljača to Loznica. Moreover, an Austrian garrison was stationed in Branjevo.[50]

The commerce and trading between Serbia and Bosnia-Hercegovina was made difficult by a variety of restrictions reducing the trading to the lowest measure. The regime did not spare material means to monitor the political situation in Serbia and the whereabouts of its leaders. In addition, a number of 'confidantes,' special agents and reporters had been engaged to provide needed information from Belgrade, when needed.[51]

Other measures included a strict passport control between Montenegro, Serbia, Turkey, and Bulgaria. Already in September of 1883, new passport regulations were approved by the Joint Ministry of Finance. The Government admitted that some regulations were "draconian." Nevertheless, the regulations were approved due to the overriding concern for peace and order. Kállay was warned that some "very severe" regulations could cause unfavorable impression abroad." [52]

Over all, Kállay proved that he could stabilize the situation and pacify the people in Bosnia-Hercegovina. His political adversaries in Vienna soon came up with a satirical comment: "Kállay versteht sich mit *seinem* (added emphasis) Volk gut aus." They obviously alluded to the fact that Kállay had Slavic ancestry on his maternal

---

49 Heinrich Renner, *Durch Bosnien und die Hercegovina kreuz und quer*, Berlin 1896, p. 450. Quoted after Kraljačić, *Kalajev režim u Bosni i Hercegovini (1882-1903)*, pp. 121-124 .

50 Kraljačić, *Kalajev rezim u Bosni i Hercegovini (1882-1903)*, pp.124- 125 .

51 Kraljačić, *Kalajev rezim u Bosni i Hercegovini (1882-1903)*, p. 125 .

52 Kraljačić, *Kalajev režim u Bosni i Hercegovini (1882-1903)*, p. 102.

side. His mother, Amalie von Kállay née Blašković de Ebetska, was of Serbian descent. Moreover, Kállay had started his political career by running for the position of a representative of the Serbian minority in Hungary. Above all, Kállay was a born Hungarian educated at the Budapest University; in Viennese political circles he befitted the image of the "other."

Kállay's long time friend and biographer, L. Thallóczy, was aware of the difficult position that Kállay occupied during his lifetime as a native Hungarian serving in Vienna but also as an Austrian official in his native Hungary. Kállay was accepted in Vienna as a high ranking servant of the Habsburg Monarchy, but never as an Austrian, which he indeed was not and did not pretend to be. He had opponents among the officials of the government, but also among the members of the opposition party in Vienna and likewise in Budapest. [53]

In reality, Kállay had a deeper understanding of the historical, political and demographic interdependence of Balkan nations. In particular, he was aware of the delicate balance that was needed to maintain the peaceful coexistence and improve the situation for the population in the countries of the region.

In 1883, Kállay was elected to the ranks of a member of the Hungarian Academy of Science. His acceptance speech was titled: "Hungary on the Border between the East and West." Kállay's speech was later translated into Serbian, and published in Sarajevo, *Ugarska na granici istoka i zapada*, in 1905.

Kállay intended to use this splendid occasion to elucidate his understanding of Hungary's historic role as a mediator between the Eastern and Western civilizations. While explaining Hungary's position, he explained his own predicament and political course that he was to follow as the highest ranking official of the Austro-Hungarian administration in charge of Bosnia -Hercegovina.

Kállay believed that Hungary was ideally suited to facilitate an understanding between the East and the West due to its geographic position, and historical role as a guardian of Europe from the time of

[53] Thalloczy, Einleitung, p. XXXII.

the Turkish invasion. Hungarian people had embraced both the Eastern and the Western paradigms in their culture and therefore were called upon to provide a civilizing mission. Hungary had participated in the Christians' crusades to recover the Holy Land from the Muslims. These events promoted closer contact with the Christians of Western Europe. Moreover, the Hungarian people had defended the Christian Europe from further Turkish expansion in the 16th century. Therefore, Hungary was justly called to fulfill its historic mission.[54]

Kállay expounded his understanding of the differences between the Eastern and Western civilization, aiming to justify the Hungarian intervention in Balkan affairs. Most of all, Kállay wanted to provide additional credence for his own long term plans as the highest official in charge of the political, economic, cultural, and educational development in Bosnia-Hercegovina.

Kállay argued that the Eastern spirit evolved in the ancient East comprising Africa, Asia, and old Greece. In Europe, the Eastern spirit encompassed the Baltic states and reached over the Eastern Carpathian Mountains to the East shores of the Adriatic. Russia and the Balkan peoples had been included in the Eastern domain.

Kállay purported that the character of the East was manifested in the exaggerated individualism that presented a hindrance for creating a cohesive and powerful state entity. The West, on the other hand, inherited the Roman idea of statehood uniting different nationalities, customs and points of view.

Interestingly enough, Kállay thought that Turkey did not belong to the Eastern domain from the start. The change occurred later and Turkey eventually succumbed to the Eastern spirit. Very likely that due to the policy of deference for Muslims in Bosnia-Hercegovina, Kállay placed Turkey outside the Eastern domain in opposition to

---

54 Kállay, *Ugarska na granici istoka i zapada*, Sarajevo 1905, pp. 61-62 and p. 68.

the historical and cultural grounds to the contrary. On the other hand, Kállay placed old Greece in the domain of the Eastern spirit.[55]

It would be difficult to accept Kállay's classification having in mind the exceptional role played by both Greece and Rome in medieval Europe and the civilization of the Renaissance.[56]

All in all, it is apparent that Kállay did not consider the Eastern and Western civilizations as equal. Kállay's dichotomy, of the ethnically divisive East versus united civic West, disregarded the fact that both civilizations contained ethnic and civic components. The existence of regional diversities, and the drive of centrifugal forces fostering independence, precipitated the fall of historic empires in the East and in the West throughout history. [57]

Kállay bemoaned the fact that the East lacked cohesion and an overriding *Staatsidee.* Therefore, Kállay considered as his most important task to instill the spirit of statehood in the newly acquired regions of Bosnia-Hercegovina.

Kállay's generous assessment of the role of the Dual Monarchy, as a consolidated entity, misinterpreted the reality of rising regional movements for independence of the historical-political entities throughout the provinces of Austria-Hungary, including Bosnia-Hercegovina. The resistance to colonial exploitation of the natural resources and riches of the land strengthened the drive for self determination.

In the course of the 1890s, the Serbian Orthodox Church and School Councils demands for autonomy for their schools had a decisive impact on the strengthening of the national consciousness in Bosnia-Hercegovina. The Serbian communities managed by sheer persistence to achieve their coveted goals. A unique testimony of this

---

[55] Kállay, *Ugarska na granici istoka i zapada,* p. 64.

[56] Jacob Burckhardt, *The Civilization of the Renaissance in Italy,* New York, Harper, 1958, pp. 177-178.

[57] Karen Barkey, "Thinking about Consequences of Empire, " p. 108. Compare also Solomon Wank, "The Habsburg Empire,"pp. 48-49, *After Empire,* Eds. Karen Barkey, and Marc von Hagen, Westview Press, Boulder 1997.

struggle had been presented in the three *Memoranda* submitted to the Emperor Franz Joseph. Starting from the first *Memorandum* submitted to the Emperor in 1896, and pursuing their demands with dogged determination, the Council finally had received the desired religious and educational autonomy in 1905.

It was a long struggle and many excellent supporters had been habitually persecuted, imprisoned and/or fired from their respective professional positions. The three Memoranda had preserved the fundamental facts of this disturbing confrontations. Each of these documents specified the confining rules and regulations that provoked wide-spread concerns. The signatories named the individuals, schools, teachers, and headmasters who suffered harsh consequences due to their demands for necessary improvements of education. In the process, their demands grew in strength and became a veritable movement supported by the population at large and their elected leaders. Moreover, the ongoing debate, known as *Sprachenkampf,* helped to subside the efforts of the Austro-Hungarian government in inventing a Bosnian language and creating an imagined Bosnian nation .[58]

Kállay tried to shrug off the voices for cultural independence as lack of understanding for his endeavors promoting an imagined *Staatsidee* that would bring Bosnia-Hercegovina under the sway of the Western world. He repeatedly stated that he did not expect understanding, but that he truly appreciated the people of Bosnia-Hercegovina and did his utmost to improve their lot. Kállay explained his position in a speech delivered in Budapest in front of an Austrian delegation:

> I am proud that I am able to govern in Bosnia and I feel close to this land. I do not know anything more honorable than to bring this land on the road of progress to the benefit of the land and its

---

58 *Bosansko-hercegovački zbornik, Tri carska memoranduma,* Novi Sad, Miletićeva štamparija, 1902. Compare also, Mirko Maksimović, Crkvena borba i pokreti, *Napori Bosne i Hercegovina za oslobodjenje i ujedinjenje,* Ed. Pero Slijepčevi Kraljačić et al., Sarajevo, 1929, pp. 70-106.

people, but also to the great advantage of the Austro-Hungarian Monarchy, once the significance and the value of these lands in the Monarchy are correctly understood. [59]

Kállay did not count on gratitude and he was equally aware that he could not accomplish all that he wanted. He tried to establish a precarious balance between leading political parties in both Austria and Hungary, in addition to providing a viable agenda for his rule in Bosnia-Hercegovina.

Thalloczy pointed out that Kállay's dedicated work was not appreciated enough. Even his successes were downplayed and observed "with a tyrannical disinterest." [60] He was not sufficiently appreciated in Hungary nor in Austria although he carried out the given mandate the best that he could. On the whole, the public opinion reflected the general malaise and lack of cohesion questioning Kállay's political credence and turning against him often with vengeance.

Kállay tried in vain to uphold the policy of Bosnian specificity *(Bosniankentum)* and create a rift between the neighboring ethnically and historically related peoples. He trusted that a strong idea of statehood *(Staatsidee)* would bring Bosnia and Hercegovina under the dominion of the Dual Monarchy, and help solve the Eastern Question. These policies produced an opposite effect by strengthening the resistance to colonial exploitation fueling the drive for national independence.

Although Kállay seemed to believe that the Habsburg Monarchy was exemplifying a firmly established idea of statehood, some leading politicians did not share this opinion. The weakening of the centripetal forces binding the provinces with the capital of the Dual Monarchy was well known and often enough discussed by those in power. Count Gustav Kalnoky, Foreign Minister to Francis Joseph,

---

[59]Thalloczy, Einleitung, p. XXXIII.

[60] "Man betrachtete seine sogennanten Erfolge mit tyranischem Gleichmut."Thallóczy, Einleitung, p. XXIV.

realized with regrets that Austria's glory depended on military power of the Habsburg monarchy from the very beginning:

> Since the time when the Habsburg territorial possessions were first united, the monarchy had developed more in the sense of a power *(Macht)* than in the sense of a state *(Staat)*. Power and purpose in external matters were more recognizable than its purpose as a state.

In the same memorandum to Francis Joseph written in the mid 1880s, Kalnoky stated that there existed no cohesion within the Empire and that the former states were steadily drifting away. [61]

Observed from a vantage point, there is no contradiction between Kállay's awareness of the existing tensions between Austro-Hungarian prerogatives of political and economic subjugation and the perceptions of the regional national elite advocating dissolution of imposed political and economic bonds. By the turn of the 20th century the Habsburg empire as a historic entity was bordering on disintegration. Francis Joseph came to comprehend the growing strength of the national movements for independence and the inevitability of the demise of the Dual Monarchy. In the midst of World War I, he declared that he was aware for a long time that the Dual Monarchy presented an anomaly in the world of his days.[62] The events following the turmoil of World War I proved the truthfulness of these perceptions.

---

[61] Quoted after Salomon Wank: *After Empire*, p. 48.

[62] Salomon Wank, "The Habsburg Empire", *After Empire*, p. 48.

Chapter 4

CULTURE IN AN OCCUPIED TERRITORY: BOSNIA-HERCEGOVINA IN THE AFTERMATH OF THE BERLIN CONGRESS

In the aftermath of the Berlin Congress of 1878, the Austro-Hungarian Monarchy sought to assure the world community at large that the occupation of Bosnia-Hercegovina would provide a better life for the population by enhancing a general economic and cultural development.

In reality, Austro-Hungarian policies had attempted to secure a stronghold in Bosnia-Hercegovina in order to ensure further expansion into the Balkans and along the Adriatic Littoral. Thus, both Bosnia and Hercegovina had a considerable strategic importance for achieving the coveted colonial aspirations. Vienna also hoped that Sarajevo, as a regional cultural center, might helped counterbalance centrifugal forces among some segments of the population, notably young intellectuals, and curtail their respective attachments to Belgrade or Zagreb.[1]

The newly installed Provincial Government *(Landesregierung)* aimed to strengthen its rule by introducing educational reforms that would facilitate creation of an invented Bosnian entity. Already in June 1879 a new ordinance was posted announcing the introduction

---

[1] Valeria Heuberger and Hans Ilming explained, in retrospect, the Austrian understanding of these manifest colonial policies: "Für Österreich galten die beiden Provinzen als strategisches unverzichtbares Hinterland zu Dalmatien sowie als Ausgangspunkt fur ein weiteres Vordringen auf dem Balkan." Valeria Heuberger, Hans Ilming, *Bosnien-Herzegovina 1878-1918, Alte Ansichten vom gelungenen Zusammenleben*, Vienna, Christian Brandstaeter Verlag, 1994, p. 22.

of a so called Land language *(Landessprache—zemaljski jezik)* subsequently renamed Bosnian language, into the school curriculum. In addition, the study of German language for a minimum of eight years was made obligatory.[2]

Habsburg authorities soon realized that many teachers were reluctant to teach the officially prescribed *zemaljski jezik (Landessprache);* they would not in good faith teach a language that was not recognized or embraced by the native population or professional educators. Even when faced with the prospect of losing their teaching positions, they did not wish to submit to the new language ordinances. The introduction of the official Land language was even more questionable due to the well known fact that the Hercegovinian dialect was widely spoken and appreciated for its semantic richness, purity and eloquence. In the spring of 1850, several decades before Austro-Hungarian troops marched into Bosnia-Hercegovina, eight distinguished Serbian and Croatian scholars had met in Vienna and signed the historic *Književni dogovor* (Literary Agreement), which adopted the dialect spoken in Hercegovina as the common Serbian and Croatian literary language.

The participants of the Agreement gave the following reasons for their decision: the Hercegovinian dialect was spoken by the majority of the people and it was closer to other Slavic languages than any other dialect. Most importantly, the vast bulk of the folk epic and lyric poetry was transmitted orally and recorded in the Herzegovinian dialect. The celebrated writers of medieval Dubrovnik had written in it. Subsequently, the Hercegovinian dialect had been accepted by the majority of the Serbian and Croatian writers. The same scholars chose the *ijekavski* variant of the *štokavski* dialect as spoken in Hercegovina and charged Vuk

---

2Šćepan Grdjić "Prosvetna borba," Pero Slijepčević, Ed., *Napori Bosne i Hercegovine,* Sarajevo 1929, p. 114. The ordinance, No. 8876, was posted on June 6, 1879 .

Stefanović-Karadžić with writing "The Principal Rules of the Southern Dialect." [3]

The upshot of this agreement was that in 1867 a law was passed in Croatia establishing "the Croatian or Serbian language" as official and making it free for anyone to use either the Latin or Cyrillic alphabet. In Serbia, the new orthography was officially accepted in 1868.[4]

To be sure, the Land language insisted upon by Austro-Hungarian authorities was also based on the Hercegovinian or Southern dialect that had been accepted as the common Serbo-Croatian literary language. The name change, *Landessprache,* was introduced in 1879 in order to suppress Serbian or Croatian ethnic consciousness. Some five years later, in 1884, the Provincial government proffered guidelines for a grammar of the Land language and suggested that "special attention should be paid to the creation of a selection of special expressions that were not originally Bosnian, but became familiar and could not be replaced with other words used elsewhere."[5]

The Land language course was offered first in elementary schools. The authorities hoped that the future graduates would eventually be employed as teaching assistants *(Aspiranten)* and thus perpetuate

---

[3] Jovan Skerlić, *Istorija srpske književnosti*, Belgrade, Prosveta, 1967, p. 265.

[4] Paul Joseph Šafarik: *Geschichte der Slavischen Sprache und Literatur*, Prague, 1869, pp. 23-27. R. Aleksić et al., *Pravopis srpsko-hrvatskog književnog jezika*, 1960 Matica srpska, Matica hrvatska, Novi Sad and Zagreb, pp. 5-6. Michael Boro Petrović: "Karadžić and Nationalism," *Serbian Studies*, Vol. 4, No. 3, Spring, 1986, pp. 53-54. Thomas Butler, *Monumenta Serbocroatica*, Ann Arbor, Michigan Slavic Publications, 1980, pp. XXI-XXII. Compare also, Jelena Milojković-Djurić, *Panslavism and National Identity in Russia and in the Balkans 1830-1880: Images of the Self and Others*, East European Monographs, Columbia University Press, New York, 1994, pp. 46-47.

[5] Archive of Bosnia-Hercegovina, BH, No. 5514/1885, quoted after Tomislav Kraljačić, *Kalajev režim u Bosni i Hercegovini 1882-1903*, Sarajevo, Veselin Masleša, 1987, pp. 230-236. These "special expressions" must have been words of Turkish and/or Persian origin. Compare: R. Aleksić et al., *Pravopis*, p. 148.

the instruction of this newly forged language. This plan was very hard to implement as the population in both provinces did not want their children to attend schools offering classes in an invented language. Because of the shortage of teachers willing to teach the Land language Habsburg officials recruited low-ranking officers *(Unteroffiziere)* or auxiliary military personnel advancing them to the position of a "teaching candidate" *(Lehramtskandidat)*. In addition, they hired a number of "intelligent lay persons" who would teach the so called *zemaljski jezik (Landessprache)* in compliance with suggested guidelines. The level of literacy among the low ranking teaching personnel must have been very modest, very likely reaching only that of an elementary education. Many newly appointed teaching candidates probably had a greater proficiency in the German language since their secondary education was in German military middle schools and, eventually for the selected few, in military academies. Their knowledge of their maternal language was limited to usage in everyday life and probably did not include any extensive reading of literary or professional studies. The inexperience and clumsiness of newly employed soldiers teaching elementary school children must have impressed observers as somewhat bizarre.[6]

Šćepan Grdjić discussed also in retrospect the lack of teachers and mentioned that the teachers were recruited from the young soldiers of lower military ranks *(podčasnici)*. The Provincial government did not provide for a school budget: the respective counties were responsible for the teachers salaries, as well as for the upkeep of old facilities or for the building of new schools including the costs of heating and lighting.[7]

Resistance to the Austro-Hungarian educational policies came mostly from the intellectual elite who discerned the true nature of the government's efforts, namely that the obligatory teaching of the *zemaljski jezik* (Land language), later termed the "Bosnian"

---

[6] According to Heuberger and Ilming: "Die rauhbeinigen Militärs beim Umgang mit den Kindern zu erleben muss auf den Beobachter leicht skurill gewirkt haben." Heuberger, Ilming, *Bosnien-Hercegovina 1878-1918*, p. 35.

[7] Grdjić, "Prosvetna borba," p. 114.

language aimed to facilitate the development of a distinct "Bosnian culture" leading to eventual creation of a "Bosnian nation". Habsburg policies aspired to weaken the historic and cultural ties that existed between the Serbian and Croatian population and their respective cultural centers in Belgrade and Zagreb. Interestingly enough, their efforts produced the opposite effect by strengthening the national consciousness of both Serbs and Croats.

Many Serbian and Croatian intellectuals were drawn to the notion of a union of South Slavs embodied in the Yugoslav idea. The rapprochement gained in momentum and strengthened in the course of the 1860s and 1870s. In particular, during the 1875-1878 uprising in Bosnia-Hercegovina against Ottoman-Turkish rule, both Serbs and Croats engaged in helping the refugees from the embattled regions. In response to the uprising, an International Relief Committee was formed in Paris in August 1875. Chosen as its head was the Serbian Metropolitan Mihail Jovanović to lead the Committee. Metropolitan Mihail promptly invited the Croatian Bishop Josip Strosmayer to lead with him jointly these humanitarian efforts. [8]

In the wake of the Austro-Hungarian occupation of Bosnia-Hercegovina political activities of any kind were strictly forbidden. In short order, a number of ordinances were posted establishing rules and regulations in regard to the civic and cultural life. As might be expected, Habsburg authorities kept a watchful eye over the few selected and sanctioned cultural and intellectual activities of the populace. The authorities were well aware of the existing rapprochement between the Serbian and Croatian people and feared most of all the possibility of the assimilation of the Muslims by either the Serbs or Croats. [9]

---

[8] Jelena Milojković-Djurić, "The Eastern Question and the Voices of Reason: Panslav Aspirations in Russia and in the Balkans 1875-1878," *Balkanistica,* Vol. 11, 1998, p. 55.

[9] Heuberger, Ilming, *Bosnien-Hercegovina 1878-1918:* Dazu kamen weitere Vereinnahmungsversuche von südslavischer Seite, dem dritten grossen Bestandteil des Habsburgerreiches. Kroaten und Serben wollten sich nach jahrhundertlanger aufgezwungener Separation wieder mit ihren "slawischen Brüdern" vereinigen, die nur infolge "turkischen Zwanges" den

The Provincial Government issued In January 1879 an ordinance (No. 257) stipulating that all meetings were forbidden unless the authorities have issued a permit: "Assemblies and meetings of any kind are forbidden until a permit is secured from the political or military authorities. A representative of the government must attend such meetings."[10]

This order remained in force for the duration of the occupation contributing to considerable cultural stagnation. Moreover, literary meetings, theater plays, and choral concerts had to be reported two weeks in advance. Any violation of this ordinance was punishable by substantial monetary fines.

Such restrictions curtailing the freedom of speech and peaceful assembly clearly belied the official assurances about the projected improvements in the field of educational and cultural endeavors. These documents testified most of all to the determination of authorities to maintain their presence in the occupied provinces at all cost.[11]

The cultural activities of the population at large during this period developed around reading halls and singing clubs. At first, these societies were formed mainly on the basis of confessional affiliations but not exclusively. The singers societies and reading halls managed to attract a large membership. The petitions for the foundation of reading halls, singers groups and staging of theatrical productions were studied with care by local authorities and almost always forwarded to the higher authorities in Vienna for final approval. Even the regular meetings of local singers societies required permissions and were posted in advance. Similarly, applications to

---

Islam angenommen hatten, in Wirklichkeit aber doch "echte" Kroaten oder Serben waren." pp. 22-23. It seems as if Heuberger and Ilming were not aware of the occasional conversions of the population to Islam a fact well established in Balkan historiography.

10 Dušan Vasiljević, *O Bosni i Hercegovini*, Belgrade, Nova štamparija Davidović, 1909, p. 13.

11 Risto Besarović, Editor, *Kultura i Umjetnost u Bosni i Hercegovini pod Austrougarskom Upravom*. Gradja za proučavanje političkih, kulturnih i socijalno-ekonomskih pitanja iz proslosti Bosne i Hercegovine (XIX i XX vijek). Sarajevo, Arhiv BiH, 1968, p. 8

publish newspapers and journals were discouraged and often denied in the course of a lengthy bureaucratic process.

Cultural life centered mostly around Sarajevo, Mostar and few other larger towns such as Nevesinje and Travnik. Choral concerts of singers societies and occasional guest appearances of theatrical groups enjoyed great popularity. Moreover, a network of modest reference libraries sponsored by these literary and educational societies had a considerable impact on the cultural periphery. Interestingly enough, during the 1880s and 1890s, Mostar became a literary center overshadowing Sarajevo in certain respects.

These organizations played a remarkable role in enriching the cultural life in Bosnia-Hercegovina and took the roles of a host of cultural institutions elsewhere. Their premises functioned as concert halls, community centers and make-shift theaters for occasional drama or comedy productions. Most had a modest reference library and a reading hall. [12]

Thus, the singers societies and reading halls became important focal point of cultural life and entertainment. These organization proliferated throughout the region and developed many worthwhile activities. Their cultural manifestations were infused at times with an added political context that apparently escaped the watchful eyes of the administration. During Benjamin von Kállay's long tenure, as Austro-Hungarian Joint Minister of Finance responsible for the administration of Bosnia-Hercegovina, a degree of freedom was sometimes tolerated in regard to the cultural aspirations and repertory choices provided that the main objectives of Habsburg administration were not adversely affected.

In the course of time, a number of new reading halls were opened. In the long run, the reading halls *(Lesevereine)* and reference libraries of various cultural associations preceded and facilitated the formation of public libraries.

---

12 Dušan Kecmanović, "Naša pjevačka društva i knjižnice," *Srpska Riječ* Sarajevo, 21. June 1905, No. 87, p. 3. Kecmanović wrote: "All the cultural life of the population centered around the small world of literary- and singers societies." Quoted after Risto Besarović, *Iz kulturne i političke istorije Bosne i Hercegovine,* Sarajevo, Svjetlost, 1966, p. 19.

The Bihać City Council was the first to address the Interior Department of the Austro-Hungarian Provincial Government in Sarajevo requesting the permission to open a reading hall for the office workers *(Beamten Leseverein)* in Bihać. In August of 1880, the Bihać City Council submitted a request to open a reading hall for the office workers *(Beamten Leseverein)* in Bihać. The Bihać petition was forwarded to Vienna together with a report by the Chief of the Austro-Hungarian administration in Sarajevo Hörmann von Orlaburg Dahlen. The report asked for additional guidelines in order to determine whether such reading halls should be allowed to open in the occupied territory. This was the first petition of the kind and the authorities in Sarajevo pointed out that such provision was not foreseen in the available guidelines.[13]

Furthermore, the question was entertained whether reading halls in Bihać or elsewhere in Bosnia should be allowed if a similar request was put forward. In a classic case of Habsburg bureaucratic indecision, clarification of this issue took more than a year, and involved authorities in Vienna and their subordinates in Sarajevo. In the process, the authorities in Vienna determined that the chief officer and his staff in Sarajevo should decide whether such reading halls should be allowed provided that these organizations did not harbor any political agenda. In the pending case of the Bihać City Council, permission for the reading hall was not granted outright as additional corrections seemed to be necessary.

The last published document pertaining to the Bihać reading hall suggested another revision of the proposed statute. The authorities of the Provincial Government in Sarajevo criticized the purported deficiencies of the revised statute referring to the rights and privileges of the membership of the proposed reading hall. The authorities advised the Bihać petitioners that the statute be reworked and submitted again in duplicates.[14]

---

[13] Besarović, *Kultura i Umjetnost u Bosni i Hercegovini.*; p. 25. The date of the request, as stated in the document, was August 12, 1880.

[14] The date of this last document pertaining to the delayed opening of the reading hall was 22. September 1881. Besarović, *Kultura i Umjetnost u Bosni i Hercegovini*, pp. 27-28.

Subsequent quests for the opening of reading halls elsewhere Bosnia-Hercegovina, were carefully scrutinized by the Austrian authorities in Sarajevo and also in Vienna. Such were the evaluations of the requests for the reading halls in Visoko, Prijedor, Livno, Sarajevo, Brčko, Tešanj, Travnik, Donji Vakuf and Tuzla among other places. Austro-Hungarian authorities both in Sarajevo and Vienna invariably demanded additional information about the programs, personnel in charge, and rules and regulations of the proposed reading halls as stipulated in their draft statutes.[15] This delaying tactic was another way of discouraging further requests of similar kind.

Habsburg obstructionism notwithstanding, the reading halls enjoyed great popularity and were founded in many cities and townships with the motivation to cultivate the interest in literary discourse and fine arts appreciation. The towns people and young intellectuals alike frequented these places in order to meet and discuss various literary and educational issues. At times, these discussions transcended literary boundaries and touched on covert political questions and aspirations.

Reading hall members frequently organized meetings with literary and musical programs known as *besjede.* These meetings featured writers, or young composers and performers. Music, especially the vocal forms such as choral- and solo songs, enhanced the rising popularity of *besjede* meetings. A special musical form called *budnice* (wake-up songs) became very popular. The poetic texts and appropriate musical accompaniments enhanced the feeling of working together, safeguarding the cultural heritage.[16]

---

[15] Besarović, *Kultura i Umjetnost u Bosni i Hercegovini,* pp. 28-53

[16] The reading halls were founded also in Croatia, Serbia and Slovenia. Count Janko Drašković was instrumental in establishing the first reading halls in Varaždin and Karlovac in 1836. The first reading hall in Zagreb was opened in 1841. Drašković took active part in the Illyrian Revival aiming to awaken interest in the historical past. Wayne Vucinich, "Croatian Illyrism: Its Background and Genesis,"*Intellectual and Social Developments in the Habsburg Empire from Maria Theresa to World War I,* Ed. by St. B. Winters, East European Monographs 1975. In Slovenia, *čitalnice* (reading halls) enjoyed increased popularity during the 1860s. Soon after *čitalnice* appeared

On 8 January, 1888 the *Zvonimir* Association of Croatian Students at the University of Vienna decided to celebrate the 300 anniversary of birth of the poet Ivan Gundulić by organizing a special *besjeda*. Although the intention of the students was ostensibly to honor the memory of a long-dead poet, the authorities nonetheless deemed it necessary to monitor the celebration with great scrutiny.

Accordingly, the Finance Ministry in Vienna requested additional information from the Provincial Government in Sarajevo about those students from Bosnia-Hercegovina participating in the Gundulić celebration. The Austrian chief officer in Sarajevo, Johann Appel, responded with a lengthy report dated 19 January 1888. Appel even supplied copies of telegrams mailed from Sarajevo and Mostar to the students in question. The report was forwarded to the Austrian government officials in Vienna in response to their earlier request.[17]

The Austrian authorities in Sarajevo obviously read these telegrams. Furthermore, a selection of these telegrams was translated into German and supplied with short biographies of the respective signatories. Most telegrams contained short congratulatory messages honoring the poet Gundulić and expressing solidarity with the students' initiative. An exception presented an extended telegram dispatched by Ivan Lepušić, a teacher of the elementary school in Sarajevo. Lepušić had singled out Gundulić's poetic merits which were equally appreciated and celebrated by Serbs and Croats alike. Lepušić aimed to point to the growing

---

in all major cities although the reading hall in Ljubljana preserved its leading position. Dragotin Cvetko, *Histoire de la Musique Slovene*, Maribor 1967, pp. 203-204. In Serbia, musical and literary performances called *besede* were initiated during the 1847 and 1848 and grew in importance during the 1860s. Jelena Milojković-Djurić, "The Role of Choral Societies in the 19th Century Among the South Slavs," *National Movements in the Baltic Countries*, Stockholm, Acta Universitatis Stockholmiensis, 1985, p. 475.

17 Besarović,*Kultura i Umjetnost u Bosni i Hercegovini*, pp. 249-250. The request from Vienna addressed to Appel was dated 11 January 1888.

cultural and political rapprochement between the Serbs and Croats.[18]

In 1892 Metropolitan Djordje Nikolajević submitted a request to open a Serbian Reading Room on behalf of the Orthodox Church community and Serbian parochial schools in Sarajevo. As the Metropolitan was the highest church dignitary in the region of Bosnia-Hercegovina, his request was subjected to very extensive scrutiny regarding the feasibility of such an institution. Subsequently, Habsburg authorities in Sarajevo forwarded Nikolajević's request to Vienna with a lengthy explanation of their understanding of the situation in the Serbian community in Sarajevo and the existing needs for a reading hall. The report was signed by the deputy of the chief Hugo Kutschera and was dated 21 April 1892. 19

The report probed the validity of Metropolitan's request and included an extensive evaluation of the Serbian cultural milieu in Sarajevo as well as of its prominent personalities. Obviously, the authorities have been keeping a keen eye on Serb cultural events, including the recent Saint Sava school celebration. The program of the celebration was scrutinized as well.

Saint Sava was celebrated as the patron saint of educational and scholastic endeavors and as the protector of school children. He was the first Serbian archbishop who translated the *Nomokanon* and a number of important liturgical canons. He also wrote about the life and humanitarian deeds of his father king Stefan Nemanja. His writings marked the beginning of Serbian literacy and literary endeavors.

In order to mark the celebration of Saint Sava's holiday, the Church Choral Society, *Sloga,* had performed an appropriate musical program. Kutschera's report questioned the role of *Sloga* during the celebration. The report did not criticize the musical selection, *per sé,* performed at the Saint Sava celebration. The main objection seemed to be the ideological profile of a number of members of the choir. Kutchera mentioned that he had received

---

18 Besarović, *Kultura i Umjetnost u Bosni i Hercegovini,* p. 250. Appel's report was dated 19 January 1888.

19 Besarović, *Kultura i Umjetnost u Bosni i Hercegovini* pp. 32-35.

pertinent information about a number of members of the choir *Sloga*. According to Kutchera's evaluation, some young people supported the program of the well known Serbian youth association *Ujedinjena omladina srpska (Union of Serbian Youth).* The Austrian authorities suspected that these members promoted the preservation of Serb national identity by nurturing the cultural heritage. The celebration of their patron saint Sveti Sava presented the case in point; the *Omladina* association supported similar cultural events closely related to important religious holidays. It was concluded that the Choral Society *Sloga* consisted ... mostly from the younger radical orthodox citizens of Sarajevo, belonging to the *Omladina* ."

In the end, Metropolitan Djordje's request for a reading hall was turned down. The deputy of the chief Kutschera claimed that the petition violated constitutional procedures. Kutschera, singled out the fact that the motion for the foundation of the reading hall had been raised and approved at a membership meeting of *Sloga*. The minutes of the Society referred to paragraphs 10 and 12 of the Society's Statute in support of their petition. Kutschera declared that this procedure was not valid and that the Society exceeded its jurisdiction and the motion for a reading hall was denied. According to Kutschera's opinion, the motion presented a reckless and willful interpretation of the Statute by the Church Choral Society *Sloga*:

> Da dieser Beschluss des genannten Gesangsvereines eine eclatante Ueberschreitung der genehmigten Vereinsstatuten involvirte und offenbar darauf ausging, auf nicht legalem Wege eine serbische Lesehalle entstehen zu lassen, hat die Landes-Regierung ... diesen auf einer vollkommen willkürlichen Auslegung der Statuten basierten Beschluss als ungultig zu erklaren.[20]

Another argument against approving the reading hall provided was its suggested name *Srpska čitaonica—Serbische Lesehalle (Serbian Reading Room)*. Kutschera's objection was in line with the established policy of systematic suppression of any organization

20 Besarović, *Kultura i Umjetnost u Bosni i Hercegovini*, p. 14.

referring even remotely to a specific nationality. There was a fear that such a reading hall would serve in addition to cultural goals the covert goals of Serbian national aspirations:" ... neben den vorgeschützten kulturellen Aufgaben auch verkappte serbische nationale Ziele vorgesteckt werden sollen." [21]

Kutchera's interpretation of this policy went so far as to even restrict the use of ethnic designations, such as *Srpski* or *Hrvatski,* only to specific religious events or practices. Kutchera would allow the use *srpski (Serbian)* with the religious denomination *pravoslavni (orthodox)* only in connection with activities conducted by the Church. The report reiterated this policy by stating:

> "... die Landesregierung daran festgehalten hat, dass die Bezeichnung "srpski" nur im Zusammenhang mit dem Worte "pravoslavni" und zwar nur für religiöse Anstalten und Einrichtungen angewendet werden dürfe und da die Landesregierung auch bisher keinem der nun entstandenen Vereinen aller Art, die Belegung nationaler Titeln *(Hrvatsko* oder *Srpsko)* gestattet hat, so wäre, wenn es überhaupt zur Gründung eines Lesevereines aus orthodoxen Sarajevoer Kreisen kommen soll, nur ein indifferenter Name wie z.B. "Gradjanska citaonica" zuzulassen." [22]

The report reiterated that national denomination, be it *Croatian* or *Serbian*, should be only used in connection with religious practices. Any other use of these terms, be it in reference to reading halls or fine arts associations, should be avoided since it could help propagate "pernicious nationalistic goals." In conclusion, it was decided that the permission for the reading hall could not be granted. Any further request for the reading hall would have to be submitted

---

[21] Besarović, *Kultura i Umjetnost u Bosni i Hercegovini,* p. 34

Milorad Ekmečić noted that the authorities objected to the use of *Serbian* in connection with the Singers Societies. They insisted that the denomination Serbian be always followed by Orthodox and that such titles be strictly limited to church a for his summer residence.

[22] Besarović, *Kultura i Umjetnost u Bosni i Hercegovini,* p. 599. Kutschera report was dated 5 July 1892.

with the name of the proposed reading hall changed to *Gradjanska čitaonica (Civic reading hall).* [23]

Kutschera's report was then forwarded to Benjamin von Kállay, the influential Minister of Finance in Vienna. Kállay supported Kutschera's decision and suggested that Metropolitan Nikolajević should be informed about the denial of his request. He was in agreement that, " ... the request for the opening of the reading hall of the Oriental Orthodox Church and school district in Sarajevo had to be denied ... due to the incompetence of the mentioned (church) community." It was not specifically explained how it was determined that the Society was incompetent and how this incompetence was manifested, if at all.

> Mit der Absicht der Landesregierung, das Gesuch der orient. orthod. Kirchen und Schulgemeinde von Sarajevo um Bewilligung zur Errichtung des geplanten serbischen Lesevereines wegen Incompetenz der genannten Gemeinde zu einem solchen Schritte abzuweisen und den Metropoliten Nikolajević in gleichem Sinne verständigen, bin ich volkommen einverstanden. [24]

In his correspondence with Kutschera, Kallay used the terms *Orientalische Orthodoxe Kirche, Orientalishe Orthodoxe Gemeinde, Orientalische Orthodoxe Confession* in order to avoid the denomination *Serbian Orthodox Church, Serbian Orthodox Community, Serbian Orthodox Religion.* The highly inappropriate term *orientalische orthodoxe (oriental orthodox)* was invented in order to replace the universally accepted by all other ecclesiastic and civil authorities: *Srpska pravoslavna crkva, (Serbian orthodox church)* or *Srpska pravoslavna vera (Serbian orthodox religion).*

These policies remained to be enforced and subsequent requests were again discussed at length and submitted for final approval to

---

23 Besarović, *Kultura i Umjetnost u Bosni i Hercegovini,* p. 34. The report was dated 21 April 1892 and signed by Hugo Kutschera.

24 Besarović, *Kultura i Umjetnost u Bosni i Hercegovini,* p. 35. Kállay answered in a writ dated 14 May 1892.

the central government offices in Vienna. As a rule, the local communities were advised to revise the submitted requests producing an inordinate amount of documentation and requiring a sustained and almost dogged persistence from the petitioners. Even some fourteen years after the beginning of the occupation of Bosnia-Hercegovina, in 1892, the bureaucracy did not function any smoother; such permissions were delayed, repeatedly scrutinized and, as a rule, forwarded to higher authorities in Vienna with requests for additional clarification.

Another example of the thoroughness investigation of religious celebrations was presented in another report of the deputy Kutschera, this time in connection with the annual celebration of *Vidovdan* (St. Vitus day). In June of 1892 the members of the Singers' Society *Sloga* in Sarajevo planned to commemorate *Vidovdan* with appropriate riverside entertainment on the banks of the Bosna river at Ilidza. *Vidovdan* was observed as the society's *slava* commemorating Saint Vitus, *Sloga's* patron saint.[25]

The program of the celebration was submitted for official sanction. The deputy of the chief of the government in Sarajevo, Hugo Kutschera, rejected both the proposed featured speaker and his keynote address entitled "Gusle moje od suva javora" ("My *Gusle* from Old Maple"). Kutschera thought that the speech had an outspoken "Serbian nationalist character." He also censored the choral song bearing the same title that was supposed to be performed after the speech.

Judging by the title, the speech very likely referred to the events of the past, celebrating the endurance of the Serbian people under difficult conditions. The choral song, with the same title, was chosen to enhance the message of historical continuity. The *gusle*, a stringed instrument, accompanied the reciting of epic poetry and therefore was often used as a metaphor for the historic memory of a people.

Kutschera also insisted that the following sentence be stricken from the announcement: "Na ovu zabavu poziva društvo svakog brata Srbina i sestru Srpkinju, kao i svakog prijatelja srpskog naroda." (The Society invites to this party all Serbian brothers and sisters as well as all the friends of the Serbian people). The second

---

[25] Besarović, *Kultura i Umjetnost u Bosni i Hercegovini,* p. 599

part of the invitation clearly referred to members of the Croatian and Muslim communities regardless of their ethnic or religious denomination, as a manifest gesture of good will.

It is regrettable that Kutchera did not have on his agenda the fostering of friendly relations and the well-being of the population under his jurisdiction. He obviously wanted to keep the people divided forbidding even an open invitation of Serbian citizens to the community at large. Kutschera dispatched his deputy, the Superintendent Ra[eta, to attend the celebration and submit a written report with his evaluation of the St. Vitus *slava* celebration.

Rašeta's report centered on the description of the *slava* as a folk custom. He probably was impressed by the pageantry of the festivity while the innermost meaning of the *Vidovdan* celebration escaped his observation. Rašeta reported that the celebration began in the Serbian church with the festive liturgy and the communion. The religious ritual closed with a requiem for the deceased members of the Society. In the afternoon a festival was planned with a musical program on the river Bosna at the popular spa, Ilidža.[26]

In truth, the celebration of *Vidovdan* had a much more profound meaning and was not only a memorial for the deceased members of the Society. The major historic events and the many known and unknown soldiers who fought throughout the historic times were remembered. The program contained well understood reminiscences of all that constituted the Serbian people as a national entity.

As mentioned before, the meaning of *Vidovdan* and its historic context obviously escaped Rašeta. In his written report to the deputy Kutschera, he described the celebration as a folk custom or *slava*. The report had no references to the *Vidovdan* commemoration as an homage to the Serbian historical past. The Serbian people observed *Vidovdan* celebration as a homage to the Serbian historical past and a remembrance of the famous defeat at Kosovo in 1389. Subsequently, *Vidovdan* presented a memorial to all fallen soldiers defending their country from foreign intruders. In any event,

---

26 The Joint Finance Minister in charge of Bosnia-Hercegovina, Benjamin von Kállay, chose the spa Ilidža for his summer residence.

Kutschera forwarded Rašeta's observations as an attachment to his own report to the superiors in Vienna.[27]

The previous year, in the early winter of 1891, the *Narodno* pjevačko društvo (Folk Singers Society) in Mostar had prepared an interesting program celebrating Croatian history at the time of reign of king Zvonimir. The opening number featured the hymn "Zvonimir" as a prelude for the play "Zvonimir, the King of Croats." It is noteworthy that this play was written by the prominent Serbian writer and statesman Milan Subotić. The program and information about the performance schedule was submitted in advance to the district chief Baron Isidor Benko seeking his approval.

Benko routinely notified the higher authorities in Vienna. Interestingly enough, the Joint Finance Minister Kállay took note of the planned performance and raised a number of objections. Kállay criticized the lay-out of the program design with the Croatian crest entwined with a garland of names of all South Slav lands including Montenegro. He warned Benko about the nationalistic tendencies contained in the concept of the program, seeing in the chosen hymn and play dedicated to king Zvonimir the glorification of the idea of Greater Croatia.[28]

Benko responded by expressing circumspectly his great pleasure at Kállay's interest in the cultural life of Mostar. He confirmed that national tendencies of Serbs and Croats were often an integral part of many cultural programs in Mostar. In a somewhat patronizing manner, he contended that the literary style of such poems was most of all metaphorical and elaborate and that the simple people would surely never comprehend the real message. In addition, he had never observed that these performances caused any factual damage to the regime. It was his opinion that both Serbs and Croats should

---

27 Besarović, *Kultura i Umjetnost u Bosni i Hercegovini,* p. 599. Kutschera report was dated 5 July 1892.

28 It should be noted that the play was written by Subotić, a Serbian writer who admired the Croatian king but did not subscribe to any nationalistic tendencies be it Serbian or Croatian. Compare, J. Milojković-Djurić, *Panslavism and National Identity in Russia and in the Balkans 1830-1880: Images of the Self and Others,* East European Monographs, Columbia University Press, 1994, pp. 51-53.

be free to arrange their respective programs since it would be impossible to ban all public performances. Benko therefore decided to give equal opportunities to both ethnic groups of the population. 29

In February of 1892, the newly elected board members of the same *Folk Singers Society* in Mostar requested permission to solicit funds for the erection of a building to serve the needs of the Society's membership. The petition mentioned that the Society was founded in 1888 by a group of Catholic citizens. The goal of the *Folk Singers Society* was the cultivation of folk singing for the enjoyment of their members and mutual entertainment *(Geselligkeit)*. Although the society was composed mostly of Croats, the petition omitted any reference to ethnic affiliation because of the prevailing regulations. Any ethnic denomination was allowed only if the group was associated with a religious group or activity.

The petition stated that there was a scarcity of adequate buildings and that the available concert halls had a capacity of approximately 150 seats. The larger halls in Mostar were expensive to rent. The Society hoped to benefit from a building of its own to be used for rehearsals, performances and entertainment of the membership and public at large. 30

As was typically the case, the Society's request met with hostility on the part of the Habsburg authorities. In forwarding the petition to Vienna, Johann Appel, the chief of the Austro-Hungarian government in Sarajevo, argued that permission for the solicitation of funds could be only granted only to support humanitarian endeavors helping the needy and destitute. It was his contention that a music hall would not provide such services but serve only for social and musical purposes and entertainment of the membership. Kállay promptly seconded Appel's opinion and permission to construct a building was denied. It should be noted that no

29 Archive for Bosnia and Hercegovina, ZV, Res 1/1891; quoted after Tomislav Kraljačić, *Kalajev* režim *u Bosni i Hercegovini 1882-1903*, Sarajevo, Veselin Masleša, 1987, pp. 165-166.

30 Appel's report was dated 23 February 1892. Besarović, *Kultura i Umjetnost u Bosni i Hercegovini*, p. 596.

additional funds were solicited from the Provincial Government, and the Society's eventual building would have been in all likelihood erected with private funds.[31]

Throughout Bosnia-Hercegovina, singers societies played a leading role in musical life, cultivating the tradition of choral singing. In this respect *Sloga* and *Trebević* in Sarajevo, *Gusle* and *Hrvoje* in Mostar achieved a very high level of musical artistry. At times, the programs of these societies also included instrumental music such as the popular *tamburice* ensembles.

In 1896 two Serbian choral Societies *Sloga* and *Gusle* gave a joint gala performance. Under the pretext of a simple meeting of two choral societies, their special concert in fact celebrated the coronation of Nicholas II, the Emperor of Russia. This historic event rekindled the covert notions of Slavic solidarity and national consciousness.[32]

The attempt to found a reading hall in Donji Vakuf in 1896 presented an interesting case. The Reading Hall Association petitioned the Austro-Hungarian Provincial Government in Sarajevo to allow the opening of the proposed reading hall in accordance with the submitted statute. The first petition was denied due to "the suspicion that the Association would harbor dissidents*(Malcontenten)* and would also favor a religious outlook." Then the Association provided a membership roster showing that all three religions would be represented. Thus, it seemed that such a reading hall would have been advantageous and desirable in promoting good will and civility among the citizens of Donji Vakuf. In spite of all stated good intentions of the organizers, Appel cautioned that political tendencies should be barred in accordance with the second paragraph of the Statute. Appel was obviously not in favor of the growing collaboration among the Catholics,

---

31 Besarović, *Kultura i Umjetnost u Bosni i Hercegovini,* p. 598. Kallay wrote on February 29, 1892.

32 Besarović, *Kultura i Umjetnost u Bosni i Hercegovini,* p. 20.

Orthodox and Muslim populations in Bosnia-Hercegovina, in particular in Donji Vakuf.[33]

On the whole, the Muslim communities seemed to be less inclined to petition for the opening of reading halls as reflected in the paucity of such requests in the official archives. Moreover, as Serbo-Croatian was the prevailing common tongue throughout Bosnia-Hercegovina, such petitions by Muslims rarely requested the permission to use Turkish as an official language. In 1904, however, one such petition on behalf of the Bugojno reading hall called for the opening of a *Turska Kiraethana.* In handling the unusual request István Burián, Kállay's eventual successor as Austro-Hungarian Finance Minister, commented that it was unknown whether other Muslim reading halls had chosen Turkish as their official language. In the case that they had not done so, which was very likely, he saw no reason to permit the use of Turkish as the official language in Bugojno.

In any case, Burián concluded that his decision would have little practical effect, because in his view the number of literate Muslims was rather limited. Moreover, Burián thought that the usage of Turkish language in official business matters would pose unnecessary difficulties for local Habsburg administration. On the other hand, he raised no objection to the proposed title *Turska Kiraethana* as such, since there were reading halls with similar titles in other cities such as Prijedor and Zenica.[34]

Among the periodicals published during the Austro-Hungarian occupation, the journal *Nada* (Hope) deserved special mention. Among other things, it was founded under the auspices of Benjamin von Kállay, the Joint Finance Minister in charge of Bosnia-Hercegovina. Kállay decided that an illustrated literary and educational journal should be published in Sarajevo. Kállay envisioned a number of wide-ranging political and cultural benefits

---

33 Besarović, *Kultura i Umjetnost u Bosni i Hercegovini.* The report was dated 2 November 1896 and signed by Appel. p. 52.

34 Besarović, *Kultura i Umjetnost u Bosni i Hercegovini,* pp. 57-58. Signed by Istvan Burian, *Finanzminister.* His opinion was dated 13 December 1904.

that such a journal could perform. While on an official visit to Bosnia-Hercegovina in 1893, Kállay formalized his request for a journal in a report addressed to the Provincial Government *(Landesregierung)* in Sarajevo dated 14 February 1894:

> Already at the time of my visit to Sarajevo last year, I informed the Provincial Government about my decision to start a literary-educational journal in *Bosnian language* (emphasis added). The task of the journal should be to provide interesting material from different fields of knowledge and education presented to the native reading public in a simple and persuasive manner befitting their educational horizon and level of understanding. On the other hand the journal should depict in word and picture the cultural development in Bosnia-Hercegovina in an objective and trustworthy manner in order to further such information abroad. [35]

Kállay saw the role of the journal as two-fold; firstly, the journal should inform the population of Bosnia-Hercegovina about the new developments in "all fields of human endeavors." In a patronizing manner Kállay suggested that the submitted articles should be adjusted and simplified to match the level of comprehension of the reading public. Secondly, the journal should inform readers abroad about cultural development in Bosnia-Hercegovina. Kállay stated that he was also considering the political benefits that such information may bring: he obviously wanted to present Bosnia-Hercegovina as an independent cultural entity with a specific scholarly, artistic and literary profile.

Appointed *Nada's* editor-in-chief was Crown Counsel Constantine Hörmann. Hoping to encourage widespread collaboration, Hörmann extended various invitations and published announcements in the press actively soliciting manuscripts. Not everyone embraced the officially sponsored project. On 17 November 1994, the renowned writer and public figure Jovan

---

35 Besarović, *Kultura i Umjetnost u Bosni i Hercegovini*, p.91.

Jovanović-Zmaj wrote an open letter which was published in the journal *Obzor*. [36]

Jovanović-Zmaj flatly refused to collaborate with the editors of the new journal:

> I wrote quite a lot for Serbian papers, I worked as well for Croatian papers. But you did not mention in the invitation or the announcement which language would be used Serbian or Croatian. It must be that *Nada* like the Provencial government itself will chose to publish articles written in the so called Land language. I cannot support the notion of inventing such an unsuitable name for our beautiful language instead of its real, ancient and beautiful name. [37]

The venerable prince Lujo Vojnović from Dubrovnik wrote in support of Jovanović's refusal for collaboration on 1 December 1894:

> Allow me Counselor (Hörmann) to use this opportunity and voice my concern. The letter of Zmaj Jovanović had excited and agitated all the writers be it Serbian or Croatian. I could not bring it in concordance with your earlier statement issued at the meeting in Sarajevo. You stressed that the writers may use freely the name Serbian or Croatian, while the editorial office would remain impartial in accordance with the current system in Bosnia. [38]

In any event, the first issue of *Nada* appeared on news stands on New Years Day, 1895. The journal was lavishly produced with numerous illustrations and drawings. The front page had a number of symbolic figures. At the top of the first page was the image of an old bard—*guslar*. The *Guslar* was regarded as the keeper of historic memory safeguarding the knowledge of important events. He was

---

[36] The letter appeared in *Obzor*, No. 264, on 17 November 1894.

[37] Todor Kruševac, *Bosansko Hercegovački listovi u XIX veku*, Sarajevo, 1978, p. 348.

[38] Kruševac, *Bosansko* Hercegovački *listovi u XIX veku*, p. 348.

depicted with the stringed instrument *gusle* in his hands since he always recited the epic renditions of historic events with the accompaniment of the stringed instrument. The title *Nada* was itself surrounded by a star and a crescent reminding of Muslim escutcheons. According to the heading, the journal was dedicated to learning, entertainment and fine arts explorations. The Provincial Museum was listed as the editorial office of the journal and Constantine Hörmann the editor-in-chief. *Nada's* inaugural editorial explained the advantages of journals dealing with learning and entertainment:

> These journals take care of the spiritual life of a people, they collect the golden nuggets of wisdom from the people as well as from elsewhere. *Our people are united as an entity by their language regardless of the name and alphabet they use. They have developed a fine literary style reflecting their well known talents and spiritual values* (emphasis added). Earlier there were such journals but they did not last long. These considerations created the idea to start a journal in Sarajevo that would serve as a mirror reflecting the spiritual culture of the South Slav peoples. [39]

Obviously, the editors aspired to attract writers from Bosnia-Hercegovina as well as from neighboring Slavic countries by encouraging collaboration in the literary field. Most importantly, they emphasized the communality of the spoken language as well as the use of both the Cyrillic or Latin alphabet, contrary to previous statements in various reports and announcements. Prior to the founding of the journal the invitations for collaboration emphasized the usage of the so called Land- or Bosnian language. In all likelihood, the unwillingness of many writers to participate in a project utilizing the officially sanctioned Bosnian- or Land language influenced the significant change of policy. The responses of Jovanović-Zmaj and Vojnović had undoubtedly played a decisive role in the editorial board's realization that its earlier insistence on the

---

[39] *Nada*, Sarajevo, Zemaljski muzej, No. 1, 1895, p. 1.

use of what many considered to be an invented Bosnian language was a self defeating proposition.

Most importantly, the editorial pointed to the well-known fact that the same language was used by all the peoples in Bosnia-Hercegovina regardless of their ethnic identity: "Our people have been united as an entity due to their common language regardless of the name and alphabet they use." The editorial obviously acknowledged the shared common language and thus reversed its earlier course.

As the leading cultural journal *Nada* published reviews of theatrical productions when such performances occurred. Plays were well attended and several literary or choral societies also had their own drama sections. The members gave dramatic performances and helped to generate interest for more formal theatrical productions. Under Habsburg rule, professional and dilettante theater companies from Serbia and Croatia were permitted to make guest appearances.

The first traveling theater performed in Sarajevo in 1881. Heinrich Spira and his troupe of actors received the needed permission from the authorities to stage performances in the German language. The daily *Sarajevski list* furnished this description of the public attending the German theater, "The public consisted of Austro-Hungarian merchants and workers, a smaller number of military officers and clerks and two or three Spaniards." [40] After the new Provincial Government was well established, additional military personnel and civilians arrived to make their fortunes in the occupied provinces.

After the trials and tribulations associated with the Austro-Hungarian occupation and the great fire that had ruined much of Sarajevo the people again started going to the theater. The increased attendance and frequency of staged plays did not escape the watchful eyes of the authorities who saw in these cultural manifestations a potential source of income. The theater companies were confronted with considerably higher taxation.

---

40 *Sarajevski list*, !8 November 1881, No. 108, p. 3. Quoted after Besarović, *Kultura i Umjetnost u Bosni i Hercegovini*, , p. 159.

In due time, the Austro-Hungarian Board of Finance in Sarajevo determined the amount of taxation to be paid by a theater company. A report, dated 15 January 1884, was dispatched to the Joint Ministry in Vienna including the fixed scale of payments since the beginning of the implementation of this policy. The report stated that, at first, the taxation *(Stempelpauschale)* amounted to six gulden, starting from 25 July to October 20, 1881. The authorities increased the tax to thirty gulden starting from October 1981 to the end of September 1882. In 1884 the tax was raised again to twenty four gulden monthly altough payable only when theaters were actually open and plays were staged. [41]

As might be expected, the rapid rise in the tax met with protest on the part of theater companies. Heinrich Spira petitioned the Finance Department of the Provincial Government to reduce the taxation to 12 gulden per month. The established price was 24 gulden. Spira's petition was supported by the Austrian authorities in Sarajevo pointing to the humanitarian and educational missions that the theater was performing. Since there were in average 20 to 22 performances each month, the amount due for the tax *(Stempelgebühr)* presented one fourth of the gross income. Gradually the financial situation of the company became difficult: the theater management had to curtail expenditures as well as the artists salaries. Even the number of performances had to be reduced to four per week. The authorities eventually condescended that the tax should be lowered to 15 gulden, having in mind the difficult position of the company and the reduced number of performances. The amount was still 3 gulden more than Spira's request.[42]

Permission for traveling theaters to perform in Bosnia-Hercegovina was not always easy to obtain. On three different occasions, Fotije Z. Iličić had sought permission for his *Traveling National Theater* to perform in Sarajevo. He petitioned the authorities three times but was not granted the needed permit.

In January of 1881 Iličić closed his guest appearances in Bosnian-Kostajnica (Bosanska Kostajnica), Iličić again sought permission to

---

41 Besarović, *Kultura i Umjetnost u Bosni i Hercegovini pod Austrougarskom Upravom,* p. 702

42 Besarović, *Kultura i Umjetnost u Bosni i Hercegovini,* p. 702

tour elsewhere in Bosnia-Hercegovina with his fellow actors, beginning with the township of Dubica.

Local officials stationed in the Austrian section of Kostajnica, reluctant to approve Iličić's request on their own, turned to the Interior Department in Vienna for guidance. According to information at hand, Iličić wanted to stay four weeks in Dubica. His repertory included plays written by Iličić himself such as *Uprising in Bosnia, Uprising in Hercegovina, Battle at Grahovo, Battle at Kosovo Polje.* These plays did not seem appropriate to the government officials in Kostajnica, who hypothesized that Iličić might have been assigned to fulfill some sort of political mission. He was known to be a friend of the former Serbian prime minister Ristić. 43

The request by authorities in Kostajnica, marked as confidential, made an impression in Vienna and an official query about Iličić's whereabouts was dispatched to Baron Herbert, who was at the time in Belgrade on an official visit. Herbert gathered the needed intelligence and responded shortly after. According to his information, Iličić was born in Szerb-Canad in Hungary. Iličić, like the majority of his troupe, was a Habsburg subject. At one time, Iličić was a member of the National Theater in Belgrade. Prior to the Turkish-Serbian war, he had toured with a small company throughout Serbia. He had also toured Slavonia, Croatia and the regions of the Military Border (Militärgrenze, Vojna Krajina). On that occasion, Iličić had received the requested concessions for his theatrical productions from authorities in Zagreb.

Herbert concluded that although Iličić often presented himself as an ardent Serbian patriot, his demeanor had more to do with his professional posture as a seasoned actor. According to Herbert's sources, Iličić did not have any political connections with the Serbs in Belgrade, and was not charged with any political mission for the

---

43 Besarović, *Kultura i Umjetnost u Bosni i Hercegovini,* p. 685. The confidential note was dated 20 January 1881 in Kostajnica.

Serbian government. His financial situation was explained as difficult.[44]

In any event, Austro-Hungarian officials in Sarajevo turned down Iličić's request to tour Bosnia-Hercegovina. The redoubtable Iličić, however, refused to accept the latest rejection and turned to the ultimate authority in the Habsburg Empire, the emperor himself. Iličić decided to write to Emperor Franz Joseph explaining his situation. His petition, dated 31 July 1881, was concise and written well in German language.

With obvious pride Iličić stated that his *Traveling National Theater* had already toured all the larger cities in Croatia, Slavonia, Dalmatia and the Military Border as well as parts of Hungary proper. He explained that in turning down three previous requests to tour Bosnia-Hercegovina, the Provincial Government in Sarajevo had cited the impoverishment of the population and the dire state of economy. This situation was caused by the devastation and burning of Sarajevo during the fighting of the Austro-Hungarian forces leading to the occupation of the Bosnia-Hercegovina.

Iličić pointed out, however, that since that time a considerable number of singers, musicians, and artists had passed through Bosnia-Hercegovina serving the people in their own way while earning their living. If His Majesty would grant him a permission *(Genehmigung)* to tour it would not only benefit the petitioner but equally thousands of men and women who would receive needed spiritual sustenance. This would all be accomplished if the Emperor would grant permission *(Genehmigung)* to Iličić's company to perform in Bosnia-Hercegovina. The letter was dated 30 July 1881 and signed by Fotije Z. Iličić *"Director des wandernden National-Theaters."* [45]

The petition apparently did some good, as Iličić received permission to tour Bosnia-Hercegovina and conduct performances for a period of three months. On the other hand, he was not granted permission to stage any plays in Sarajevo itself.

---

44 Besarović, *Kultura i Umjetnost u Bosni i Hercegovini,* pp. 685-686. The report was dated 26 February 1881.

45 Besarović, *Kultura i Umjetnost u Bosni i Hercegovini,* p. 692

Some fourteen years later, in 1895, Fotije Z. Iličić addressed another plea to Emperor Franz Joseph, this time written in Serbian language. Whereas his 1881 petition had been written in German, concise and up to the point, the new plea was redundant and included many tangential biographical details. Precisely this redundancy and added episodes provided an interesting personal account of the perils of a traveling company, even one with a high-sounding name, *Serbo-Croatian National Theater*.

Iličić began by stating that he had been born in 1845 in Srpska Csand, Veliko Sent Mikloski county, Torontal parish in Banat. His father had been a soldier in the Austrian army who defended the "Emperor's crown from the Hungarian uprising" during the revolution of 1848-1849.

After the end of the fighting, Iličić's father returned home but he was treated harshly and unjustly prosecuted by vengeful Hungarian officials. In consequence, he had decided to resettle his family and young children in Serbia having in mind their well being and hoping to protect them. After taking care of his family, he had returned to the battlefield and helped to assure victory for the Habsburg Crown. With the final suppression of the Hungarian revolt, he returned to Srpska Csand only to find that his house burned down and his estate in ruins. Therefore, he had crossed the border again and rejoined his family in Serbia, where he eventually died in 1865. Just as his father had remained a Habsburg subject all his life, Iličić argued that he too has been a loyal Austrian subject.

Iličić continued his letter to Franz Joseph by stating that he had devoted his life to the theater, first as an actor in various companies. In 1870 he had become director of the Serbian-Croatian Traveling Theater, in which capacity he had visited many places where Serbs and Croats lived. He then recalled, at considerable length, an unpleasant episode in the township of Veliki Zvornik in Bosnia, which had resulted in his expulsion from Habsburg territory.

In February 1892, after staging several performances with his company for some fourteen days, Iličić requested for an extension of his passport. The officer in charge, one Franjo Brodnik, declared that Iličić's passport had expired and was therefore invalid anymore, fining Iličić 50 forints. Although Iličić paid the fine, he was told he could not proceed elsewhere in Bosnia. Iličić returned to his appartment where he was confronted by seven soldiers with rifles and bayonets. The soldiers ordered him to leave the Austro-Hungarian territory and return to Serbia with his family and fellow actors. They asked Iličić to cross the Drina river immediately. It was already past five o'clock and the Muslim *mujezin* had started the evening prayer. The skies were getting dark and night was setting in. The Drina river, which formed the border between Bosnia and Serbia, had risen perilously high, pushing boulders and tree trunks from eroded shores. Because of the hazardous conditions, the ferry that normally connected the two banks had been out of operation for five days.

Iličić pleaded with Brodnik, reminding him that he was an Austrian citizen and therefore should be treated in a civil way to allow at least an overnight stay. Brodnik could send him under guard, if necessary, to Donja Tuzla or to some other town. Brodnik, however, ordered Iličić and his party, including the children, into the ferry. While crossing the turbulent river Drina, they almost drowned. It was only with the help of another ferry, from the Serbian side, that they were able to reach the Serbian territory.

Iličić complained to the authorities in Sarajevo about Brodnik's behavior. Instead of receiving any kind of satisfaction, Iličić had an unfavorable report logged against him in Zagreb. Iličić was distressed that the authorities in Zagreb denied a concession for his traveling theater since he had enjoyed this privilege for some 22 years. He thought that an unfavorable report also caused the cancellation of needed permissions for appearances in Budim and Pest.

In his new petition, Iličić initially asked the Emperor for forgiveness, if he had made any mistake, and thus offended the "mad and arrogant officer Brodnik" *(besnog i oholog činovnika Brodnika).* He asked the Emperor to let him return to his native country where his ancestors lived and shed their blood. He also asked for the return of his confiscated permit *(dozvola).* Even if he had been declared guilty, he had already spent four years in exile far from his homeland. He stated that he had been careless for not applying more promptly for an extension of his passport. At this juncture, however, the tone of Iličić's petition changed abruptly. Instead of continuing in a conciliatory fashion, Iličić gave vent to hurt feelings and wounded pride, pointing to various injustices that he had been obliged to endure. He asked that Brodnik be punished for his willful and rude behavior. Furthermore, Iličić asked to be compensated for the losses that he incurred while living abroad in exile. Ever the thespian, he concluded on a flowery high note, somewhat reminiscent of a theatrical ending pronounced by the hero of a play: "Expecting justice—happiness—and satisfaction, kissing your mighty Imperial and Royal right hand, I am the obedient subject of your Highness." The petition was signed by. Iličić on 13 October 1895 in Smederevo.[46]

Iličić's second petition obviously did not reach the desk of Franz Joseph, as it was eventually deposited in the Provencial Archive in Sarajevo. In fact, it is not clear whether Iličić received any reply whatsoever from any authorities.

Over a decade later, Iličić and his theater company did finally make it to Sarajevo. On 23 May 1909, an article in the daily *Srpska riječ* informed the readers that the Theatrical Group led by Fotije Iličić was scheduled to appear in Sarajevo and entertain the public. The writer of the article stated that a Serbian troupe would finally perform a repertory that would be easily understood by the public. Earlier, numerous guest appearances of foreign troupes had featured German and Hungarian theatrical groups which apparently traveled often to Bosnia-Hercegovina. The reviewer had the impression that all available German actors were paraded in Sarajevo at one time or another. [47]

---

46 Besarović, *Kultura i Umjetnost u Bosni i Hercegovini,* pp. 713-714 . .According to this petition, Iličić must have renamed his theater troupe to Serbo-Croatian National Theatre. Obviously that Iličić's petition was not forwarded to the highest authority since it was filed and deposited in the Archive in Sarajevo. It is also not clear whether Iličić received any reply from the authorities any time later.

47 *Srpska rije č* of 23 May 1909, god. V, No. 23, p. 3. Quoted after Risto Besarović, *Iz kulturne i politicke istorije Bosne i Hercegovine,* Sarajevo, Svjetlost, 1966. Besarović, "Specifičnosti kulturnog razvitka u Bosni i Hercegovini 1878-1918," in *Iz Kulturne i* političke istorije *Bosne i Hercegovine* , p. 12.

In retrospect, Iličić's efforts could be compared with the idealistic enthusiasm of Don Quixote. In the course of his long career, Iličić bravely faced many obstacles but doggedly kept to his chosen path, which at times seemed to be doomed. Moreover, Iličić had a vision that the theater should not only entertain but also help advance the knowledge of historic events of national importance. In spite of the Habsburg censorship and restrictions, Iličić managed to write or adapt several historical plays for his troupe to suit his repertory. He obviously had a high respect for his mission and therefore proudly named his company the *National Theater Company*. Iličić directed his life-long aspiration with dignity, advancing the art of dramatic performance with tenacity and worthwhile endurance in disregard of limited resources, maltreatment and hardship.

In March of 1913, Iličić wrote another letter from Mostar where he was apparently residing at the time. In it he asked his friend Dragutin Ilić to help find employment for his children with the National Theater in Belgrade. It seems that Iličić's enthusiasm for the theater was shared by his children. Iličić pointed out that the stage in Belgrade needed new and young talents. He volunteered his handsome younger son who had a fine demeanor and appearance and was especially deserving of appointment. Other companies would fight for him since he was talented and understood theatrical production. Iličić also added with a note of bitterness that despite his son's obvious merits, he had been refused a similar position the previous year.[48]

A wealthy benefactor, Dimitrije Jeftanović, appreciated the role that a theater could play in the cultural life of a people. Not satisfied with the short term engagement of traveling troupes in Sarajevo, Jeftanović offered to build privately a theater in the Bosnian capital. Initially, Austro-Hungarian authorities publicly praised Jeftanović for this generous offer. His proposed theater, however, was never built. Ever so suspicious, the authorities eventually decided that a permanent theater with a repertory of plays in Serbian language may easily became a stronghold of national aspirations. They

48 Besarović, *Kultura i Umjetnost u Bosni i Hercegovini,* pp. 740-1.

therefore, prevented its realization by raising a host of bureaucratic obstacles.[49]

In conclusion, the archival holdings of the Austro-Hungarian administration in Bosnia-Hercegovina provide a veritable treasure trove of information about the cultural policies carried out during the thirty-year-long Habsgurg administration in the two provinces.[50]

These documents offer a unique insight into imposed directives and restrictions influencing the shaping and fruition of some cultural activities as well as curtailing or denial of others. The censorship criteria and most of all the so-called "preventive censoring" testified to efforts to control the population in the occupied provinces and to safeguard the Habsburg authority. Some documents offer unexpected insights into personal lives and tribulations which personified the voices of a legion searching for some semblance of human dignity

Most importantly, these documents reveal some of the realities of life under foreign rule. The testimonies and judgments of administrative officers as well as supplications and responses of numerous petitioners reflect, in an oblique way, the struggle of the population to assert a measure of cultural independence.

---

49 Marko Marković, *članci i ogledi,* Vol. II, Sarajevo, Veselin Masleša 1961, p. 40.

50 Risto Besarović provided a unique service by publishing the bulk of the documentation from the Archive of Bosnia-Hercegovina. Besarović compiled also a selection of documents from the State Archive in Vienna, Archive of the Serbian Academy of Arts and Sciences in Belgrade and the Archive of the City of Sarajevo. *Kultura i Umjetnost u Bosni i Hercegovini pod Austrougarskom Upravom*. Sarajevo, Arhiv Bosne i Hercegovine, 1968, 790 pp.

Chapter 5

ARTICULATING CULTURAL POLICIES IN BOSNIA-HERCEGOVINA: AUSTRO-HUNGARIAN CENSORSHIP OF THE DAILY PRESS AND LITERARY JOURNALS

Prior to the Austro-Hungarian occupation of Bosnia-Hercegovina, there existed already a modest body of achievements produced by the native intellectual elite. A number of dailies and journals were published by locally owned presses. Several private collectors boasted rich depositories of books and manuscripts. From time to time, theatrical performances took place organized by the traveling theater companies. During special holidays several church singers societies gave choral recitals. These results were achieved by individual efforts and were not the outcome of an established cultural policy of Turkish overlords. The low level of literacy of the population, comprising only three percent, illustrated the lack of concerted efforts in regard to educational policies. Prior to the Austro-Hungarian occupation, during the period of reforms during the 1850s and leading to the early 1870s, the Turkish administration showed an increased initiative in the field of general enlightenment. However, Bosnia-Hercegovina was not influenced to a great extent by this late awakening of the cultural progress since it remained to be on the periphery of the Turkish Empire.[1]

---

[1] Milorad Ekmečić *Stvaranje Jugoslavije 1790-1918*, Belgrade, Prosveta, 1989, p. 100. Todor Kruševac, *Bosansko-hercegovački listovi u XIX veku*, Sarajevo 1978, p. 10. Risto Besarović, "Specifičnosti kulturnog razvitka u

The new administration *(Landesregierung)* paid great attention in controlling the public opinion keeping a watch over the reporting of current events. The publication of previously established papers and journals was not allowed to resume. The publishers were informed that special permissions and concessions had to be secured before any publication of journals and dailies could resume.

The first concessions for the publications of journals were granted as late as 1881—some three years after the Austro-Hungarian occupation of Bosnia-Hercegovina. These concessions were given to the editors of officially sanctioned dailies and periodicals which served as the mouthpiece of the administration. Among the first was the journal *Bosnische Post* which started its publication in 1883. The journal was published in the German language and served as a vehicle of the Provincial Government *(Landesregierung)* throughout the Austro-Hungarian occupation and subsequent annexation of Bosnia-Hercegovina.[2]

It was not easy to receive a concession for the publication of a journal: the wait for the approval could be a long time, often requiring additional corroboration. There was also the required submission of the journal prior to its distribution for the so called "preventive censoring." Any article that was declared as unsuitable had to be replaced by previously approved material, so that no blank places would show in the final version of the issue. Yet the persistence of the interested writers and editors in pursuing their mission paid off: the literary journals managed to mobilize the talents of a number of creative individuals.

Over the years, the journals *Zora, Bosanska vila, Behar, Razvitak, Pregled,* the dailies like the *Srpska Riječ, Hrvatski dnevnik, Musavat, Otadžbina, Glas slobode* distinguished themselves

---

Bosni i Hercegovini 1878-1918," *Iz kulturne i političke istorije Bosne i Hercegovine,* Sarajevo, Svjetlost, 1966, pp. 7-9.

2 Todor Kruševac, "Periodika bosanska u prvom austriskom periodu," *Zavisni politički listovi, Prilog za proučavanje istorije Sarajeva,* Sarajevo, 1974, p. 135.

performing a valuable service for the growing number of their devoted readers.

In September of 1884, the first number of the Turkish journal *Vatan* appeared in Sarajevo. The local authorities forwarded two copies of the journal with the German translation of the editorial article to the authorities in Vienna. The accompanying report stated that the permission for the publication of this journal was given in May of 1884, in accordance with the established procedures.[3]

Vatan's lead editorial article contained a very valuable assessment of the early years of Austro-Hungarian occupation. The unnamed writer stated that seven years had passed since the last issue of the Turkish newspaper *Vatan* has been published. The journal had previously enjoyed the prestige as the official newspaper of the Turkish administration. The present journal was no longer an official newspaper. This time *Vatan* was founded thanks to the joint efforts of several outstanding members of the Muslim community. The need was felt to inform the public about the important current events as well as about the newly formulated laws and regulations. The past historic events still loomed large in the memory of the Turkish population and the onslaught of the Russian army during the Russo-Turkish war was still remembered. [4]

The editorial reminded the readers that the Muslim population in Bosnia-Hercegovina was presently in a better position than Muslims in other Balkan countries. The Emperor of Austria-Hungary safeguarded the dignity of Muslim social standing. The unnamed writer based this opinion very likely on the fact that the Provincial Government choose not to proceed with the anticipated land reforms and the large land holdings remained as before in the hands of a few rich land lords, mostly Muslims.

---

[3] Risto Besarović, Editor, *Kultura i Umjetnost u Bosni i Hercegovini pod Austrougarskom Upravom. Gradja za proučavanje političkih, kulturnih i socijalno-ekonomskih pitanja iz prošlosti Bosne i Hercegovine (XIX i XX vijek).* Sarajevo, Arhiv BiH, 1968, p. 426.

[4] Besarović, *Kultura i Umjetnost u Bosni i Hercegovini,* p. 427.

Moreover, the Emperor introduced many advantages, acquired from progressive developments elsewhere, that was coupled with the benefits of a peaceful situation in both provinces. In Bulgaria, on the other hand, the Muslims were ruled by former serfs *(kmetovi)* who appropriated the wealth of their former overlords. The editor thought that religious freedom did not existed for Muslims in Bulgaria.[5]

The writer recalled the early days of Austro-Hungarian occupation of Bosnia-Hercegovina. At first, the occupation did not proceed in an orderly fashion and in peaceful cooperation with the population of Bosnia-Hercegovina. Instead, the Austrian forces were confronted with a fierce upheaval of the renegades. The occupiers reacted with military force using repressive measures in order to enforce their rule.[6]

The writer expressed his satisfaction that the Austrians treated all the population in Bosnia with an even hand. They did not single out or castigate the Muslims since the Austrians treated equally all nationalities from the very beginning of the occupation.

The writer pointed out that the Muslim population was not pleased with the arrival of Austro-Hungarian military might: they feared that the occupation would not bring betterment and would instead introduce other forms of exploitation. The Muslims were obviously surprised that the Provincial Government did not exercise special humanitarian concerns for the Christian population. In addition, agrarian reforms had not been introduced, as previously discussed and agreed upon at the Berlin Congress. Most of all, the Austrian forces aspired to extend their occupation of the region for a

---

5 Besarović, *Kultura i Umjetnost u Bosni i Hercegovini,* p. 428.

6 Besarović, *Kultura i Umjetnost u Bosni i Hercegovini,* p. 428. Interestingly enough, some Austrian historians acknowledged the heavy fighting of the population resisting with all their might the advancing army. Compare, Valeria Heuberger, Hans Ilming, *Bosnien-Herzegovina 1878-1918, Alte Ansichten vom gelungenen Zusammenleben,* Vienna, Christian Brandstaeter Verlag, 1994, pp. 19-20.

long time. In order to keep their rule, they sought support from the rich Muslim landowners, as the influential social class .

According to *Vatan's* editorial, the existing taxation and various regulations were respected and even supplemented *(ergänzt)* with new taxes and regulations. Obviously *Vatan's* editors were well informed about the increased burden of taxation as the main complaint of the population.

The editorial praised the building of the railroad linking Sarajevo with Austria-Hungary as well as the planned railroad connection between Mostar and the port of Metković.[7]

The Muslims were satisfied that their religious cannons were respected and their *kadis* (judges) were allowed to continue the practice of *sheriat*. In comparison, the Muslim population in Cypress did not enjoy the same privileges. The English government did not try to improve the situation on the island, and railroads were not built. The English overlords were only interested in exploiting the riches of the island for themselves.

The editorial concluded that the Berlin Treaty brought, in fact, advantages to the Muslim brethren. Turkey had again preserved its presence in Europe. The peace agreement was strengthened by the intentions and actions of the three Emperors of Austria-Hungary, Germany, and Russia. Even France had approached the Great Powers, although until recently France abstained from collaboration with them due to long-standing animosity directed against Germany. The Serbian government showed good faith in various negotiations. Even Montenegro, the staunch enemy of the Turks, promised to offer compensation for some former Turkish estates.[8]

Obviously, the Muslims were pleased that the Provincial Government was responsive to their needs and demands. The official policy relied on the support of the Muslim landowners, much

---

7 Besarović, *Kultura i Umjetnost u Bosni i Hercegovini,* p. 429.

8 Besarović, *Kultura i Umjetnost u Bosni i Hercegovini,* p.427.

to the woe and growing resentment of the vast majority of the rural population.[9]

In 1884, the chief of the Austro-Hungarian government in Sarajevo, Johann Appel, decided to blacklist a number of newspapers and journals and stop their distribution in Bosnia-Hercegovina, fearing their influence. He informed the Finance minister in Vienna of his decision to censor a number of publications, not allowing their distribution in Bosnia-Hercegovina. These publications were mailed from Hungary directly to a post office box in Sarajevo. Most of these journals have been published in Serbia or in the Serbian and Croatian regions under Hungarian jurisdiction. The following newspapers were mentioned as undesirable: *Dio, Istok, Jedinstvo, Mlada Srbadija, Narodna misao, Nova Srbija, Radnik, Ujedinjenje* and *Zvono*. The same was suggested for the journal of the Radical party in Serbia *Odjek* which replaced the former *Samouprava*. [10]

In fact, the authorities imposed further limitation of the freedom of speech by opposing the distribution of journals and papers published in Serbia and Voivodina. Moreover, they curtailed the publications of journals and daily papers in many devious ways imposing the obligatory examination of every issue of any paper before its publication *(Bürstenauszug)*. This procedure, dubbed as "preventive censoring," continued to be observed during the entire Austro-Hungarian occupation of Bosnia-Hercegovina.

Even editors and publishers of various journals dealing with theological and educational matters had to request permissions for publication. In May of 1887, the Serbian Metropolitan Djordje Nikolajević submitted the request for publication of a journal entitled, *Dabro-Bosanski i*Istočnik. The Metropolitan pointed to the need for a religious and educational journal. Such a journal would facilitate the duties of the priests serving in the Dabro-Bosnian Dioceses by helping them to address the needs of parishioners. The

---

9 Ekmečić, *Stvaranje Jugoslavije 1790-1918*, p. 83 and p. 95.

10 Besarović, *Kultura i Umjetnost u Bosni i Hercegovini* , p. 431. Appel's report was dated 18 December 1884.

journal would deal with topics of general enlightenment, educational issues, discussions of selected sermons, articles about the history of church, religious customs and literary news. The journal would also help explain the new governmental regulations pertaining to the church, and inform about the religious events. It would explain the meaning of holidays by explicating the lives of the saints and elucidate the rules by which the church should abide. The journal would be published monthly. [11]

The petition was forwarded to the Joint Ministry in Vienna supplied with a commentary by Johann Appel and dated 4 June 1887. The reply came swiftly from Vienna, signed by the Finance Minister, Benjamin von Kállay, granting the permission for publication of the *Dabro-Bosanski Istočnik*. Kállay's reply stressed the need for the continuing surveillance of the journal in order to safeguard its ecclesiastical character. He also posited that the editor of the journal, Nikola Lalić should be informed that the permission could be revoked at any time. Kállay added, in a conciliatory tone lessening the implied threat of a closure, that a similar provision was already in place for the two catholic church journals published at the time in Sarajevo.

The Austrian authorities in Sarajevo informed Metropolitan Nikolajević that the permission for publication of the *Dabro-Bosanski Istočnik* had been granted. Moreover, the letter addressed to Metropolitan Nikolajević specified five requirements that the journal should meet:

1. The Government may revoke the privilege of the publication of the journal at any time.

2. The journal was due for "preventive censoring," and it could not be published prior to the submission to the government for evaluation.

3. The spaces left blank after an article was stricken should be substituted with an appropriate text.

---

[11] Besarović, *Kultura i Umjetnost u Bosni i Hercegovini,* pp. 435-436. Nikolajević submitted the request on May 15, 1887.

4. The Government should receive two additional copies immediately after the publication of the journal.

5. Any change in the program, title or personnel employed by the journal could be allowed only by a special permission of the Government. [12]

The formulation of these requirements presents valuable insight into the editorial policies that the Austro-Hungarian government intended to enforce. The candid disclosure of their policies presented the authorities as stern and adamant rulers suppressing any possible free exchange of ideas.

In October 1887, the Franciscan Brotherhood requested a name change of their journal from *Glasnik Bosanskih i Hercegovačkih Franjevaca* to *Glasnik Yugoslovenskih Franjevaca* (The Herald of Yugoslav Franciscans). The Franciscan monks argued that the changed title would enlarge their readership by attracting readers outside of Bosnia-Hercegovina to include the neighboring regions as well. Although the Austrian authorities upheld a policy of suppressing the use of national denominations in any titles of journals, societies, libraries, or reading halls, an exception was made in the case of the Franciscan request. However, the chief of the Sarajevo office, Johann Appel, posited that the change of name would not alter the editorial policies. The appointed preventive measures would continue to ensure that the established policies regarding the journal's publication would stay in place.[13]

Appel forwarded the petition and his report to the Joint Finance Ministry in Vienna. The Finance Minister in charge of Bosnia-

---

[12] Besarović, *Kultura i Umjetnost u Bosni i Hercegovini,* pp. 437-438. Kállay's permission was dated 13 June 1887.

[13] Besarović, *Kultura i Umjetnost u Bosni i Hercegovini,* p. 441. Appel recommended that the name change be granted. Appel's report was dated 25 November 1887: Die von der Redaction des Glasnik bos. herceg. franjevaca geplante Titeländerung bliebe im Ubrigen ohne Einfluss auf das Programm der Zeitschrift selbst, in den vorgeschriebenen Präventivmassregeln liegt aber die volle Gewahr dafür, dass sie Seitungsunternehemen die bisher verfolgten Bahnen nicht verlassen werde.

Hercegovina, Benjamin von Kállay, replied granting permission if certain conditions were met.[14] He supported Appel's recommendation for the approval of the name change. He warned that it would be necessary to watch and exercise judiciously a discreet "preventive censorship" of the journal; all that could endanger Austria's interests should be avoided. Great attention should be paid that under the name 'South Slavic' (Yugoslav) no special Croatian tendencies would be introduced. Kállay's permission, dated 14 December 1887, was marked as 'confidential'*(Vertraulich)*.[15]

Although Kállay himself had misgivings about the name change, it seemed that the Austrian officials in Sarajevo were not informed about the evolving Yugoslav rapprochement fostering cultural cooperation. It should be remembered that in 1867 the Croatian Academy of Science chose to rename their prestigious institution to Yugoslav Academy. Bishop Strosmayer was a staunch supporter of Croatian and Serbian collaboration and promoted a united Yugoslav ideological platform. The motivation of the Franciscans for the insertion of the denomination *Yugoslav* could be understood as part of the same notion.

In August of 1890 Eduard Spindler, the owner of the book printing shop in Sarajevo, submitted the petition for the publication of a weekly magazine *Napredak* published in Cyrillic alphabet. Antonije A. Stražičić was suggested for the position of the editor. Since Stražičić was born in Dalmatia, the Austrian authorities requested information about Stražičić from the authorities in Zadar. According to the furnished data, Stražičić was a catholic although his

---

[14] Benjamin von Kállay started his illustrious political career in 1868 as an Austro-Hungarian consul and diplomatic agent at the court of Prince MIhailo Obrenović. In 1882 he was appointed to the position of a Joint Minister of Finance in charge of Bosnia-Hercegovina. Kállay's mother, Amalia Blašković de Ebetska was of Serbian descent.

[15] Besarović, *Kultura i Umjetnost u Bosni i Hercegovini,* p. 442. The subsequent permission, granting the name change, was handed over to Friar Ante Đurić on 18 December 1887.

cultural and political interests were aligned with the Serbian party. Very likely that Stražičić was a Serb belonging to the Old Catholic faith, *staro-katolička veroispovest.* He took active part in the political campaign on behalf of the Serbs in Dalmatia, and in Dubrovnik. Stražičić was described as a decent man and there was no reason to oppose his nomination. Stražičić wrote articles for the journal *Srpski glas* reporting often about events in Dubrovnik as a regular corespondent from this city. Stražičić wrote also articles on literary topics which were published in the prestigious journal *Bosanska vila.* He enjoyed a reputation of a fine journalist. The journal was scheduled to start appearing on the 1 of September, 1890.[16]

The permission for the publication of *Napredak* was finally granted and Stražičić was confirmed as the editor of the magazine. Additional information were forwarded to Vienna only three days prior to the scheduled publication of the first issue. The report was signed by the chief of the Austrian government in Sarajevo Kutschera and was dated 28 August 1890.

The Chief of the Provincial Government Appel reported to the Joint Ministry of Finance about the questionable editorial policy of the journal *Vrhbosna.* This journal was published under the auspices of the local Catholic Bishopric. In the issue of 1 October 1892, *Vrhbosna* had published the poem "Ideja za zivot" (An Idea for Life). The issue was duly presented to the Interior Department of the Provincial Government for preventive censoring.

Appel was not prepared to encounter any difficulties with this journal. Yet, he became very surprised by the tendentious tenor of the newly published poem: he declared the content to be infused with inflammatory political overtones. Appel could not understand why the editor chose to publish a poem that did not correspond to the established program of a religious periodical. Therefore, Appel summoned the editor to his office questioning his motivation for publishing such a poem. He reported with obvious relief that the

---

16 Besarović, *Kultura i Umjetnost u Bosni i Hercegovini,* pp. 442-444.

editor eventually agreed that the poem was not suitable for dissemination in *Vrhbosna*— a journal sponsored by the Catholic church. Appel was clearly ill at ease about the whole incident and he decided to file a report addressed to the Joint Ministry of Finance in Vienna. He appended the mentioned poem to his report.[17]

The examiners kept a watchful eye on the journals and newspapers published in Bosnia and Hercegovina as well as on those published abroad. In 1908 the number of censored titles reached 187 according to the documentation referring to the censoring of newspapers and journals.[18]

Kállay's Role in the Publication of the Journal *Nada* and the Status of the Journal *Bosnische Post*

The journal *Nada (Hope)* deserves a special place among the periodicals published during the Austro-Hungarian occupation. The Finance Minister Benjamin von Kállay suggested the idea of an illustrated literary and educational journal to be published in Sarajevo. Kállay envisioned that such a journal should bring many benefits. While on an official visit to Bosnia-Hercegovina in 1893, Kállay formalized his request for a journal in a writ addressed to the Provincial Government *(Landesregierung)* in Sarajevo, dated 14 February 1894. Kállay stated that he had previously informed the Provincial Government about his decision to start a literary-educational journal in Bosnian language. The task of the journal would be to provide interesting material from different fields of knowledge and education presented to the native reading public in a

[17] Besarović, *Kultura i Umjetnost u Bosni i Hercegovini,* p. 71.

[18] Arhive Bosne i Hercegovine, Fond Zemaljske Vlade, No. 1627, res/1908. Quoted after Besarović, *Kultura i Umjetnost u Bosni i Hercegovini,* p. 33.

simple and convincing manner appropriate to their educational horizon and level of understanding. On the other hand, the journal should depict in word and picture, the cultural development in Bosnia-Hercgovina in an objective and trustworthy manner in order to advance such information abroad. [19]

Kállay projected the role of the journal as two-fold: firstly, the journal should inform the population of Bosnia-Hercegovina about the new developments in "all fields of human endeavor." Kállay indicated that," the submitted articles should be adjusted and simplified to match the level of comprehension of the reading public." Secondly, the journal should inform the readers abroad about cultural developments in Bosnia-Hercegovina. Kállay established that he was also considering the political benefits that such information might bring: he obviously wanted to present Bosnia-Hercegovina as an independent cultural reality with a distinct scholarly, artistic and literary profile.

Kállay reasoned that the Croatian and Serbian journals of this kind were mostly nurturing their own respective national tendencies. The new journal should aim to be impartial and concentrate on belles-lettres and the enlightenment of the population in Bosnia-Hercegovina. Kállay hoped that the journal would find many readers among the native population and among the civil servants of the Austro-Hungarian government in Sarajevo. Kállay asked Constantine Hörmann to closely examine the feasibility of a journal aimed to highlight the specificity of Bosnia-Hercegovina. Hörmann was the Counsel to the Provincial Government in Sarajevo and he was charged with the implementation of cultural and educational policies in Bosnia-Hercegovina. In the end, Kállay decided to delegate the responsibilities of the founding of the journal to Hörmann. [20]

Hörmann took his newly assigned task seriously and proceeded to examine the current periodicals in other Slavic countries,

---

19 Besarović, *Kultura i Umjetnost u Bosni i Hercegovini* , p. 91.

20 Besarović, *Kultura i Umjetnost u Bosni i Hercegovini,* pp. 91- 93.

including Russia. He strongly supported the idea of a literary and educational journal since he believed that there existed a real need for such a journal in Bosnia-Hercegovina.

On 4 February 1894, Hörmann submitted a detailed report suggesting the format of the journal and a list of possible collaborators. He supplied the names of writers and illustrators from Bosnia-Hercegovina, Croatia, Slavonia, Serbia, Montenegro, and Bulgaria. He included the expected costs for the publication of the journal and honoraria for the contributors. Hörmann anticipated that the journal would very likely receive around 1400 subscriptions. Roughly 950 copies of the journal should be printed in the Latin alphabet and 440 copies in the Cyrillic alphabet. The single issue had a price of 6 florins and it was calculated that the subscription should bring 8400 florins, while the overall cost of publication would amount to 10600 florins. The suggested name for the journal was *Nada* (Hope). Hörmann's report was dated 4 February 1894.[21]

In order to ensure the collaboration of eminent South Slav writers and artists, Hörmann decided to personally visit and invite a number of writers and journalists to contribute. For this purpose he traveled to Belgrade, Sofia and Zagreb in May of 1894. More importantly, Hörmann recorded his impressions of places and personalities he had visited leaving a valuable report and a unique travelogue. He managed to visit not only the writers and artists but also the Serbian King Alexander and a number of high ranking politicians. Hörmann's Travelogue very likely served as a *bona fide* information for Kállay and other high ranking officials. Kállay might have even suggested the travel to Hörmann.

Hörmann arrived in Belgrade on May 6, 1894. He called on his former acquaintance Dr. Nikola Petrović whom he had met earlier in Sarajevo. At the time of their first meeting in Sarajevo, Petrović had guided a group of senior high school students from Belgrade on a study tour to Sarajevo. Similar guided tours to interesting locations

---

21 Besarović, *Kultura i Umjetnost u Bosni i Hercegovini,* pp. 74-79.

were, as a rule, offered to graduating seniors and have remained a cherished tradition of the high school programs in Serbia up to the present day. Petrović was serving as the headmaster of the famous Second High-School for Boys in Belgrade. He obviously wanted his young charges to visit Sarajevo and possibly to establish contact with their Serbian and Croatian counterparts. Petrović was very likely trying to cultivate friendly contacts and cultural collaboration among the neighboring young people.

Hörmann learned, that in the meantime, Petrović had become the director of the National Theater in Belgrade. Petrović was pleased to invite Hörmann to attend two performances in the National Theater the same day. Hörmann noted that he saw the matinee performance of the play *Djido* by Janko Veselinović depicting the life in a Serbian village. In the evening, he attended the play *Pribislav i* Božana which was based on Slavic mythology.

The next day he visited the Archeological Museum and its director Valter Valterović. Valterović complained about the insufficiency of funds allocated for the museum. The Museum was founded by Janko Šafarik, whose efforts have laid a solid foundation for a good start. After his death, the acquisition of artifacts have gradually ceded. The numismatic collection, given to the Museum by King Milan, was in poor shape, with many gold pieces missing. Valterović explained that Queen Natalie gave these coins as gifts to her many god-children at baptism.[22]

Hörmann paid a visit to the Serbian Prime Minister Svetomir Nikolajević and was introduced to the members of his cabinet. Hörmann was very impressed with the Minister for Education Djordjević, who was a well educated man. Djordjević presented Hörmann with the new issue of the journal *Prosvetni glasnik* published by the Ministry of Education. This journal was regularly sent to the Museum in Sarajevo as part of the exchange program of publications. Djordjević asked his guest to send to him the teaching curricula *(Lehrpläne)* of all middle schools in Bosnia-Hercegovina in

22 Besarović, *Kultura i Umjetnost u Bosni i Hercegovini,* p. 96-97.

particular from the vocational schools and the Theological Seminary *(Bogoslovija)* in Reljevo. Djordjević also asked for recently published textbooks in order to compare the new teaching curricula with the old ones. Djordjević felt the need for reorganization of some schools in Serbia. Djordjević thought that there were too many high schools *(Gymnasiums)* and not nearly enough vocational schools available to the students.[23]

Hörmann was granted a brief audience with the young King Alexander. The King was pleasantly surprised by Hörmann's knowledge of the Serbian language. Hörmann explained that he was born in Belova, in the region called the Military Border, and learned the language as a child.

The King wanted in particular to learn more about the Museum in Sarajevo and its archeological collection. He asked for detailed information about the number of employees, the cataloguing and display of artifacts. He was familiar with the journal *Glasnik zemaljskog muzeja* (Herald of the Provincial Museum) published by the Museum. He complained that the Museum in Belgrade was not organized as well, since it was housed in several separate buildings lacking unity. The King wanted to learn more about the newly founded workshops under the auspices of the Museum in Sarajevo. These workshops aimed to preserve a number of old handicrafts and specially the already famous art of carpet weaving. The products of the artisans employed in these workshops were in high demand due to their exceptional quality.[24]

Hörmann did not find many future contributors in Belgrade for the journal *Nada* and only a handful of writers and scholars agreed tentatively to send contributions. The writers seemed mistrustful to collaborate with a journal whose sponsor was a Counsel to the Austrian government. Some even thought that the covert political tendencies of the journal *Nada* would be eventually harmful for the Serbian cause. One writer asked whether he could submit an article

---

23 Besarović, *Kultura i Umjetnost u Bosni i Hercegovini,* p. 100.

24 Besarović, *Kultura i Umjetnost u Bosni i Hercegovini,* p. 103.

dealing with the Serbs and their language. Hörmann assured him that writing about the Serbs in the kingdom of Serbia was acceptable, provided the political or religious tendencies be omitted. Hörmann repeated that the journal aimed to publish articles about literature and education. However, the unnamed acquaintance was not satisfied since he considered that the Serbian population in Bosnia-Hercegovina should be included when discussing Serbian culture. In the end, Hörmann received a confirmation for future collaboration from Dr. Nikola Petrović, Professor Ljuba Stojanović and the writer Milorad Šapčanin. Incidental pictorial illustrations were promised by Valter Valterović, Dr. Jovan Žujović, Dr. Batut and others.

The next city on Hörmann's itinerary was Sofia. Since Hörmann did not have any previous contacts with Bulgarian writers, he asked the Austrian Consul von Burian for assistance. Taking Burian's advice, Hörmann paid a visit to the president Stefan Stambolov. While approaching the mansion, Hörmann noted that several gendarmes were guarding the locked entry of the residence. After the massive door was unlocked, Hörmann entered the foyer, and the doors were swiftly locked again. Stambolov was very kind and suggested a meeting with the minister of education, Gencev. Gencev turned to be very helpful in facilitating the meetings with writers and artists willing to contribute to the journal *Nada*.

In the course of his stay, Hörmann took walks in the pleasant park Jardin Royal. One morning, to his surprise, he noticed an approaching cavalcade consisting of a horse drawn carriage guarded on all sides by seven gendarmes on horseback: seated in the carriage was Stambolov with his wife. Hörmann was soon informed that Stambolov always appeared well-guarded after an earlier assault in front of Hotel Bulgaria that had been carried out by a political dissident named Belčev. Moreover, Stambolov, like many of the ministers in his cabinet, quickly acquired considerable fortune.

Hörmann noticed that the ladies of the high society were dressed in finery that must have exceeded their husbands salaries.[25]

Hörmann was impressed by the artist Thadeus von Ajdukiewicz, who was well known for his exquisite portraits. Ajdukiewicz invited him to his atelier. In the course of conversation, Hörmann learned that Ajdukiewicz was a versatile individual: he was a well informed and skillful painter, but also a passionate horseman. Hörmann thought that it would be desirable to invite Ajdukiewicz to establish his atelier in Sarajevo. In the case that Ajdukiewicz would arrive in Sarajevo for a visit, Hörmann wrote, he should be shown the attractive places of the city. Hörmann listed several places to be shown such as the Horse Racing Track and the State Depot for Horse Breeding, the Agricultural Station *Butimir* and the famous spa at Ilidža.[26]

All this spoke of the good life that Hörmann and other Austrian officials enjoyed in Sarajevo and its environs. Hörmann obviously appreciated all the advantages that Sarajevo had to offer. Moreover, the Horse Track, in addition to the profitable raising of full bred horses and agricultural enterprises at *Butimir* provided hefty profits for the Austrian Government. The fertile soil and a well operated farm produced a cornucopia of fruits and vegetables, meat and dairy products. In addition, there was the beauty of the countryside, mountain views, and the green valley intersected by the river Bosna. The banks of the Bosna at Ilidža were favorite places for outings among the locals. These picturesque places have been described by unknown folk singers in many songs celebrating the beauty of the clear waters and the clean air scented by the lilac and rose blossoms of the surrounding gardens. The beauty of the countryside was discovered and appreciated by many Austrian travelers, writers and journalists, who wrote travelogues and

---

25 Besarović, *Kultura i Umjetnost u Bosni i Hercegovini,* p. 106.

26 Interestingly enough, Benjamin von Kállay and his family chose Ilidža as their summer residence. A spacious house in this famous spa became the summer domicile of Kállay and his family.

articles describing the region. Even post cards with captions in German language, published during the occupation, described with great allure the beauty of Bosnia-Hercegovina.[27]

On 19 May Hörmann arrived in Zagreb where he quickly established contacts with several writers. However, the writers were not yet ready to promise collaboration; they preferred to write for Croatian journals published in Zagreb. Many excused themselves since they had obligations to write for the various publications of the literary association *Matica hrvatska*. Others were of the opinion that the main literary center should be in Zagreb and that the literary development in Bosnia-Hercegovina should be directed from Zagreb. Hörmann complained that he had to speak for hours, providing information about the journal *Nada,* in order to attract a single writer for collaboration. Hörmann felt betrayed since he was born in Belovar and spent many years serving in Croatia and subsequently in Bosnia-Hercegovina, as an Austrian governmental officer *(Beamte).* He expressed his disappointment as he had thought that his offer for collaboration would be eagerly accepted. Among the writers who agreed to send their articles was Šandor Gjalski (pen name of Ljubo Babić), Buda Budislavljević, and Eugen Kumičić.

Hörmann pointed out that his efforts in promoting interest in literary and educational collaboration were not appreciated. Yet, he thought that these efforts would help create a new "Bosnian" culture. He mentioned with obvious pleasure that he was known, in some Croatian circles, as "the Father of the Bosnian nationality and language." [28] He must have believed that he could help forge a "Bosnian" nationality from above by enhancing collaboration among the writers in Bosnia and neighboring Serbia, Bulgaria and Croatia. Such collaboration would acknowledge Bosnia as a separate entity

[27]Heuberger, Ilming, *Bosnien-Herzegovina 1878-1918.* This book includes a selection of postcards, title pages from several travelogues and various illustrations describing Bosnia-Hercegovina.

[28] Besarović, *Kultura i Umjetnost u Bosni i Hercegovini,* p. 111.

under the aegis of a benevolent and enlightened Austro-Hungarian government. Obviously, Hörmann was in agreement with the viewpoints of his superior, the Finance Minister Benjamin von Kállay, with regard to the creation of a Bosnian consciousness as well as to the invention of the Bosnian language.

Interestingly enough, both Kállay and Hörmann thought that the creation of a literary and educational journal would help to create a new cultural entity "Bosnian culture." This new culture would create an artificially homogenized Bosnian consciousness that would produce, in the process, a historic amnesia. Both Kállay and Hörmann hoped to obscure the existence of distinct cultural entities in Bosnia-Hercegovina, which produced their own cultural and religious edifices, in addition to rich folklore: epic and lyric poetry, tales, songs, dances, including exquisite artifacts. Since Hörmann resided in Sarajevo, he must have been aware of the importance of religious denominations that united and also separated the respective population in Bosnia-Hercegovina. He wrote numerous opinions himself while settling the requests of all three religious groups comprised of Orthodox Christians, Catholics and Muslims. These groups lived side by side for centuries preserving their own respective cultures and way of life.

Kállay was overall in agreement with Hörmann's extensive report about his travels and meetings with possible collaborators of the journal. He dubbed Hörmann's report as *Promemoria* and found it useful in securing needed funds for the publication of the journal *Nada*. Kállay repeated his hope that the journal would enlighten and stimulate the reading public in Bosnia-Hercegovina. The journal should also inform the readers abroad about the cultural events in Bosnia-Hercegovina. Kállay had a number of suggestions referring to the publishing and illustration of the journal. He suggested that the painter Ewald Arndt should be hired in order to take charge of the pictorial aspects of the journal. A copy of Kállay' s report to the Joint Finance Ministry in Vienna was also forwarded to the Austro-Hungarian government in Sarajevo. The first issue of the journal *Nada* was scheduled for October 1894. The journal was to appear twice a month.[29]

Hörmann extended an invitation encouraging collaboration with the journal *Nada* by publishing announcements in the press and soliciting manuscripts. In response to Hörmann's announcements Jovan Jovanović-Zmaj wrote an open letter which was published in the journal *Obzor*. Jovanović refused to collaborate with the editors of the new journal since it was not mentioned in the invitation or the announcement which language would be used Serbian or Croatian. Jovanović-Zmaj disclosed that he had written quite a bit for Serbian papers, and also for Croatian papers as well. He suspected that *Nada*, like the Provincial Government itself, would choose to publish articles written in the so called 'Land language.' Jovanović-Zmaj emphasized that he cannot support the notion of inventing such an unsuitable name for "our beautiful language instead of its real, ancient and beautiful name." [30]

The esteemed prince Lujo Vojnović from Dubrovnik wrote in support of Jovanović's refusal for collaboration on 1 December 1894. He stated that the letter of Jovanović-Zmaj has excited and agitated all the writers, Serbian or Croatian since Hörmann's earlier statement issued at the meeting in Sarajevo stressed that the writers may use freely the name Serbian or Croatian. The editorial office would remain impartial in accordance with the current system in Bosnia. [31]

The first issue of *Nada* appeared on the news stands on 1 January 1895. The journal was generously produced and included numerous befitting illustrations and drawings. On the

---

29 Besarović, *Kultura i Umjetnost u Bosni i Hercegovini*, p. 91. Kállay's report was dated 14 February 1894, Vienna.

30 Kruševac, *Bosansko Hercegovacki listovi u XIX veku*, p. 348. The letter appeared in *Obzor*, No. 264, on 17 November 1894.

31 Kruševac, *Bosansko Hercegovački listovi u XIX veku*, p. 348.

top of the first page the image of an old bard - *guslar* was depicted. The *guslar* was perceived as the valued interpret of historic memory safeguarding the knowledge of important events. He was portrayed with the stringed instrument—the*gusle*—in his hands since he always recited the epic renditions of historic events with the accompaniment of *gusle*. The title *Nada* was surrounded by a star and a crescent reminding of Muslim insignia. According to the title, the journal was dedicated to learning, entertainment and fine arts explorations. The Provincial Museum was listed as the editorial office of the journal and Constantine Hörmann was the editor in chief.

The editorial published in the first issue of the journal explained the advantages of journals dealing with learning and entertainment. These journals nourish and enrich the spiritual life of a people. Furthermore, the editorial established that: " Our people are united as an entity by their language, regardless of the name and alphabet they use. They have developed a fine literary writing reflecting their well known talents and spiritual values. Earlier, comparable journals were published but they did not last long. These considerations created the idea to start the journal *Nada* in Sarajevo that would serve as a mirror reflecting the spiritual culture of the South Slav peoples." [32]

Evidently, the editors strove to attract writers from neighboring Slavic countries by encouraging collaboration in the literary realm. Most importantly, the mutuality of the spoken language was emphasized contrary to the previous statements in various reports and announcements. Prior to the founding of the journal, the invitations for collaboration emphasized the usage of the so called *Land-* or *Bosnian* language. However, the unwillingness of the writers to use the invented *Land-* or *Bosnian* language influenced this change. The responses of Jovanović-Zmaj and Vojnović must

---

[32] *Nada*, No 1, 1895, Sarajevo, Zemaljski muzej, p. 1.

have had a decisive input in the realization that the creation of an invented language was a self defeating proposition.

Most importantly, the editorial pointed to the well known fact that the same language was used by all the peoples in Bosnia-Hercegovina regardless of their ethnic provenance: "Our people have been united as an entity due to their common language regardless of the name and alphabet they use."

The editorial obviously acknowledged the Hercegovinian—or Southern dialect—as the common language of the population in Bosnia-Hercegovina, regardless of their religion and ethnic background. Very likely, editors wanted to promote good will and collaboration with the writers sharing the same language in Serbia and Croatia. The Hercegovinian—or Southern dialect—was adopted as the common Serbian and Croatian literary language following the signing of the renown *Književni dogovor* (Literary Agreement). In 1850, leading Slavic scholars signed the Literary Agreement in Vienna finalizing this historic decision.[33]

The illustrations included in the first issue of the journal *Nada* presented some scenes from the ordinary life of the people in Bosnia-Hercegovina. The chosen scenes depicted most often Muslim edifices and Muslim people dressed in traditional clothes. Such was the drawing marked with the caption *Povratak s pazara* (Return from the market).[34] The scene depicted an old man with a *fes* on his head riding a donkey. He was crossing an open field with dilapidated gravestones defining this desolate space as an old and abandoned Muslim cemetery overgrown with grass. The illustration was signed by E. A. Ceplin. The same artist provided another illustration depicting a Muslim women with a veil in front of a

---

[33] R. Aleksić et al., *Pravopis srpsko-hrvatskog književnog jezika*, Novi Sad and Zagreb, Matica srpska, Matica hrvatska, 1960, pp. 5-6. Compare also, J. Milojković-Djurić, *Panslavism and National Identity in Russia and in the Balkans 1830-1880* , New York and Boulder, Columbia University Press, 1994, pp. 46-47.

[34] *Nada*, No 1, 1895, p. 5.

dzamija - a Muslim religious edifice. [35] On the next page another Muslim religious edifice was depicted with a passing man wearing a Turkish turban on his head. Interestingly enough, the appended illustrations depicted Bosnia as an exotic oriental land accentuating the unusual and picturesque as if cast in another time and a far away space. Most often the scenes portrayed Muslim men and women as if the majority of the population in Bosnia were Muslims which was not the case. According to the polls conducted in 1879, the total population was 1,158.164. Orthodox numbered 496,485, Catholics 209,391 and Muslims comprised and 448,613. [36]

The journal *Nada* aimed as well to provide information about the cultural life in Bosnia-Hercegovina by publishing literary essays, articles with historical themes, short travelogues and occasional reviews of theatrical plays. The journal hoped to influence and stimulate the literary works of Bosnian writers. The pictorial supplements were commissioned specially for this journal and often depicted picturesque landscapes and old townships projecting a feeling of abandonment and nostalgia for a time gone by.

Bosnian scenes were also presented in the pictorial works of several Austrian, Czech and Hungarian artists centered around *Nada*. Gradually a style developed, bordering on mannerism, depicting Bosnia and Hercegovina with a false romantic aura. The artists used a selective approach trying to portray with an exaggerated pathos picturesque corners of the old urban dwellings or the austere and imposing countryside. Obviously Bosnia-Hercegovina was perceived most of all as "an exotic colony" of the Habsburg Empire.[37]

---

[35] *Nada*, No 1, 1895, p. 8.

[36] Milorad Ekmečić, *Radovi iz Bosne i Hercegovine*, Belgrade, BIGZ, 1997, p. 206.

[37] Ljubica Mladenović: "Staro Sarajevo vidjeno kroz bilježnicu jednog slikara," *Prilozi za proučavanje istorije Sarajeva*, Vol. 1, Muzej grada Sarajeva, Sarajevo 1963, p. 133.

The commissioned art works for the journal *Nada* enjoyed apparently great appeal abroad. Therefore, the Provincial Government in Sarajevo suggested that an exhibit of these drawings and paintings be presented at specially arranged exhibits. The main contributor to *Nada* , Ewald Arndt, had been already invited to participate with his drawings at the exhibit organized in Berlin by the *Verein Berliner Künstler.* The exhibit turned to be very successful. Arndt received fine reviews in the Berlin newspapers for his motives and landscapes from Bosnia-Hercegovina. The Austrian artist Maximilian Lieberwein and the Slovenian painter Ivan Kobilica were mentioned as possible contributors for the future exhibits. These artists already submitted a number of drawings for the journal *Nada.* The mentioned artists decided to form an artistic club dubbed "Die Sarajewoer."

The journal *Nada* was chosen to help commemorate fifty years of the rule of Francis Joseph. In December of 1898, the Provincial Government in Sarajevo approached the Finance Ministry in Vienna in reference to this anniversary. Johann Appel suggested that the 24th issue of the journal *Nada* should mark this event. This special issue should celebrate the life and achievements of Francis Joseph. Again it was suggested that the articles should be written "with great care and in popular form" having in view the local reading public. The patronizing manner did not change over the years: the Bosnian readership was consistently observed as if requiring special considerations and necessary simplifications of published materials *(mit grossem Sorgfalt in populärer Form).* [38]

It was suggested that the solicited articles should describe the Monarch as a ruler and as a family man. Even the title of a prospective article was suggested: *Des Herrschers Herz* (The Heart of the Ruler). This article should describe the personality of the Emperor, as well as the origin of the Habsburg dynasty. Another article could describe the stately residences and country estates of the "beloved Monarch." This special volume should be in the form of

38 Besarović, *Kultura i Umjetnost u Bosni i Hercegovini,* p. 147.

a keepsake, *Gedenkbuch,* to be distributed to the students in local middle schools, police departments, military camps, customs officials in Bosnia-Hercegovina, Vienna, Graz and Budapest. Finally this special issue of *Nada* should be given to the libraries and to the pupils of private religious schools. Even the Central Prison in Zenica should receive copies of the journal.

Kállay accepted this proposition and informed duly the Provincial Government in Sarajevo. Kállay's opinion was dated 28 December 1898. [39]

However, the publication of *Nada* was becoming a financial burden to the editorial office of the Provincial Museum. The journal did not attract the projected number of readers, and the subsidies to the journal increased over the years. In spite of the carefully selected editorial board the journal folded before the decade from its inception was over.

Another paper sanctioned by the Provincial Government, *Bosnische Post*, continued to be published throughout the occupation. Early in 1896 it became known that the current Editor, Milena Mrazović, was ready to sell the journal *Bosnische Post* including the concession for its publication. Mrazović decided to sell the journal for personal reasons, although the journal was well established and had a sound financial balance. Dr. Vladislav Niec, who was until recently associated with this journal, petitioned the government in Sarajevo for the transfer of the concession in view of the anticipated change of ownership. Niec had two partners for this deal: Dr. Vošnjak and Djuro Vrinjanin. The Chief of the Austro-Hungarian government in Sarajevo, Johann Appel, forwarded the petition for the transfer of the concession attached to his own lengthy report.[40]

Appel established that Mrazović was in close touch with Dr. Vošnjak during the past year and a half. Vošnjak had a good salary and a well to do family. Yet, Appel thought that Vošnjak probably would not have the required 40,000 florins, the amount worth a third

---

[39] Besarović, *Kultura i Umjetnost u Bosni i Hercegovini,* p. 147.

[40] Besarović, *Kultura i Umjetnost u Bosni i Hercegovini,* p. 459.

of the asking price. Vošnjak was the leader of the Slovenian Party. Appel proceeded to provide biographical and professional data for both Niec and Vrinjanin. According to Appel, Dr. Niec was son of a Ruthenian priest. He had a profitable law office but very likely did not have enough savings for his share of ownership amounting to 40,000 florins. The third partner, Djuro Vrinjanin, worked as the bookkeeper for the journal *Bosnische Post,* and was in a poor financial position. It was Appel's opinion that the prospective owners did not have enough capital to establish a well organized journalistic enterprise. Their joint financial situation would not allow for the engagement of renown personalities as contributors to the journal. The collaboration of prominent notables in any important project was a goal that the Provincial Government seemed not to be able to accomplish.[41]

The prospective owners promised a better and more competent editorial approach in the sections of the journal dealing with the economy, agriculture, finance and jurisprudence. Appel thought that these assurances were given in order to secure the concession rights. Most importantly, the political affiliations of the partners should be scrutinized. Dr. Niec, an ethnic Ruthenian, had a good reputation as a lawyer. He was careful in his demeanor and very likely he did not see clearly his political role. Yet, there was no doubt that his central orientation was Panslavic: as a Ruthenian, he presumably sympathized with the Russians. His social contacts pointed to the same conclusion, although Niec was very careful while conducting his private affairs. Appel pointed out that these observations were compiled on the basis of a solid surveillance lasting several years.

According to Appel's evaluation, Djuro Vrinjanin was a "pronounced Croatian poltroon of the Starčević party." Moreover, he was ill-bred *(unerzogen)* and had no professional education. For many years, he was a supporter of the Great Croatian Party in the occupied territory. He used every opportunity to represent the

---

41 Besarović, *Kultura i Umjetnost u Bosni i Hercegovini,* p. 460.

Croats from Bosnia in Zagreb and in other places. Vrinjanin tried to point to the interdependence *(Zusammenhörigkeit)* of Bosnia-Hercegovina and Croatia. In these efforts he was helped by one Bobić who was a local iron dealer *(Eisenhandler)*.[42]

Dr. Vošnjak was a well known representative of the Slovenian and Panslavic orientation. He traveled widely through the occupied region in order to get the needed political recognition; Appel noted that all this was already reported to the Government. Thus, the coalition Niec-Vrinjanin-Vošnjak would embody a Ruthenian-Great Croatian-Slovenian-, and most of all, a Panslavic school of thought. The viewpoints of the prospective new owners were not desirable and therefore "needed no further justification." The journal was well received abroad and enjoyed a good reputation. Therefore, Milena Mrazović should be advised to return the concession to the state. Dr. Niec, Dr. Vošnjak and Vrinjanin should not receive the concession for the publication of the journal.

Appel concluded that the real reason for the denial of the concession should not be openly stated. Instead, Dr. Niec should be informed that his request for ownership, as a partner or editor of a political journal was incompatible with his position as a licensed state lawyer. Therefore, he was not eligible for a concession of a journal such as *Bosnische Post*. More importantly, the concession for the journal *Bosnische Post* should be safeguarded for a more appropriate company with a larger investment capital.[43]

The Journal *Bosanska Vila* and its Editors Kašiković and Nikašinović

The reports of Provincial Government officials in Sarajevo reflected occasionally the struggle for prestige of the petty

---

42 Besarović, *Kultura i Umjetnost u Bosni i Hercegovini*, p. 460.

43 Besarović, *Kultura i Umjetnost u Bosni i Hercegovini*, pp. 461-462.

bureaucrats representing two contending empires, Austria-Hungary and Turkey. In the aftermath of the Berlin Peace Treaty the Turkish Sultan and his government remained formally the highest authority in Bosnia-Hercegovina, in spite of the fact that they were obliged to relinquish the administration and economic exploitation of these provinces.

The former Turkish overlords continued to cultivate personal ties with some of their outstanding former subjects. The Austrian authorities were surprised to learn from a Turkish newspaper that Nikola Kašiković, the long time editor of the journal *Bosanska Vila,* received a decoration, the Medžidije*Orden,* from the Turkish Government.

Kašiković received the decoration in 1896, upon the recommendation of Ali Paša Rizvanbegović, although it was not clear why Kašiković deserved this decoration. It was speculated that it might have been due to Kašiković's interest in the Muslim population, and his reports about the Muslims in the journal *Bosanska Vila* and other literary and political journals published in Serbia.[44]

The Austrian officials were disturbed and annoyed by this allegedly disrespectful diplomatic procedure. They were not informed that a decoration was brought to Sarajevo and given to Kašiković. This gesture from the Turkish government seemed to belittle their sovereignty. Moreover, Kašiković never asked for permission to wear this decoration in public. It was reported that Kašiković wore openly the decoration, and even informed the post-office of his new title, "Ritter des ottomanischen Medžidije-Ordens."

The officer in charge, Johann Appel, reported to the authorities in Vienna asking for a permission to call Kašiković for a hearing. He even suggested that the Chief of Police should personally admonish Kašiković not to wear a decoration from a foreign country without an expressed permission of the Austrian authorities. Kašiković should be warned that if he continued to do so he might receive a fine

---

44 Besarović, *Kultura i Umjetnost u Bosni i Hercegovini,* p. 143.

(Bestrafung).[45] Certainly, the demands of the Austrian authorities were redundant, reminiscent of a comic opera plot bordering on impertinence.

The Journal *Bosanska Vila* was founded in 1885 under the auspices of the Serbian Teachers Association in Sarajevo. At first, the editors paid special attention to the collection of folklore most notably orally transmitted epic and lyric poetry, short stories, and traditional customs. Later on *Bosanska Vila* became a journal with literary tendencies and served as a forum for young poets and writers. Nikola Kašiković, a teacher, writer, and folklore collector, became the Editor of the journal in 1887. Kašiković was very successful, and his editorial policies brought recognition and prestige to the journal *Bosanska Vila*. Kašiković managed to attract a number of fine writers not only from Bosnia-Hercegovina but also from Serbia and Croatia. The Austro-Hungarian police paid special attention to the editorial office of the journal, which was even declared, at one time, as the "den of rebels." Over the years, numerous reports testified to the confidential monitoring of Nikola Kašiković since he became well known as the influential editor of *Bosanska Vila*.

Kašiković continued to be closely followed by the Austrian authorities even when visiting the neighboring countries. A case in point was a report referring to Nikola Kašiković and his participation during the Vuk Stefanović-Karadžić anniversary in Belgrade. In early September 1888, Nikola Kašiković and one high school pupil, Simo Jeremić, attended the one hundredth anniversary celebration of the birth of Vuk Stefanović-Karadžić The report stated that Nikola Kašiković was "politically unreliable" and therefore should be monitored during his stay in Belgrade. [46]

Moreover, the authorities thought that Kašiković and his close friend, the orthodox priest Stjepo Trifković, played an important role in the Serbian movement for autonomy. Kašiković's occasional

---

45 Besarović, *Kultura i Umjetnost u Bosni i Hercegovini,* p. 145.

46 Besarović, *Kultura i Umjetnost u Bosni i Hercegovini,* p. 252.

travels to Serbia were questioned: he purportedly went on official business as the editor of *Bosanska Vila* in order to promote his journal. In fact, most of the journal's subscribers and a number of contributors were from Serbia, and Kašiković had legitimate reasons to cultivate contacts with his readership. Nevertheless, the Austro-Hungarian officials thought that Kašiković's travels to Serbia also served his covert actions involving local dissidents*(Malcontenten)* and their counterparts in Serbia. [47]

Interestingly enough, in October of 1912 a detailed report supplied information about Kašiković's family. The report stated that he was married and that his wife, a former teacher, was of Serbian descent born in the Serbian regions of southern Hungary. Their three sons received scholarships and pursued their university education in Belgrade. After the graduation they remained in Belgrade were they received employment in their respective professions. Kašiković's daughter attended schools in Sarajevo and afterwards in Montenegro where she studied at the Cetinje High School for Girls. It is believed that all four children were educated at the expense of the Serbian government. The same lengthy report listed the people that had remained in contact with Kašiković. Obviously, Kašiković was very closely watched. [48]

The report singled out Kašiković's meeting with councilmen Jovo Pešut, Živojin Dačić and Dr. Milorad Pavlović during the celebration of the tenth anniversary of the association *Prosvjeta* in Sarajevo, in 1912. The members of the *Prosvjeta* association aspired to promote educational goals. Pavlović was blacklisted since he was an outspoken critic of the Austrian annexation of Bosnia-Hercegovina. The police reported that the meeting took place in the hotel *Europa*. After the meeting, the report mentioned the purported disappearance of Kašiković from the hotel. The police were puzzled since Kašiković was nowhere to be found in spite of a diligent search.

---

[47] Besarović, *Kultura i Umjetnost u Bosni i Hercegovini,* p. 175. The report was dated 2 August 1911 and signed by Franjo Brodnik.

[48] Besarović, *Kultura i Umjetnost u Bosni i Hercegovini,* pp. 175-176.

The report ended, on a deflated note, as if too much was done about nothing: Kašiković very likely went afterwards directly to his home since he was not seen anywhere else in the city. [49]

The correspondence between Kašiković and Dr. Milorad Pavlović was a matter of another query. Although nothing suspicious was found at the time, Pavlović was not forgotten, but followed further. Thus, four years later, in 1916, in the midst of the World War I, the Austrian police searched Pavlović's apartment in Belgrade and seized his correspondence. Pavlović's correspondence was scrutinized, and a listing of his contacts and friends was added to the report. This report was forwarded to the military headquarters. Kašiković's letters, addressed to Pavlović, were singled out and translated into German. On the basis of these letters it was concluded that Kašiković was an Austrian enemy and therefore should be taken into custody. The censors claimed that the seized letters showed that he was a proven threat to the Austrian security. Kašiković's letters dating from 1908, 1911, 1912, and 1913 were translated into German and attached to the report. [50]

In spite of restrictions and obstacles created by the Provincial Government, Kašiković remained at the helm of the journal *Bosanska Vila* for 26 years. The efforts to control the population in Bosnia-Hercegovina could be well illustrated by the documentation preserved in the archives pertaining to Nikola Kašiković his associates and his family members.

The petition of Božidar Nikašinović supplied a very special point of view in regard to the current situation in Bosnia -Hercegovina. In 1898, Nikašinović a former editor of the journal *Bosanska Vila*, submitted a petition for the foundation of a new weekly journal entitled *Srpski Balkan*.. He saw the role of his journal primarily as a

---

[49] Besarović, *Kultura i Umjetnost u Bosni i Hercegovini*, p. 177. The report was dated 2. October 1912 in Sarajevo and signed by commissioner Karl Collas.

[50] Besarović, *Kultura i Umjetnost u Bosni i Hercegovini*, p.180 The report was dated 11 March 1916.

vehicle helping the improvement of the situation in Bosnia-Hercegovina. Moreover, Nikašinović presented an extensive evaluation of the Austro-Hungarian role in the Balkans in his petition.

Nikašinović recalled that in 1878 Austria-Hungary had a leading position in the European political theater especially in the negotiations dealing with the Eastern Question. Nikašinović thought that Slavic solidarity and Panslavism seemed to have gained momentum during the upheavals in Bosnia-Hercegovina. Russia and the whole of Slavdom seemed to present a threat to the Western Powers. Consequently, the autonomy of Bosnia-Hercegovina, envisioned by the San Stefano Treaty, could not be realized. The ensuing Berlin Treaty brought the occupation of Bosnia-Hercegovina, dashing all hopes for the much desired autonomy.[51]

Nikašinović posited that the occupation of Bosnia-Hercegovina did not proceed as it was expected. The much needed agrarian reform could have been the basis for Austro-Hungarian staying power in the Balkans. Instead of reforms, Austria-Hungary preserved the existing feudal bondage, showing great deference for the Muslims, especially for the rich landowners. They became the spoiled children of the *Landesregierung,* and everything was done for them, harming the rest of the country. The feudal burdens had been even increased and the relation between the serfs and landholders *(kmet—aga)* subverted beyond repair. Nikašinović warned that the special treatment that the Muslims enjoyed would not help the impending annexation plans of Bosnia-Hercegovina. The Provincial Government should not count on the Muslim support for the annexation, as that was not likely to be the case.[52]

Nikašinović stressed that the agrarian question was of paramount importance. The government had burdened the peasants far more than the previous Turkish government. Yet the sources of their income were not increased and some benefits had even been

51 Besarović, *Kultura i Umjetnost u Bosni i Hercegovini,* p. 485.

52 Besarović, *Kultura i Umjetnost u Bosni i Hercegovini,* p. 485.

curtailed. The peasants could not make a living from agriculture alone but any other options, such as working on a highway, paid only the minimum wages *(nadničenje).* Moreover, the people were often insulted by inhuman behavior of police and finance officers. Nikašinović thought that the police and tax authorities should not keep the people in a permanent state of fear and still expect allegiance for such a government. The simple people did not know their civic rights and much less the governmental laws and they sometimes acted out of ignorance or fear. Nikašinović deplored the fact that the native citizens were not asked to participate in the Provincial Government. There was not even one native individual working for the government, not even in a consulting capacity. [53]

The goal of the occupation should have been humanitarian concern for the vast majority of peasantry and not the appeasement of the rich overlords—beys. If the Provincial Government acted in such a way, it would have perhaps lost the support of 200- to 300 beys but gained support of one and a half million of citizens. Besides the agrarian reforms, the development of an industrial base should have been expanded.[54]

The Monarchy should not have acted like England did in India, having mainly material exploitation in mind. The Austro-Hungarian Empire should have been cognizant that the constituent Slavic population encompassed two thirds of the total population of the Monarchy. Nikašinović correctly pointed out that Bosnia-Hercegovina was a decisive factor in preserving the viability of Monarchy's future.[55]

Nikašinović addressed his petition to baron Kutschera. In turn, Kutschera decided to forward Nikašinović's petition to his superior, Benjamin von Kállay.

Kállay thought that Nikašinović projected "wild political misconceptions" *(fantastische politische Abirrungen).* Kállay did not

---

[53] Besarović, *Kultura i Umjetnost u Bosni i Hercegovini,* pp. 483-485.

[54] Besarović, *Kultura i Umjetnost u Bosni i Hercegovini,* p. 486.

[55] Besarović, *Kultura i Umjetnost u Bosni i Hercegovini,* p. 481.

agree that the healing of the Monarchy should begin with the improvements and reforms in Sarajevo. The Monarchy included, in addition to the Slavs also numerous Germans, Italians, Romanians and Hungarians. [56] However, the fact remained that the Slavs constituted the majority of the population of Austria-Hungary.

On a conciliatory note, Kállay recognized that the governmental rules and regulations *(Regierungsmassregeln)* should be criticized if they were perceived as unlawful. Also, some governmental officials should be criticized if they deserve a legitimate reprimand. Kállay admitted that he was personally ready to tolerate such criticism. However, such criticism should not appear too often in the journal.[57]

Nikašinović predicted correctly that the annexation would not proceed easily, and most importantly, that the precarious situation in Bosnia-Hercegovina could gravely endanger the existence of the Monarchy. Nikašinović was aware of the underlying resistance of the population to the colonial exploitation of the Austro-Hungarian Monarchy. He offered a valuable critique of the difficult reality of living under occupation. Although aware of the existing tensions he obviously hoped that his assessment would help to introduce needed changes and to improve the lives of the population in Bosnia-Hercegovina. Nikašinović still trusted that the Monarchy could summon the strength to incorporate some reforms and provide for a better and just government.

Some form of reorganization within the Habsburg state might have prolonged the Monarchy's rule and also improved the situation in Bosnia-Hercegovina. Nonetheless, this would only have been a temporary respite since the Habsburg Empire was permeated with inherent weaknesses that would have inevitably led to its demise. The Habsburg Empire, like all historical empires, provided intermittent stability and power, despite the fact that it was in a long

---

56 Besarović, *Kultura i Umjetnost u Bosni i Hercegovini*, p. 488.

57 Besarović,*Kultura i Umjetnost u Bosni i Hercegovini*, p. 489. Kállay replied on 15 March 1898.

decline. Even the Emperor Frances Joseph was aware that the Habsburg Empire was an anomaly in the modern world of his days.[58] Furthermore, the effects of a enlivened national consciousness in occupied provinces, as well as the rising role of the regional elite, accelerated the process of Monarchy's demise. Prior to World War I the Habsburg Empire and its imperial concept was approaching its end.

Founding of the Provincial Museum and its Journal *Glasnik Zemaljskog Muzeja*

One of the enduring legacies of Kállay's administration was the founding of the *Zemaljski muzej—Landesmuseum* (Provincial Museum) in Sarajevo. Kállay had deserved to be credited for his foresight in acknowledging the importance of the preservation of the archeological artifacts and for his initiative leading to the foundation of the Museum. In addition to his diplomatic and political career, Kállay was an astute historian with great appreciation for the monuments of the past. While serving as the Austro-Hungarian Consul in Belgrade, he used every opportunity to visit the historical locations throughout Serbia.[59]

During his tenure as the Joint Minister of Finance, he had traveled extensively through Bosnia-Hercegovina exploring the land and its people. Kállay's summer residence was located in the spa Ilidža not far from Sarajevo. He often stated that he cared

[58] Solomon Wank, "The Habsburg Empire," *After the Empire*, Boulder, Westview Press, Eds. K. Barkey and M. von Hagen, 1997, p. 45 and p. 48.

[59] Compare Chapter 3 for more information about Kállay's travels throughout Serbia and his collecting of artifacts.

deeply for Bosnia and its population.[60] Moreover, as a wise politician, he had rightly appreciated the inherent importance of Bosnia-Hercegovina within the realm of the Austro-Hungarian Empire.

Under Kállay's personal supervision the Museum Association, *Musealenverein,* was formed in 1884. Dr. liro Truhelka was charged to guide the newly founded Association and generate public interest for the preservation of archeological sights *in situ,* and valuable artifacts from the past. In 1887 the Museum Association gained in importance since it was designated as a research institution charged to promote the idea of a future *Landesmuseum.* Within the same year, Kállay drew a resolution granting the foundation of the *Landesmuseum—Zemaljski muzej* (Provincial Museum), and Truhelka was named as its first curator. The festive opening of the Museum took place on February 1 of 1888. Constantine Hörmann was appointed to the position of the director of Provincial Museum as well as to the editorial post of the planned *Glasnik Zemaljskog muzeja (The Herald of the Provincial Museum).*

In 1892 the Joint Ministry of Finance, headed by Kállay, had prepared a draft for a bill regulating the upkeep of the monuments of the past.[61] In 1894 an international archeological congress was organized, and in 1910 a symposium of Austrian museums had its

---

60 Ludwig Thallóczy, *Die Geschichte des Serbischen Aufstandes 1807-1810,* Einleitung, Vienna, Holzhausen, 1910, p. XXXIII.

61 Very likely that not much was done in this respect. The provision set by Kállay was apparently unknown some ten years later to the members of the newly established Bosnian-Hercegovinian Assembly. The Assembly showed a praiseworthy awareness of the importance of safeguarding the monuments of the historical past. A resolution to this effect was submitted by Josip pl. Vancas and passed at the second session of the Assembly in 1911. The Provincial Government *(Landesregierung)* replied expressing readiness to establish necessary regulations concerning the conservation of historical monuments. The reply was dated 28 October 1911. *Staatsarchiv,* Vienna, Cabinet Kanzelei No. 2078/1892. Quoted after Besarović "Specifičnosti kulturnog razvitka u Bosni i Hercegovini 1878-1918," in *Iz kulturne i političke istorije Bosne i Hercegovine,* Sarajevo, Svjetlost, 1966, pp. 16-17.

meeting in Sarajevo. The culmination of these efforts led to the construction of the new impressive building to house the collections of the Museum.

The Museum had a number of publications referring to its activities and achievements in respective fields of endeavors. Most of all, the Museum continued to promote the preservation of archaeological sights *in situ* and collecting of archeological- and folk artifacts. In addition, special workshops gained considerable prestige with their programs advocating the preservation of indigenous handicrafts and artistic creations of the region. Very useful material pertaining to these activities was published in the *Glasnik Zemaljskog Muzeja* (The Herald of the Provincial Museum).[62]

Constantine Hörmann was closely associated with cultural policies pursued by the Austro-Hungarian finance minister Benjamin von Kállay. Hörmann served as a special counsel to Kállay before assuming the position of the director of the Provincial Museum. Hörmann was aware of the privileged position that Kállay granted to the native Muslim population. The given situation must have influenced his decision to start a collection of Muslim folk poetry. Upon completion of his task, Hörmann presented the collection to Kállay asking for additional financial support for the preparation and publication of the submitted volume. Kállay expressed his satisfaction with Hörmann's collection of Muslim poetry. In January of 1888 Kállay officially approved the publication of the collection pointing most of all to the favorable impression that such a collection would impart on the interested readership at home and abroad. Kállay even recommended that the collection be printed on good paper and that the cost of printing be financed by the government.

Kállay obviously appreciated, next to the inherent ethnographic merit, the political value of Hörmann's collection. Moreover, Kállay

---

62 Risto Besarović, "Specifičnosti kulturnog razvitka u Bosni i Hercegovini 1878-1918," in *Iz kulturne i političke istorije Bosne i Hercegovine*, p. 17.

noted that it should be mentioned, in the Introduction to the volume, that the poetry of Christians in Bosnia-Hercegovina had already been published.[63]

The worthwhile activities of the Provincial Museum sparked interest of the Czech ethno-musicologist Ludvik Kuba. He received the necessary permission of the Provincial Government to collect folk songs in Bosnia-Hercegovina. He garnered financial support for his endeavors from the Provincial Museum. According to the plans, the folk song collection was scheduled for publication in 1892 under the auspices of the Provincial Museum. Soon enough, Kuba became aware of the exceptional richness of the native folklore and the abundance of the collected material made it difficult to meet the given deadline. In September of 1892, Kuba asked for additional financial support for his work in the amount of 300 gulden.[64] He asked for more time postponing the date of publication to 1893.[65]

Finally, in 1894, Kuba concluded his work and submitted his collection of folk songs comprising some 1126 folk melodies.[66] Kuba wrote a lengthy Preface of 96 pages, in Czech language, with a note of an impending translation into Serbo-Croatian and German. In January of 1896, Appel suggested that Franz Vilhar, teacher in a middle school in Zagreb, should serve as a reviewer. Franz Kubai, a German music teacher, was suggested as a second reviewer. Kubai

---

63 Archive BiH, Fond ZMF, Präs br. 17/1888. Quoted after Besarović, "Specifičnosti kulturnog razvitka u Bosni i Hercegovini 1878-1918," *Iz kulturne i političke istorije Bosne i Hercegovine,* p. 24.

64 Ibid., p. 552.

65 Risto Besarović, Ed., *Kultura i umjetnost u Bosni i Hercegovini pod Austrougarskom Upravom,* p. 545.

66 Zija Kučukalić praised, in retrospect, Kuba's work that managed to safeguard a valuable treasury of folk songs. Kuba's collection enabled many readers throughout Europe to became acquainted with the folk songs of Bosnia-Hercegovina. Compare, Z. Kučukalić, *The Development of Musical Culture in Bosnia-Hercegovina,* Sarajevo, Association of Composers, 1967, p. 34.

himself was a folk song collector of South Slav folk songs and enjoyed a fine reputation. [67]

In April of 1896 the chief of the Austro-Hungarian government in Sarajevo, Johann Appel, evaluated the reviewers reports of Kuba's folk song collection including the appended Preface. He suggested that the Preface be omitted since Kuba's classification of folk songs was not acceptable to the reviewers. The collection in itself was valuable, as it recorded a rich treasury of melodic material and should be published, albeit with a new Preface. Appel suggested that the Preface should be penned by someone on the staff of the Provincial Museum. He even suggested the title page of Kuba's collection: *Volksmelodien in Bosnien und der Hercegovina,* gesammelt von Ludwig Kuba, herausgegeben vom Bosnia-Hercegovina Landes-Museum in Sarajevo.[68]

While the achievements of the Museum had been recognized, the political overtone of the official patronage of the Museum was criticized in the daily *Srpska riječ* [69] The expensive and lavishly illustrated publications of the Museum, the congresses and costly entertainment of visiting scientists sparked criticism. Such tendentious patronage served as an advertisement for the governmental goals degrading the sciences and arts to an organized planned propaganda: "The science approached the denigrating barbaric role comparable to the horse races and shooting of the doves."[70] The Provincial Government did establish a race track at Butimir as an added attraction enhancing the social life of the few wealthy horse race lovers. Moreover, shooting of the doves was a

---

67 Besarović, Ed., *Kultura i umjetnost u Bosni i Hercegovini pod Austrougarskom Upravom,* pp. 554-555.

68 Ibid., pp. 555-558.

69 *Srpska riječ* of 27 March 1908, god. IV, No. 59, p.1. Quoted after Besarović, "Specifičnosti kulturnog razvitka u Bosni i Hercegovini 1878-1918," in *Iz kulturne i političke istorije Bosne i Hercegovine,*. .p. 11.

70 Ibid.

popular distraction of foreign bureaucrats serving in Bosnia and their special guests.

The writer of the article objected that large sums of money were spent for the Museum in the past and that this policy would very likely continue in the future. Attention should be paid also to other institutions even more useful for the population at large. Strange as it may sound, the authorities claimed that there was not enough money for such an important institution as the public library. The government supported some preferred cultural institutions even though according to personal opinions and one-sided evaluations. *Zemaljski muzej* was the case in point.

It seemed that the authorities were taking care only of the cultural institutions that "served as political advertising and were spectacular in appearance." The article finished with a plea for the foundation of a much needed Public Library.[71]

One year later, in 1909, an editorial in *Srpska Riječ* commented on the construction of the new building for the Museum costing two million crowns:

> If the people were better informed about such a great expenditure burdening our fatherland, they would have protested. There were times in Bosnia-Hercegovina when governmental revenues were used without any discretion in order to show to the world the cultural progress of the occupied territory. There were races at Butimir, shooting of the doves, receptions for tourists, various congresses, the publication of the journal *Nada,* new buildings on prominent places. *Zemaljski muzej* should be also included to this list.

---

71 Ibid.

The writer acknowledged that the Museum was a valuable cultural edifice although it was not needed in the present situation. The allotted money could have been far better used.[72]

Most of all, the plans for the building of *Zemaljski muzej* were sharply criticized in the Serbian press. Many writers reacted adversely to the building of a museum considering the very high cost of its construction. The new imposing building should serve as a formidable representation of Austrian stewardship in front of enlightened European circles. The extremely high cost of the new Museum building was also pointed out. The cost of the building was calculated to be over two million crowns, definitively too much for an impoverished country with an urgent need for overdue and unresolved agrarian reforms.[73]

The museum was financed with the revenues generated in Bosnia-Hercegovina. The Museum had two main departments concentrating respectively on the archeological-historical research and on natural sciences. Both departments became very successful and achieved from the very start considerable results. The collection of archeological and ethnographic artifacts was impressive in many respects. Kállay continued to support and encourage the collections of artifacts from prehistoric times as well as Roman archeological remains. In 1903, the prehistoric collection alone comprised over 3000 objects. Both the prehistoric remains and Roman artifacts had been displayed in grand style. Far less attention was bestowed on the preservation of the vestiges of the medieval Slavic past. Any connections with the neighboring Slavs, beyond the borders of

---

[72] *Srpska Riječ,* Sarajevo, 20 March 1909, Vol. V, No. 63 pp. 1-2. Quoted after Besarović, "Specifičnosti kulturnog razvitka u Bosni i Hercegovini 1878-1918," *Iz kulturne i političke istorije Bosne i Hercegovine,* p. 35-37.

[73] Besarović, "Specifičnosti kulturnog razvitka u Bosni i Hercegovini 1878-1918," *Iz kulturne i političke istorije Bosne i Hercegovine,* p. 55

Bosnia-Hercegovina, were readily omitted in order to obscure the common historic past.[74]

A major accomplishment of the Museum was the publication of the journal *Glasnik Zemaljskog Muzeja (The Herald of the Provincial Museum).* The journal was started in March of 1889 and the editorial board encouraged submission of Museum associates and even specialists abroad. In addition to articles covering a wide range of interests, the journal published professional news highlighting the research conducted at the Museum. Over the years very useful material pertaining to archeology, history of Bosnia, and ethnography was published in this journal.[75]

Constantine Hörmann had been appointed to the editorial post of the journal *Glasnik Zemaljskog muzeja (Herald of the Provincial Museum)* . The journal was the vehicle of the Provincial Museum. The *Herald of the Provincial Museum* became in due time a valuable professional voice, advocating the preservation of the archeological sites and artifacts as well as the cultivation of indigenous arts and crafts. The first issue of the journal was published in March of 1889.

The Editor's Foreword for the first issue, titled "To the Readers of the Herald," intended to explain the goals that this journal wanted to achieve. Firstly, the journal aspired to publish articles documenting the research conducted by archeologists, historians and Museum's research personnel. The Museum had managed to collect valuable vestiges of the past including Illyrian and Roman artifacts. Secondly, the Museum strove to be an educational institution, promoting also the traditional folk arts and crafts. The Museum had arranged a display of the newly established collections of coins, seals, heraldry, manuscripts, and ethnographic material. In the course of time, the Provincial Museum had sponsored several

---

74 Vladimir Ćorović, *Bosna i Hercegovina,* Belgrade, Srpska književna zadruga, 1925, p. 12.

75 Besarović, "Specifičnosti kulturnog razvitka u Bosni i Hercegovini 1878-1918,". *Iz kulturne i političke istorije Bosne i Hercegovine,* p. 17.

workshops promoting the already famous silver smithy, carpet weaving, and fine embroidery.

Over the years, the Museum had published a number of publications referring to the activities and achievements sponsored by the Museum in various fields of research. The Museum continued to promote preservation of archaeological sights and collecting of folk artifacts. In addition, special workshops were established that gained considerable prestige with their programs cultivating the indigenous handicrafts of the region. In due time these workshops were independently operated and employed native workers men and women alike. The production of hand woven rugs increased with time and became a recognized industrial enterprise. The sales of newly produced artifacts in these workshops, in particular the hand-crafted rugs, generated considerable monetary gains and earned recognition by connoisseurs and public at large.[76]

These promising results encouraged the idea of an eventual transformation of the Museum into a Center for Archeological Research of the entire Balkan region at an opportune moment in the future. Obviously, that all these efforts were also motivated by the wish to show that the Austro-Hungarian Monarchy was capable of fulfilling the promised cultural mission in Bosnia-Hercegovina. The role of the Monarchy was even projected in a broader geopolitical framework encompassing the whole Balkan peninsula.

The achievements of the Museum had been recognized, while the political overtone of the official patronage of the Museum was often criticized in the daily press. Thus, the daily *Srpska riječ* chastised the expensive and lavishly illustrated special publications, as well as exceptional scientific excursions and the meetings of scientists. Such tendentious patronage served as an advertisement

---

76 Todor Kruševac, "Privredne prilike grada Sarajeva za vreme Austro-Ugarske uprave," *Godišnjak Istorijskog društva Bosne i Hercegovine*, 1958, p. 199. Kruševac noted that the wages were low for women. Girls, as young as 14, earned only 0.40 to 1 crown daily. Experienced women made 2 to 2.40 crowns a day.

for the governmental goals degrading the sciences and arts to an organized planned propaganda.[77]

In spite of occasional misapplication of cultural policies pursued by the Provincial Government, the Museum played an important role raising awareness of valuable historical repositories. The Museum instigated various worthwhile projects that mobilized the talents of outstanding scholars such as Franjo Miklošić, Konstantin Jireček, Vatroslav Jagić, Lajoš Thallóczy, Ćiro Truhelka, Svetozar Ćorović and many others. Both the Museum and its journal *Glasnik Zemaljskog Muzeja* provided a very valuable platform for the publication of archeological and ethnographic research. Most of all, the preservation of invaluable artifacts under the auspices of the Provincial Museum presented a lasting legacy of Kállay's tenure in Bosnia-Hercegovina as the Austro-Hungarian Joint Minister of Finance.

---

77 *Srpska riječ* from the 27 March 1908, Vol. IV, No. 59, p. 1. Quoted after Besarović, "Specifi]nosti kulturnog razvitka u Bosni i Hercegovini 1878-1918," *Iz kulturne i političke istorije Bosne i Hercegovine*, p. 11.

Chapter 6

THE FOUNDING OF SOCIETIES FOR SUPPORT OF EDUCATION: PROSVJETA, NAPREDAK, AND GAJRET

The beginning of the twentieth century brought the foundation of several influential educational societies into the cultural life of Bosnia-Hercegovina. The importance of education was on the mind of many concerned citizens and so was the necessity of helping students requiring financial assistance. These societies intended to offer scholarships to aid the young students pursuing their respective education in high schools and universities.

A group of prominent citizens in Sarajevo decided to request a permission from the Austro-Hungarian Provincial Government *(Landesregierung)* to found a society titled *Prosvjeta, Društvo za pomaganje Srba djaka iz Bosne i Hercegovine koji* uče *u srednjim i velikijem školama Bosne i Hercegovine i Austrougarske monarhije* *(Prosvjeta,* Society for Support of Serbian Students in High Schools and Universities in Bosnia-Hercegovina and in the Austro-Hungarian Monarchy). In 1901 the petitioners submitted the statute of the new Society to the Provincial Government stating their educational goals. The society intended to aid education of the Serbian youths enrolled in high schools in Bosnia-Hercegovina as well as in the institutions of higher learning in the Austro-Hungarian Monarchy. The petitioners explained that the proposed program offering financial aid became a necessity since the number of high school students requiring financial help had consequently increased. Many talented youngsters were left without economic means to pursue higher education and the Provincial Government was not in position to help them all. The Society wanted to offer support to students from poor families since the existing situation caused concerns to all in favor of education. A petition was signed by a group of prominent individuals from Sarajevo, mostly from the ranks of the intellectual elite comprising teachers, medical doctors, well-to-do merchants, priests and law clerks. A number of signatories pointed out that they were at one time grateful recipients of governmental stipends. The petition was dated 20 December 1901, and forwarded to the Provincial Government in Sarajevo.[1]

A similar effort was organized by Croatian citizens in Mostar. A group of leading citizens had decided to form the Union for Support of Croatian Students *(Unterstützungs-Verein)*. An article written for the paper *Osvit* intended to inform fellow citizens about this highly motivated group and their worthwhile goals. The article, in form of an open letter, was written in early December of 1901. Very likely that the publication of this letter was planned to coincide with the beginning of Christmas season trusting in the good will of the authorities in charge. Nevertheless, the article was apparently expunged in the process of the so called "preventive censoring" prior to the distribution of the paper *Osvit* and was never published. However, the letter itself was duly filed and preserved in the Archives of Bosnia-Hercegovina.

The article stated that all classes of the society, from the peasants to the merchants, were united in the wish to support education, there was a repeated outcry: "Give us schools."[2] The great interest for education should embolden all with a vision to help in these efforts. The education of the young presented the first step towards the well being of a people. However, the economic

---

[1] Risto Besarović, *Kultura i Umjetnost u Bosni i Hercegovini pod Austrougarskom Upravom, Gradja za proudavanje političkih, kulturnih i socijalno-ekonomskih pitanja iz prošlosti Bosne i Hercegovine, (XIX i XX vijek).*, Sarajevo, Arhiv BiH, 1968, pp. 335-337.

[2] Besarović, *Kultura i Umjetnost u Bosni i Hercegovini*, p. 339.

conditions in the region were getting more difficult, especially for the peasants, when considering education of their children. The number of pupils and students had slowly risen but the economic conditions became progressively worse. The education at the university level demanded great material expenditures and could present an insurmountable obstacle for many. The unknown writer stated that a citizens committee was formed in order to take necessary steps in organizing the Union for Support of Croatian Students. Moreover, bishop Paskal Buconjić offered his patronage.

The conclusion was printed in bold letters: "A dobro činiti ne može nam i neće nitko zabraniti." (Nobody will or can prevent us from doing a good thing.) The unknown writer trusted that nobody could go so far as to ban an altruistic and civic-minded action. Yet the article was censored and was not published, but nevertheless preserved in the Archives of the Provincial Government in Sarajevo.[3]

Soon enough the indefatigable members of the Union for Support *Napredak* addressed again the authorities requesting the permission for the inaugural meeting of the membership. Deputy Karl Pittner informed the Joint Finance Ministry for Bosnia and Hercegovina in Vienna that a group of Catholic citizens in Mostar had decided to organize a Union for Support *(Unterstützungsverein)* to help needy students. The officials were reluctant to approve the petition of the newly formed group having in mind the previously censored article in the journal *Osvit*. The censored article announced the intention of Catholic citizens to constitute the Union for Support of Croatian Students. [4]

In his response, Benjamin von Kállay, the Joint Finance Minister, informed the Provincial Government in Sarajevo that he had evaluated the report about the foundation of the

---

[3] Besarović, *Kultura i Umjetnost u Bosni i Hercegovini*, pp. 339-340.

[4] The report was signed by Karl Pittner, *Kreisvorsteher*, and dated 26 December 1901. Besarović, *Kultura i Umjetnost u Bosni i Hercegovini*, pp. 341-342.

Unterstüzungsverein offering support to Croatian students from Mostar. Kállay advised the officers in charge to keep the interested parties at bay and to postpone the foundation of the union as long as possible. Kállay suggested that the permission be granted if the Orthodox citizens should submit a similar petition and the action of both associations could not be arrested. [5]

In the meantime, the high school teacher Vladimir Škarić had filed the petition for approval of the Statute of the newly formed society *Prosvjeta.* The goal of the Society was to financially assist the Serbian middle- and high school students from Bosnia-Hercegovina and also from some other Serbian regions ruled by the Austro-Hungarian Monarchy.

The Statute was examined by the officials of the Provincial Government and specific changes were suggested. Thus, the Society must remain under the supervision and control of the local authorities in order to comply with the ordinance regulating public meetings. All the meetings had to be announced at least three days in advance in order that a deputy of the government could be present. Furthermore, the programs of performances and literary readings should be submitted eight days in advance and should include the texts of the poems and plays. In the case that a performance should take place in another city, or if the Society had planned a joint program with the participation of another group, the respective programs should be submitted to the authorities in Sarajevo and to

---

5 Besarović, *Kultura i Umjetnost u Bosni i Hercegovini*, p. 343. It seems that the Petition of the Society Prosvjeta was not yet forwarded to Vienna and Kállay was only anticipating the move of the Serbian leaders when he wrote his opinion which was dated 29 January 1902: "Betreffend die beabsichtige Gründung eines Unterstützungs-Vereins für kroatische Studenten in Mostar ... Demgemäss lade ich die Landesregierung ein, die Interessenten von der Gründung des geplanten Vereines so lange als möglich zurückzuhalten. Sollten auch die Orthodoxen mit einem analogen Plane hervortreten und die Aktion hinsichtlich beider Vereine in gütlichen Wege nicht zurückgehalten werden können, so halte ich es für das richtigste, die Gründung beider Vereine ohne weiteres zu genehmigen."

the local authorities of the town hosting the guest appearance of the Society.[6]

In conclusion, the Chief of the Provincial Government Appel decided to recommend the foundation of both the Catholic and Orthodox Societies wishing to support impoverished students.[7]

Finally, the Joint Finance Minister Kállay gave his tentative approval for both the Serbian and Croatian Societies. He asked the Serbian society *Prosvjeta* to implement some minor alterations in the paragraph referring to the eligibility requirements for the membership. In regard to the Statute of the Croatian Union, Kállay suggested the following clarification in the Paragraphs 5 and 7 referring to the proper classification of citizenship: instead of "the citizen of the Austro-Hungarian Monarchy" it should read "the citizen of one of the states of the Austro-Hungarian Monarchy." *(Staatsbürger der österr.-ung. Monarchie* changed to *Staatsbürger einem des Staates der österr.-ung. Monarchie).* [8]

The authorities were duly informed about the implementation of required changes in the Constitution and Statute of the *Prosvjeta* Society. Finally, the official opening of the *Prosvjeta* Society took place on 31 August 1902 in Sarajevo. The founders of the Society repeated their desire "to help the Serbian students in middle schools and universities ... in order to produce their own intellectuals and in the largest possible number." It was a shared opinion that the education of young professionals presented the most acute need for the people under Austrian occupation. [9]

In December of 1902, the Muslim Society for the Support of Students *Gajret* (Aid) followed the example set by the Serbian and Croatian societies for support and petitioned the government in

---

[6] Besarović, *Kultura i Umjetnost u Bosni i Hercegovini*, p. 344.

[7] The permission was dated 28 April 1902 and was signed by Appel.

[8] Besarović, *Kultura i Umjetnost u Bosni i Hercegovini*, p. 352 Kállay's opinion was dated 28 June 1902.

[9] Besarović, *Kultura i Umjetnost u Bosni i Hercegovini*, p. 361 Prosvjeta existed until 1949.

Sarajevo for approval of their statute. In their petition they pointed out that two such societies were already formed: one society was organized by Catholics and the other by Orthodox citizens. In view of the situation, Appel reported to Vienna forwarding the statute of *Gajret* Society recommending an approval.[10]

The Provincial Government did not postpone to a great extent the foundation of a Muslim society since it suited their overall policy of keeping the Bosnian confessional communities divided. Moreover, with *Gajret* in existence, young Muslims would be less likely inclined to participate in the Croatian *Napredak-* or the Serbian *Prosvjeta* societies. Safet-bey Bašagić, the well known Muslim poet and historian, was at the helm of the newly established *Gajret* society. H. Hrasnica was elected as vice-president, Riza-bey Kapetanović and Edham Mulabdić joined as members at large.[11]

Nevertheless, the authorities in Vienna did not grant the permission outright and asked for the revision of the Statute of *Gajret* Society. Subsequently, the permission was granted and the newly founded *Gajret* Society convened on 20 February 1903 in Sarajevo. Many members of the Muslim Society *Omladina (Youth)* attended the inaugural meeting. A number of congratulatory telegrams were read from Tešanj, Banja Luka and Dubica.[12]

The *Prosvjeta* Society progressed well, and in June of 1906 asked for the permission to publish its own journal bearing the society's name. The journal *Prosvjeta* would endeavor to inform the members about the activities of the Society in accordance with the Statute. The journal would not entertain political issues.[13]

The authorities did not approve the choice of the editor in the person of the young writer Petar Kočić. The Society petitioned again

---

[10] Besarović, *Kultura i Umjetnost u Bosni i Hercegovini* , p. 362. The petition was dated 9 December 1902.

[11] Anita Lekić, "Gajret and the Bosnian Muslim Intelligentsia," *Serbian Studies*, Vol. 10, No. 2, 1996, p. 189.

[12] Besarović, *Kultura i Umjetnost u Bosni i Hercegovini,* p. 363.

[13] Besarović *Kultura i Umjetnost u Bosni i Hercegovini* , p. 273.

and suggested that Šćepan Grbić, the president of the Society, be approved as the editor *pro tempora*. It was emphasized that the journal *Prosvjeta* would not publish political issues. The Chief of the Provincial Government in Vienna, Eugen Albori, gave his permission to Grbić to carry out the duties of the editor of the journal *Prosvjeta* until a permanent editor was found. [14]

In 1907, the *Gajret* society launched its own monthly journal bearing the same name. At first, the journal served as an informative bulletin with an initial circulation of 2000 copies. However, the profile of the journal changed when Osman Djikić assumed the position of the editor-in-chief in 1909. Djikić, a well known journalist and writer, turned the journal *Gajret* into a literary periodical by publishing literary works and articles discussing many topics of the Bosnian life. The printed contributions were written in Serbo-Croatian language both in Cyrillic and Latin script along with the Arabic summary on the back cover of the journal. [15]

The journal *Prosvjeta* published an interesting assessment of the role of reading halls and libraries in the occupied provinces:

> ... A people threatened with the loss of national identity grow to understand the importance of public libraries as one of the strongest means for preservation of the native language and national consciousness. The proponents of new ideas understood well the importance of public libraries and always supported the foundation of such institutions.[16]

---

14 The petition was dated 8 December 1906. Besarović, *Kultura i Umjetnost u Bosni i Hercegovini* , p. 274, and p. 375.

15 Lekić, "Gajret and the Bosnian Muslim Intelligentsia," *Serbian Studies*, Vol. 10, No. 2, 1996, p. 191.

16 "Narodne knjižnice i čitaonice," Prosvjeta, Sarajevo, 1 Nov 1909, No. 11, str. 169-170." Quoted after Risto Besarović, "Specifičnosti kulturnog razvitka u Bosni i Hercegovini 1878-1918," *Iz kulturne i politi]ke istorije Bosne i Hercegovine*, Sarajevo, Svijetlost, 1966, p. 35.

The article deplored the fact that Bosnia-Hercegovina was the only European country without a public library. In spite of many shortcomings, the Society *Prosvjeta* managed to continue its activities over the years, in support of education and cultural growth.

Soon enough, *Prosvjeta* Society decided to establish ten mobile libraries supplied with a minimum of fifty books each. These mobile libraries were designated to serve the far away villages. The first mobile library was established in Puračić, according to an article in the daily *Srpska Riječ.*[17] Yet, the foundation of a public library in Sarajevo remained an unfulfilled dream for a long time to be.

The founding of educational and cultural organizations such as *Prosvjeta,* followed almost simultaneously by *Napredak* and *Gajret,* had a beneficial influence on the subsequent cultural development. At first, these societies provided financial support for the students in middle schools and universities. The societies aimed to educate the young intellectual elite in order to provide leadership for the native population. Later on, their respective activities contributed to the overall improvement of the cultural milieu.

The Role of the Prosvjeta Society in Sarajevo

At the time of the foundation of the Serbian educational society *Prosvjeta* in 1902, the Serbian population in Bosnia-Hercegovina had only 35 individuals with university education. The education of the young was evidently not a high priority of the Austro-Hungarian Provincial government (Landesregierung).

In 1906, after 28 years of occupation, the Austro-Hungarian administration had opened 251 elementary schools in Bosnia-Hercegovina using local revenues for their building and operation.

---

17 *Srspka Riječ,* 10th December 1905, No 164, pp. 1-2, quoted after Besarović, "Specifičnosti kulturnog razvitka u Bosni i Hercegovini 1878-1918," *Iz kulturne i političke istorije Bosne i Hercegovine,* p. 32

These schools were supposed to serve a population of 1,700,000 in the region with the budget of 675,790 crowns. During the same period of occupation, 266 military barracks were built with a budget of 3,753,189 crowns also realized from the locally generated revenues. Thus, the military budget exceeded the school budget almost six times.[18]

After twelve years of concerted efforts led by *Prosvjeta,* at the eve of the World War I, the situation had been greatly improved. The number of university educated individuals increased to 259 including the currently enrolled university students. These exceptional results were achieved by placing the education of the young at the top of the list of priorities: two thirds of *Prosvjeta* assets went towards the support of needy students.[19]

The intellectual elite obviously aspired to improve the cultural milieu pursuing this goal with determination. They helped to organize several educational and musical societies that often included reference libraries. These societies aimed to support interest in education and strengthen the prominence of native intelligentsia. In March of 1912, the editorial in the daily *Srpska Riječ* noted with obvious satisfaction the existence of 44 Serbian reading halls and 28 singers societies.[20] In addition to reading halls and singers societies, the network of physical fitness clubs *Soko* (Eagle) had gained recognition. However, a large number of societies did not guarantee an uniform quality of their respective

---

[18] Dušan Vasiljević, *O Bosni i Hercegovini,* Lecture presented to the Slavic Benevolent Society in St. Petersburg on April 12,1909, Belgrade, Davidović, 1909 pp. 20-21.

[19] Djordje Pejanović: "Prosvjeta, Srpsko prosvjetno i kulturno društvo u Sarajevu 1902-1949, manuscript, quoted after Besarović, Specifičnosti kulturnog razvitka u Bosni i Hercegovini 1878-1918," *Iz kulturne i* političke *istorije Bosne i Hercegovine,* pp. 22-23.

[20] *Srpska Rije'č* , Sarajevo, No 94, 2 May 1913. "Specifičnosti kulturnog razvitka u Bosni i Hercegovini 1878-1918," *Iz kulturne i* političke *istorije Bosne i Hercegovine,* p. 50.

programs and endeavors. The societies could not always fulfill their aspirations due to the difficult financial situation and lack of means to support some of the chosen activities.[21]

The celebration of the tenth anniversary of the cultural organization and publishing house *Prosvjeta* was planned to take place in Sarajevo in September of 1912. The proposed festive celebration included an appropriate program and an opening parade of all participants through the main streets of Sarajevo. An athletic meet was also scheduled, including a special musical program. The music was provided by the *Ragusa* music group from Dubrovnik, and the music group *Dušan Silni* from Belgrade.

Prior to the celebration, the main council of the *Prosvjeta* association had submitted the preliminary program of the festivities to the Austro-Hungarian authorities in Sarajevo, asking for their approval. The request was dated August 17, 1912, a month ahead from the celebration. The officer in charge scrutinized the program and apparently was not sure whether the music group *Dušan Silni* should be allowed to perform. Thus, a query about the music group *Dušan Silni* was forwarded to the Austrian police authorities in Prague. Apparently the local authorities have learned that the music group *Dušan Silni* had participated in Prague at an international *Sokol* meeting in July of 1912.[22]

The police in Prague replied the next day, 7 September 1912, under the heading *Confidential (Vertraulich)*, that the members of the music group *Dušan Silni* from Belgrade did participate during the festivities and behaved correctly giving no cause for concern. The music group accompanied the routines of the gymnasts and played during the parade through the city. Obviously, the police

---

21 "Tragom jedne inicijative," *Otdadžbina*, Sarajevo, 1 March 1912 No. 62, p. 2. Quoted after Besarović, "Specifičnosti kulturnog razvitka u Bosni i Hercegovini 1878-1918," *Iz kulturne i političke istorije Bosne i Hercegovine*, p. 29.

22 Besarović, *Kultura i Umjetnost u Bosni i Hercegovini*, pp. 381-382 and p. 387. The telegram was mailed to Prague on 6th September 1912.

officials were impressed by the musical performance since they described the musical rendition of the program as *"klingendes Spiel"* (sonorous play).[23]

Finally, the permission for the participation of the *Dušan Silni* music group was granted, provided that the members would not be suited in their uniforms but dressed in everyday street clothes. Furthermore, the report stated that the group should not appear at the head of the procession but rather be placed in the middle of the parade. Apparently, all precautions were taken to lessen the impression that the music group may impart on the captive audience with their 'sonorous play' as it was described in the Prague police report.

The same report mentioned that the organizers planned to bring eminent visitors to Sarajevo such as the former Serbian prime minister Stojan Novaković. Novaković served as the prime minister at the time of the Austrian annexation of Bosnia-Hercegovina. Moreover, the onetime premier of the Serbian government Ljuba Stojanović, in addition to Dr. Čedomilj Mitrović, a university professor from Belgrade, and Dr. Dušan Vasiljević had been invited likewise. Vasiljević, who resided in Sarajevo, stayed in close touch with Mitrović and other Serbian leaders in Belgrade during the annexation crisis. Obviously, the whereabouts of noted personalities were examined even outside the occupied territory of Bosnia-Hercegovina. The report mentioned that Mitrović was a brother-in-law of Vasiljević, and that Vasiljević stayed in Mitrović's house when visiting in Belgrade during the Annexation crises." ... *Dr. Čedo Mitrović ist Schwager des Dr. Dušan Vasiljević welcher zur Zeit der Annexionskrise bei ihm weilte."* [24]

Dr. Jovan Skerlić, a prominent literary historian and a representative in the Serbian Parliament, and Tihomir Ostojić, secretary of the *Matica Srpska* in Novi Sad, were included among the guests. Commenting the presence of these eminent participants

---

[23] Besarović, *Kultura i Umjetnost u Bosni i Hercegovini* , p. 387.

[24] Besarović, *Kultura i Umjetnost u Bosni i Hercegovini* , p. 386.

in the *Prosvjeta* celebration, the Austrian authorities concluded that Skerlić should be closely followed during his stay in Sarajevo. In the case that Skerlić would decide to present a lecture, he should be promptly removed from the premises.

Furthermore, the same report paid special attention to Dr. Jovan Cvijić. Cvijić, an internationally respected scholar and specialist on Balkan geography, was issued a permission to travel to Bosnia-Hercegovina in 1908. He was followed by the Austrian military police and because of his purportedly 'suspicious' behavior was strip-searched. However, the search did not produce any damaging evidence.[25]

The report hastened to add that the request for this search was authorized by a telegram from Vienna. Evidently, the officer in charge felt that his zealous execution of duties was an unusual and inappropriate gesture. Surprisingly, the higher authorities approved his request disregarding the dignity and civil rights of a well known visiting scholar.

During the *Prosvjeta* celebration, an athletic meeting was organized, highlighting the popular physical fitness movement of the *Sokol* association. The athletic program included several *Sokol'* organizations from the kingdom of Serbia, and the *Sokol'* members from Župa. The athletic association *Pobratim* was also invited.

The reports pertaining to the *Prosvjeta* celebration showed with how much care the Austro-Hungarian authorities monitored cultural events in Bosnia-Hercegovina. As a rule, the submitted programs of celebration as well as invited participants were thoroughly investigated. Often enough, a subsequent report instructed the local authorities who should be specially watched during the course of the

---

25 Besarović, *Kultura i Umjetnost u Bosni i Hercegovini*, pp. 386-387: "Jovan Cvijić Universitäts Professor im Jahre 1908 wurde ihm eine offene Ordre fur eine Studienreise in Bosnien-Hercegovina ausgestellt; während der Reise wurde er von militärischer Seite überwacht und infolge seines verdächtigen Verhaltens einer Leibesvisitation unterzogen, welche jedoch nichts gravierendes ergab."

event or even followed later on. Obviously that these cautious measures were not instituted to address the needs and concerns of the population in Bosnia-Hercegovina: these measures were implemented to ensure a long lasting Austrian occupation of the regions. All along, it was forgotten that the Austrian forces were supposed to protect impartially all the peoples of the territory, and not to impose additional hardship and restrictions especially in the field of cultural and educational developments.

The Founding of the Public Library in Sarajevo

In 1909 an article in the journal *Prosvjeta* voiced criticism in regard to the cultural policies in Bosnia-Hercegovina, in particular to the unresolved problem of a public library stating that "our is the only European land without a public library." The article mentioned, with regrets, that a lot of money was spent on horse races, hunting and shooting of the doves, and various lavish receptions for foreign guests. It seemed that there was always sufficient money for the building of luxurious hotels and erection of monuments in honor of some dignitaries from abroad, as well as for festive dinners for numerous foreigners.[26]

The same article questioned the statements of authorities claiming that there was not enough money available even for such an important institution as the public library. Strangely enough, the government granted funds for some cultural institutions albeit depending on personal opinions and one-sided evaluations. *Zemaljski muzej* (Landesmuseum) was the case in point; big money was spent for it in the past and this policy would very likely continue

26 *Prosvjeta*, Sarajevo, 1 November 1909, No 11, pp. 169-170. Quoted after Besarović "Specifičnosti kulturnog razvitka u Bosni i Hercegovini 1878-1918," *Iz kulturne i* političke *istorije Bosne i Hercegovine*, p. 35.

in the future. Attention should be also paid to other institutions even more useful for the population at large. It seemed that the authorities preferred the cultural institutions that could serve for political advertising. The article finished with a plea for the foundation of the future public library.[27]

Editorial in *Srpska Riječ,* commented also on the new building for the Museum costing two million crowns. The unnamed writer expressed his opinion in this editorial under the heading "Museum:"

> If the people were better informed about such a great expenditure burdening our fatherland, they would have protested. There were times in Bosnia-Hercegovina when revenues were used without any discretion in order to show to the world the cultural progress in the occupied territory. There were races at Butimir, shooting of the doves, receptions for tourists, various congresses, the publication of the lavishly illustrated journal *Nada*, new buildings on prominent locations. Zemaljski muzej should be also included to this list.

The writer concluded that in the present situation the allotted money could have been far better utilized.[28]

In December of 1909, Vladimir Ćorović pleaded again for the founding of a public library as a much needed center for serious research. The lack of a well equipped library was detrimental for any serious scholarly work. The existing libraries were established without sufficient resources aiming to serve as reference libraries for a number of cultural societies. Ćorović quoted as an example the situation in Mostar where several small libraries existed in the

---

27 Ibid.

28 Srpska Riječ Sarajevo, 20 March 1909 Vol. V, No 63, pp. 1-2. Quoted after Besarović "Specifičnosti kulturnog razvitka u Bosni i Hercegovini 1878-1918," p. 35-37.

Serbian community center, the singers society, the artisans society, and the women cooperative.

Similar situation existed in Sarajevo where several reference libraries of various societies coexisted. Ćorović suggested the merging of these libraries in order to eventually enrich the primary library funds both in Sarajevo and Mostar. Even the Library of the Provincial Museum served mainly as a reference library for its staff and was not open for the general public. Ćorović also thought that the Library of the Provincial Museum *(Zemaljski muzej)* and the Library of the Balkan Institute should be developed alongside the projected Public Library.[29]

The *Prosvjeta* Society had carefully contemplated the foundation of a Public Library in Sarajevo. This issue was on the agenda of many Society's meetings and the ongoing discussion intensified with time. The daily press and members of many other societies devoted their attention to the planning of the Library. The collecting of books was launched and various other preparations were undertaken.

Before long, the population at large encouraged a well organized action for collecting books for the future public library. This action rendered considerable results. The daily *Srpska Riječ* started publishing the names of the donors and lists of donated books. Among the first was the famed publishing cooperative *Srpska književna zadruga* setting an example by donating all its available editions in duplicates. Other institutions followed such as *Srpska državna Štamparija, Ćupićeva zadužbina, Srpska kraljevska akademija nauka*. Noted individuals supported also the action like Rista Radulović, Vladan Djordjević, Mihailo Gavrilović, Jovan

---

[29] Vladimir Ćorović, "Naučni rad u našoj sredini," *Srpska Riječ*, Sarajevo, 9 December 1909 , No 257, pp. 1-27. Quoted after Besarović, "Specifičnosti kulturnog razvitka u Bosni i Hercegovini 1878-1918," *Iz kulturne i političke istorije Bosne i Hercegovine*, p. 38.

Skerlić and the editorial board of the journal *Srpski književni glasnik*. 30

Finally, the request for the foundation of the future Public Library was submitted to the Provincial Government in Sarajevo. The request was written with great care providing all important information pertaining to the goals of the future Public Library. The authorities had been already informed since their official representatives had attended the meetings which were duly posted in advance. The authorities received also the local newspapers for "preventive censoring" and therefore must have been well-versed about the many articles of support for the proposed Library.

In spite of the information on hand referring to the *Prosvjeta* Society's efforts in creating a public library, the Great Educational Council, as the official body in charge of education, did not grant the needed approval. Many members of the *Prosvjeta* Society thought that the Council acted in blatant disregard to the real needs of the population. For some thirty years of occupation no effort was made to help create a public library and make real advancement in the cultural make up of the Bosnian capital. Instead, obstacles and delays were introduced even for modest expenditures when compared to the millions that were poured in the much criticized Provincial Museum . However, the board of *Prosvjeta* Society understood that perseverance was the only choice and decided to address the Great Council time and again restating the goals of the future library.[31]

Thus, Risto Radulović commented quickly on the surprising decision of the Great Council denying monetary assistance.

---

30 *Srpska Riječ*, Sarajevo, 3 June 1911, No 106, p. 2. Quoted after Besarović, "Specifičnosti kulturnog razvitka u Bosni i Hercegovini 1878-1918," *Iz kulturne i političke istorije Bosne i Hercegovine*, p. 42.

31 Minutes from the VIII session of the Prosvjeta Board, 11 (24) January, 1911. Quoted after Besarović, "Specifičnosti kulturnog razvitka u Bosni i Hercegovini 1878-1918," *Iz kulturne i političke istorije Bosne i Hercegovine*, pp. 43-44.

Radulović wrote about the astonishing lack of understanding that the Great Council showed denying financial aid for the Central Public Library.[32]

> It is not easy to understand the delay of support of our Great Educational Council whose primary duties are to provide ample support for such institutions. This delay is even more reprehensible considering that, in addition to a central library, a mobile library will be established to travel to all our cities and even into the villages."

Radulović thought that the mobile library should serve as a cultural forum and include occasional public lectures. The spoken word would facilitate and enhance any educational efforts directed at the broad masses of people. Radulović proposed to model such programs in accordance with the evening schools and popular universities in the West. These programs were well received providing a good example to follow. He believed that "the spoken word is the best propagator among the peasants and little people in small townships." Accordingly, such programs would help in the educational mission. Radulović was also in agreement with the initiative of the United Serbian Youth favoring the foundation of libraries in the villages.[33]

Moreover, Radulović was the first to suggest the idea of the foundation of a Serbian Central Library under the auspices of the *Prosvjeta* Society. Radulović remained consistent in his request

---

[32] R. Radulović, "Srpska narodna biblioteka," *Pregled*, Sarajevo, 15May 1911, No. 1, 2, 3. Quoted after Besarović, "Specifičnosti kulturnog razvitka u Bosni i Hercegovini 1878-1918," *Iz kulturne i političke istorije Bosne i Hercegovine*, p. 43.

[33] Quoted after Besarović, "Specifičnosti kulturnog razvitka u Bosni i Hercegovini 1878-1918," *Iz kulturne i politi]ke istorije Bosne i Hercegovine*, p. 44.

pointing to "the great role that the intellectuals should play and the necessity of their preparation for this task."[34]

The action for collecting books was also sponsored by the Croatian community. The Croatian cultural and educational society *Napredak* decided to found a library for the students and learned persons which also would serve the pupils in middle schools. The Board of the Society appealed to the friends of the Society to donate "books that would serve the education of the Croatian youth instead of remaining in the boxes covered with mildew."[35] Another appeal was published in the daily *Hrvatski Dnevnik*.

> We need help from everyone. There are many books in some private collections including books with the pages not yet cut open. We laugh at those who keep money in jugs, but our books are in bookcases or in attics under thick layers of dust. Take out these books, give them life again and the active power that are entrusted in them! A nation's literature is not represented in bookcases or dusty attics but in the heart and soul of a people. We do not shy away from work, but show to us that you understand us, that you approve of our work by giving for people's education as much as your duty and conscience will tell you. Who gives quickly gives twice as much! [36]

The Board of the *Prosvjeta* Society addressed the Great Educational and Governing Council in Sarajevo *(Veliki Prosvjetni i*

---

[34] Pero Slijepčević, Predgovor (Foreword), R. Radulović, *Rasprave i Članci*, Belgrade, SKZ, 1940. p. XXXIII. Quoted after Risto Besarović, "Specifičnosti kulturnog razvitka u Bosni i Hercegovini 1878-1918," *Iz kulturne i političke istorije Bosne i Hercegovine,* p. 39.

[35] *Hrvatski dnevnik*, Sarajevo, 30 January 1912, No. 24, p. 3. Quoted after Besarović, "Specifičnosti kulturnog razvitka u Bosni i Hercegovini 1878-1918," *Iz kulturne i političke istorije Bosne i Hercegovine*, p. 43.

[36] *Hrvatski Dnevnik,* Sarajevo, 15 March, 1913, No. 62, p. 1, Quoted after Besarović, "Specifi]nosti kulturnog razvitka u Bosni i Hercegovini 1878-1918," *Iz kulturne i* političke *istorije Bosne i Hercegovine,* p. 44.

Upravni Savjet) with a request for financial help. The Council was most of all charged to oversee the educational and general cultural issues in Bosnia and Hercegovina. The Board of the *Prosvjeta* society asked for 10 000 crowns in order to help the founding of the Central Library in Sarajevo. According to the minutes of the Society, the request was informative and carefully worded so that the members of the Great Council could easily evaluate the merits of a public library in Sarajevo and give their consent. To this effect the Board addressed the officials with a petition in March of 1911. The officials rejected the plea stating that sufficient funding was not available. However, the Great Council would be willing to reconsider the request should the goal, the composition, and the organization of the National Library be better explained.

The annual meeting of the *Prosvjeta* Society took place on 30 June 1912. The main topic of the agenda was the organization of the Central Public Library in Sarajevo. The minutes of the meeting stated that the secretary of the Society, Vladimir Ćorović, had volunteered to organize the Library's book fund. The Board stated that around 3000 books and 1700 periodicals were collected for the Library so far. The Board expressed great pleasure with this new acquisition and agreed to hire the first librarian, which was promptly advertised in the daily *Narod* on 31st July 1912. [37]

Finally, he Serbian Central Library *(Srpska centralna biblioteka)* in Sarajevo was opened for the reading public on the 8 January 1913. The January issue of the journal *Prosvjeta* repeated an appeal for more donations of books. Already in the February issue it was stated that the Singers Society *Sloga* in Sarajevo responded by donating a fine collection of 1623 books, including older books, journals and magazines. Moreover, there existed 43 Serbian reading rooms and 28 singers societies in Bosnia-Hercegovina. A great number of these societies and reading halls had their own reference libraries.

---

[37] Besarović, *Kultura i Umjetnost u Bosni i Hercegovini*, p. 49. Djordje Pejanović was aproved as the librarian and he promptly started serving in this capacity from September 1912.

According to an editorial in *Srpska riječ* the numerous supporters of the idea of a centralized library urged that all the existing libraries should merge creating a network of branch libraries under the auspices of *Prosvjeta.* [38]

The opening of the Central Library presented the highest achievement of the *Prosvjeta* Society in the field of public education and cultural development. The publications of the Society included, in addition to the journal, an almanac and various commemorative publications. The Society had also planned to publish books suitable for broad masses of readers. The founding of the Central Library was achieved by concerted efforts of many dedicated individuals from the ranks of the Serbian intelligentsia. The leadership of Risto Radulović, Vladimir Ćorović and Djordje Pejanović was singled out for their exceptional contribution. All three men were from Mostar.[39]

The Role of the University Student Associations during the Austro-Hungarian Occupation

Serbian and Croatian students enrolled at the universities abroad followed with care the cultural and political events in their homeland. At the same time, the students were monitored by the Austro-Hungarian authorities in Vienna and Graz as well as by those in charge in Sarajevo and Mostar.

---

[38] *Srpska Riječ*, No. 94, Sarajevo, 2 May 1913, p. 1. Quoted after Besarović, "Specifičnosti kulturnog razvitka u Bosni i Hercegovini 1878-1918," *Iz kulturne i političke istorije Bosne i Hercegovine*, pp. 50-51.

[39] Quoted after Besarović, "Specifičnosti kulturnog razvitka u Bosni i Hercegovini 1878-1918," *Iz kulturne i političke istorije Bosne i Hercegovine*, p. 59.

The Serbian Student Association *Zora* at the University of Vienna decided to call a special meeting of its members in May of 1901. The meeting was called in response to the recently held Congress of Journalists in Ragusa (Dubrovnik). The students expressed their concern about the proposition entertained by the Congress concerning the possibility of a Croatian annexation of Bosnia-Hercegovina. It was suggested that a Memorandum be composed stating their distress in regard to the present situation. The students felt that Austrian political, social, economic, and cultural policies in Bosnia-Hercegovina should be scrutinized. The Memorandum was at that time compiled and signed by thirty-eight members of the Student Association. Copies were dispatched to the Austrian authorities in Sarajevo as well as to various delegations that attended the Congress in Dubrovnik.

Petar Kočić, an active member of the student body, dispatched one copy of the Memorandum to Nikola Kašiković, the noted editor of the journal *Bosanska Vila*. Kočić asked for Kašiković's evaluation and for the opinion of the Serbian community in Sarajevo in regard to the memorandum.

Moreover, in June of 1901 in Vienna, two Serbian students, Gligorije Jeftanović and Vojislav Šola, gave an interview in reference to the Memorandum. The interview was conducted by the Editor of the newspaper *Deutsches Volksblatt*: and was published soon after in the same paper. The Editor of the newspaper asked for a clarification of the nature of the Memorandum. He made inquiry whether a joint action of Serbs, Muslims and members of the students associations was planned in the future. Jeftanović and Šola denied that such a concerted action was in sight.[40]

The students expressed their concern about the current situation in Bosnia-Hercegovina as stated in the Memorandum. In order to provide a better understanding of the opinions of the population

---

40 Besarović, *Kultura i Umjetnost u Bosni i Hercegovini*, p. 286. The interview appeared in the daily paper *Deutsches Volksblatt*, No. 4460, of 5 June 1901.

concerning the political and economic situation, they had decided to travel during their vacation throughout Bosnia-Hercegovina. They planned to conduct a poll among the population of both provinces in order to gather needed information. The students wanted to learn about the impact of occupation on the population of these regions. They stated that the policies of the government should be scrutinized and these findings published in newspapers and possibly in another memorandum. [41]

The Provincial Government in Sarajevo had studied with great concern the received copy of the Memorandum. In the ensuing period, the officer in charge, Johann Appel, wrote a lengthy report stating that the undersigned students had expressed a lack of loyalty as well as anti-governmental thoughts directed against Austria-Hungary. The new order and possibilities of collaboration with the governmental agencies had not been appreciated Instead, it was repeatedly pointed out that the influential and well paid positions in Bosnia-Hercegovina were time and again taken by foreigners. [42]

Appel's report singled out several students for writing the Memorandum. These individuals were carefully investigated and their respective professional affiliations as well as family situations were scrutinized in Appel's report dated 14 June 1901.[43]

On July 13th of 1901, a circular was issued addressing all precincts officials in Sarajevo. The circular was marked as *'confidential'* and signed by the chief section-officer Wenzel Czerny. This document informed the respective police precincts that the Serbian students at the Vienna University had decided to conduct a poll in regard to the political and economic situation in Bosnia-Hercegovina during the summer of 1901. The students intended to publish the results of the polls in various newspapers. Such an action reflected a new attitude that was spreading among the Serbian

---

41 Besarović, *Kultura i Umjetnost u Bosni i Hercegovini*, p. 285.

42 Besarović, *Kultura i Umjetnost u Bosni i Hercegovini*, pp. 285-289.

43 Besarović, *Kultura i Umjetnost u Bosni i Hercegovini*, pp. 286-289.

youth and therefore should be condemned as "dangerous and nationalistic."

Furthermore, the report stated that the students studying in Vienna proposed a meeting of all Serbian students in St. Thomas (Szt. Tamas), a town in Hungary with a sizable Slavic minority. The meeting was tentatively scheduled for August of 1901. A number of students at the Graz University supported the action of the Vienna Student Association.[44]

It became obvious that the aspirations advocated by students from Bosnia-Hercegovina studying in Vienna were not a singular and isolated incident. The report was signed by the Section-Chief of the government in Sarajevo, Wenzel Czerny, and dated 13 July 1901.

Moreover, the students at the Munich University suggested a meeting of Serbian youths in Belgrade. After much discussions and preparations the organizers of the meeting decided to invite delegates from neighboring Slavic countries. Subsequently, the First Congress of Southern Slav Youths did ultimately take place in Belgrade in September of 1904.[45].

Before long, in July of 1902, the Memorandum was published in Vienna, in the printing shop of Rudolf Kamus & Co., whose owner was Djordje Pejanović, a Bosnian Serb. The Memorandum was published in German language, and was signed by 38 members of the students association. The publication attracted the attention of the Austrian authorities in Sarajevo. The officer in charge, Johann Appel, informed the joint staff office in Vienna that a Serbian translation of the Memorandum was currently prepared in Belgrade. Appel feared that copies could be smuggled to Bosnia-Hercegovina, via Zemun as the point of departure. Therefore, he

---

44 Besarović, *Kultura i Umjetnost u Bosni i Hercegovini*, p. 290.

45 Jelena Milojković-Djurić, *Tradition and Avant-Garde; Literature and Art in Serbian Culture 1900-1918*, East European Monographs, Boulder, Columbia University Press, 1988, pp. 1-2.

asked the authorities to alert the Austrian police in Zemun.[46] Appel had the impression that the native population did not care about policies introduced by Austro-Hungarian administration. The population felt deprived of any meaningful choices in pursuit of their own aspirations. In comparison, it was often mentioned, that in the neighboring Bulgaria, still under Turkish occupation, many posts and offices were filled with the native workers. The Bulgarians apparently enjoyed independence and civic freedom *(Selbstständigkeit)*. to a greater extent than the people of Bosnia-Hercegovina.[47]

Evidently, the authorities were apprehensive of the current situation and continuous lack of cooperation with the population. The citizens in Bosnia-Hercegovina minded their own affairs and showed an apparent lack of interest for the new political, social, and cultural policies introduced by the *Landesregierung* after the onset of the Austro-Hungarian occupation.

---

46 The chief of the Austrian government in Sarajevo, Johann Appel, reported about the publication of the Memorandum on 10 July, 1902. Quoted after Besarović, *Kultura i Umjetnost u Bosni i Hercegovini*, pp. 291-292.

47 Ibid.

Chapter 7

LITERARY, MUSICAL, AND THESPIAN LIFE IN BOSNIA-HERCEGOVINA IN THE FIRST DECADES OF THE NEW CENTURY

Position of Writers in the Occupied Territory: Petar Kočić and Silvije Strahimir Kranjčević.

In December of 1905, the young writer Petar Kočić had petitioned the Provincial Government in Sarajevo for a concession for publication of a satirical journal titled *Jazavac (Badger).* In his petition, Kočić gave assurances that the journal would primarily publish short literary pieces by domestic and foreign writers. The journal would occasionally include suitable illustrations and would be published twice a month. Kočić defined the editorial policy of the journal as an attempt to present in an objective way "all that was rotten and sick in the contemporary social life but always commented with decorum and in a refined manner." *Sve što je trulo i bolesno u našem savremenom društvenom životu, za tim šibanje sviju mana i poroka, ali uvjek u pristojnom i otmenom tonu).* The petition was signed "Petar Kočić writer and philosopher."[1]

---

[1] Risto Besarović, Editor,*Kultura i Umjetnost u Bosni i Hercegovini, Gradja za proučavanje političkih, kulturnih i socijalno-ekonomskih pitanja iz pro[losti Bosne i Hercegovine, XIX i XX vijek,* Sarajevo, Arhiv BiH, 1968, p. 30. Kočić obviously did not anticipate that the Austrian authorities would refuse to read about their own shortcomings and inability to govern justly and honorably. His petition was dated 2 December, 1905.

Kočić' s petition was forwarded to Vienna with a report about Kočić written by Eugen Albori, the head of the government in Sarajevo. Albori supplied a short biographical sketch stating that Kočić was born in Stričić, Banja Luka county, the son of the priest Gerasim Kočić. His family was moderately wealthy. Albori believed that Kočić was politically outspoken and unreliable.[2]

Kočić was, at the time, 28 years old. Obviously he looked and acted as a mature individual. Although relatively young, he was an accomplished writer with several published and well received literary works. Kočić had distinguished himself early in his youth as a student of the renown Serbian High School in Sarajevo. He was a precocious and outspoken youngster recognized soon enough by the local authorities as a promoter of cultural rapprochement with Serbian intellectual elite. He had finished his high school education in Belgrade at the famous First High School for Boys.

In 1901, Kočić had enrolled at the Vienna University where he studied under distinguished professors such as Vatroslav Jagić and Konstantin Jireček. He accomplished his studies on time and graduated in 1904. While residing in Vienna, Kočić took active part in the Student Association *Zora* and was a cosigner of the resolution refuting the proceedings of the Congress of Journalists in Ragusa (Dubrovnik). He had opposed the suggested annexation of Bosnia-Hercegovina as proposed by the Croatian delegation at the Congress. Kočić had also been engaged in the writing of the Memorandum of the Vienna Student Association, addressing the delegates of the Ragusa congress.[3]

Albori believed that Kočić had received financial help from Belgrade. Albori mentioned a previous report, dated 13 July 1901, referring to Kočić's travels through Bosnia-Hercegovina. These travels had been planned by the students in order to collect data

---

2 Besarović, *Kultura i Umjetnost u Bosni i Hercegovini,* pp. 305-307. Kočić was born in June of 1877 and died prematurely in Belgrade in 1916. His health was aggravated by frequent imprisonment and by persecution of the Austro-Hungarian police.

3 Albori mentioned that the memorandum was discussed previously in the report of 14 June 1901 and 11 July 1901. Besarović, *Kultura i Umjetnost u Bosni i Hercegovini,* p. 305.

about the political and economic conditions in the region. Moreover, Kočić had served as a member of the editorial board of the journal *Samouprava* published in Belgrade. He had taught in the renown Serbian High School in Novi Sad until last year.

Albori posited that Kočić's purported plans for the publication of the journal were only a pretext in order to establish his residency in Sarajevo. The editing of an easy journal would allow him to work on his political agenda, and provide an opportunity to travel through the country in pursuit of nationalistic agitation. Albori even alleged that Kočić would very likely use his position of a newspaper editor to receive the benefits of free train tickets.

Albori mentioned that he had read Kočić's three books titled, *S planine i ispod planine* (From the Mountain and the Valley). Albori even stated "that these books were in possession of the government and would be separately reviewed." Albori thought that Kočić was disrespectful towards the government officials; it would suffice to state that these books were not desirable, full of disloyal tendencies, demagogic excesses, and cynicism belittling the Austro-Hungarian authorities. Kočić even dared to disparage the highest ruler of the land—His Majesty the Emperor and King, Francis Joseph. [4]

Nonetheless, Albori thought that the journal as well as Kočić's literary work would not pose danger since the preventive censoring could regulate the content, if necessary. Albori was far more fearful that Kočić's presence could provoke revolutionary upheavals. Albori concluded, that in view of all that was said, the concession for publication should not be given but no specific reason should be quoted. [5]

It was regrettable that Albori denied the editorial post to a young and upcoming writer, including some trifling fringe benefits. At the same time, Albori had been living in high style in an occupied territory that Austrian bureaucrats like himself were skillfully exploiting.

---

[4] Besarović, *Kultura i Umjetnost u Bosni i Hercegovini,* p. 306.

[5] Besarović, *Kultura i Umjetnost u Bosni i Hercegovini,* p. 307. The report was dated 29 January 1906. The government in Vienna supported Albori's position and responded with a writ of 6 Feb. 1906, that was signed by Lajos Thallóczy.

In June of 1906, *Prosvjeta* Society asked Kočić to assume the position of the editor of the journal *Prosvjeta* bearing society's name. The journal was most of all a vehicle of the Society designed to inform the membership about the goals and activities sponsored by the Society. The journal did not propose to entertain political issues. Nevertheless, the authorities did not approve the choice of the editor in the person of the young writer Petar Kočić.[6]

Kočić stayed in Sarajevo until December of 1906. During this time, the authorities watched carefully his whereabouts. Thus, the officials had heard rumors that Kočić's one act satirical play *Jazavac pred sudom* (The Badger in the Court) was performed by the *Dilettante Theater Company* in Sarajevo. *Jazavac pred sudom* was written in 1904 while Kočić was still a student in Vienna. The play gained a wide acceptance and became a precursor of the ideology of the association *Mlada Bosna* (Young Bosnia). The renown literary scholar, Pavle Popović, praised Kočić's dramatic work that, although brief, was accepted as a masterpiece of its kind: "Malo remek delo svoje vrste."

The Chief in charge, Constantine Hörmann, addressed promptly a query to all district's offices to determine who gave the permission for the play to be performed. He asked what circumstances prompted the play to be staged and where the play was performed. In the meantime, Hörmann ascertained that a permission for a future staging of the play should be denied.

Finally, the Government decided that Kočić's presence in Sarajevo was dangerous and he was ordered to leave Sarajevo in a clandestine manner. In order to lessen the impact of a forceful departure, Kočić had to leave Sarajevo at night. On 11 December 1906, he was ushered in the train leaving Sarajevo at 9:30 p.m. In spite of all these precautions, Kočić was greeted by a large number of theology students, from the Seminary at Reljevo, when the train approached the station Rajlovac. The students came to the station to greet him shouting *"Živeo"* (Long Live). Kočić answered with a short speech standing by the window of his train. The students applauded again with another tumultuous *"Živeo."* This incident

---

6 Besarović, *Kultura i Umjetnost u Bosni i Hercegovini*, p. 273.

was reported to the authorities in Vienna and it was suggested that this demonstration must have been organized from Sarajevo.[7]

In 1909, Kočić received a modest stipend from the famous geographer Jovan Cvijić and the Serbian Academy of Science in order to collect ethnographic material in Bosnia during the summer months of 1909. He also wanted to use the collected material around the region of Zmijanje in his literary work. He visited with the oldest men from renown old families and noted down their stories as well as the customs and orally transmitted narratives, *"predanja i kazivanja."* [8]

Kočić summarized his impressions of his research in a letter to Cvijić. Kočić disclosed that he felt as if he entered a living museum of his land and he delighted to find signposts of past times. He hoped to use this material in his book *Jauci sa Zmijanja* (Wailing from Zmijanje). He wrote to Cvijić that he regretted that he was not a geographer or historian, and thus better prepared to dedicate all his energies to ethnographic research. Even so, Kočić was fortunate to write down several until then unknown epic poems about the heroic exploits of the legendary Rajko from Zmijanje. He recorded two epic songs from Mile Popadić, a priest from Gornje Ratkovo, and sent them to Nikola Kašiković, editor of the journal *Bosanska Vila*. He promised to continue with his ethnographic work and even write a study about epic poetry.

Kočić was soon enough elected to the newly created Assembly in Sarajevo and he promptly decided that he would better serve his country and his people as a representative in the Assembly than as a writer. [9]

While serving as a representative in the Assembly, Kočić realized that the official announcements and legal documents were poorly written lacking the necessary clarity of meaning. The Provincial Government in Bosnia-Hercegovina was in the hands of bureaucrats who came predominantly from Austria, Germany, as well as from Hungary, Poland, and Bohemia. These bureaucrats did not speak

---

[7] Besarović, *Kultura i Umjetnost u Bosni i Hercegovini*, p. 310.

[8] Miodrag M. Vulin, *Petar Kočić Pisac i delo.*, Sarajevo, Svjetlost, 1990, p. 140.

[9] Vulin, *Petar Kočić, Pisac i delo.*, pp. 140-141.

the Serbo-Croatian language or had only some vague knowledge of it. Thus, the resulting poor writing manifested in legal writs presented an additional obstacle for proper understanding of these papers. Kočić feared that the innate clarity of the native language was obscured in official bulletins and various communications addressing the population at large. Such poor and distorted writing presented a dangerous precedent:

> This influence is so harmful and so visible that we have to fear that our beautiful language, the most beauteous among all Slavic languages, would be spoiled, fading away and loosing the crystal clarity and lovely melody of the spoken word that is unparalleled. We should not give up our language. This is our hope and consolation.[10]

Kočić ascertained that the intellectual enslavement in Bosnia-Hercegovina was introduced with the numerous appointments of a host of foreign educators, judges, and legal clerks nominated to the newly created educational and administrative posts. In time, Kočić wrote a parody of the court procedures and of the official verbiage in his narrative *Sudanija* (Judiciary). Kočić introduced in the plot the text of a verdict modeled after the original verdict handed to him by the court. The verdict censored Kočić's role as the editor of the journal *Otadžbina* during the crisis following the Annexation of Bosnia-Hercegovina in 1908. The introductory passage of the verdict in *Sudanija* presented Kočić's argument well:

> The District court in Banja Luka had ascertained, thanks to the fortitude of its regular authority, *the well known fact* (emphasis added) that Kočić ... was not only the head but also the soul of the paper *Otadžbina*.

The clumsy wording and threatening tone attested to the discovery of an already well known fact that Kočić's was indeed the head and soul of the paper *Otadžbina*. The redundancy of the verdict, validating an already established common consent, pointed

---

10 Petar Kočić "Jezik u zakonskim tekstovima," *Sabrana Djela*, 1967, III, pp. 67-71. Quoted after Vulin, *Petar Kočić, Pisac i delo*, p. 380.

to the superficiality of similar adjudication. In addition, the awkward semantic coinages such as, *krijepošću uredovne vlasti,* testified to the poor knowledge of Serbo-Croatian language of the respective authorities.[11].

Kočić's many efforts to ease the burden of the occupied population in Bosnia-Hercegovina had been monitored and often punished with undue harshness. Kočić was frequently incarcerated and his health suffered a great deal. He died prematurely in 1916 in the midst of First World War.

Even some cultural events, such as celebration of important anniversaries of famous men of letters in the neighboring states of Serbia or Croatia, drew attention of the Austro-Hungarian authorities in Sarajevo. These events were scrutinized in special reports containing the descriptions of notable participants and their speeches.

In 1902, the Croatian writer Silvije Strahimir Kranjčević was invited to deliver the key-note address at the commemoration of the thirties anniversary of death of the poet Petar Preradović. Kranjčević had been employed as a teacher and supervisor of the school district in Sarajevo and was a long time resident in this city. The commemoration of Preradović took place in the halls of the distinguished literary association *Matica hrvatska.* in Zagreb, 31 August 1902. Kranjčević's speech, with a short description of this observance, was published in Zagreb's newspaper *Obzor.*

The Austrian authorities in Sarajevo were informed about Kranjčević's travel to Zagreb. They even wrote a report about Kranjčević's participation at Preradović's commemoration. A copy of the newspaper *Obzor,* with the speech delivered by Kranjčević was appended to the report and forwarded to Vienna. The report stated that Kranjčević was employed as a teacher and supervisor of the school district in Sarajevo for the past eighteen years. Kranjčević had continued to write poetry which was well received by the public, and he was elected to the membership of the Croatian Writer's

---

11 Vulin, *Petar Kočić, Pisac i delo,* pp. 385-386: "Okružni sud u Banjoj Luci pronašao je danas krijepošću uredovne vlasti opće poznatu činjenicu da je Kočić ne samo glavom, ali i dušom lista Otadžbina."

Union. He was described as an outstanding Croatian poet ranking with the best of his peers.[12]

According to the newspaper article, Ljuba Babić Gjalski, the vice-president of the *Matica hrvatska,* opened the meeting and introduced the featured speaker. Kranjčević started his speech with a description of the post- Illyrian period and the ideas that led to the Croatian cultural revival. Preradović, and his literary output, had reflected this chapter of cultural history and the ensuing national revival was led by able men who fulfilled well their missions. Kranjčević described the 1840s as a period of great social upheaval that "erupted like a volcano." [13]

Kranjčević pointed out that he had shared, with Preradović, the belief in the importance of safeguarding the Slavic consciousness by "remaining true to the mother tongue and the Croatian lyre." Preradović had described his own return to the realm of his ancestors and to his beloved yet humble motherland in the celebrated poem *Putnik (Traveler).* Preradović's early poetry was written in German language that he had learned well as a pupil in elementary school. In the poem *Putnik,* Preradović had stressed the importance of cultivating one's own cultural heritage. This poem had marked a turning point in his poetic journey and since than he wrote literary works using his maternal language. Preradović had eventually realized that he would remain alone and without real support in a foreign milieu. He described these feelings of alienation metaphorically since "a foreign mother cannot have a true compassion for a foreigner." Preradović's symbolic return to his native realm enabled him to receive again the gift of understanding his own poetic voice celebrating faith, love and hope. [14]

Kranjčević quoted the following verses by Preradović as metaphors of these aspirations:

"Nad guslama tvoja sila gine: /Ne razum'je pjesma zapovjedi/ Slobodna je—svome glasu sljedi!" ("Your power perishes at the

---

[12] The report was signed by the officer Hugo Kutschera and dated 17 September, 1902. Quoted after Besarović, *Kultura i Umjetnost u Bosni i Hercegovini,* pp. 292-293.

[13] Besarović, *Kultura i Umjetnost u Bosni i Hercegovini,* pp. 294-295.

[14] Besarović, *Kultura i Umjetnost u Bosni i Hercegovini,* p. 294.

gusle sound:/ A song does not understand commands/ Since it is free to follow its own voice").[15] The haunting sound of the *gusle*, an ancient string instrument, was used as a musical accompaniment for the recitation of epic poems.

In his speech, Kranjčević expressed the hope for change and "a new tomorrow" alluding to the shared expectation about a new political and cultural reality in Croatia.

The commemoration had testified to the feeling of gratitude acknowledging the poet Preradović and his poetic offerings. Although thirty years have passed from Preradović's death, his poems continued to delight and inspire. Both Kranjčević and Babić-Gjalski spoke about Croatian and Slavic consciousness stressing the need to resist foreign influences. The quotations of chosen verses, expressing hope for a better tomorrow, pointed obliquely to the dissatisfaction with present conditions. Kranjčević repeatedly referred to the dismal situation in the country and existing difficult conditions causing a general malaise and "our misery." These veiled allusions could be clearly understood as Kranjčević's commentaries on the existing political and cultural circumstances. The public obviously liked Kranjčević's speech and rewarded him with a standing ovation.

Kranjčević's speech was followed by the recitation of one of the best loved poems by Preradović, "Djeda i unuk" (Grandfather and grandson). Afterwards, the choir of the typographical workers *Sloga* had performed the song "Bože živi" (God is alive), based on the poem with the same title by Preradović

The vice-president Babić-Gjalski closed the celebration with a speech positing that Preradovic's poems remained to be a source of inspiration and strength "in the midst of difficult state of affairs that surround us." Preradović's hymn "Utjeha" (Consolation) "has continued to defend us from despair and has lifted our spirits from our misery and all wrong doing." Gjalski speech contained references to the current situation which he defined as "difficult." He reminded the audience of Preradovic's inspiring vision embodied in the following "sweet words": Zora puca, bit će dana. (The dawn is breaking, the day will come).

---

15 Besarović, *Kultura i Umjetnost u Bosni i Hercegovini*, p. 296.

The celebration ended with the singing of the Croatian anthem "Lijepa nasa domovino" (Our beautiful homeland).[16] The selected poems and commentaries had obviously exerted a very powerful message stressing the importance of native language and "Slavic solidarity."

Upon his return to Sarajevo, Kranjčević was reprimanded for not applying for a permission to deliver his speech at the Preradović celebration. He was reminded that he should observe the prescribed procedures when addressing any public meeting in the future.

It should be remembered that Kranjčević was a member of the Croatian Writers Union and considered as one of the leading poets of his time. Kranjčević published his first collection of poems, *Bugarkinje,* in 1885, whose very title evokes the ancient epic elegies *bugarštice.* He published two more collections of poems, *Izabrane pjesme* (Selected Poems) in 1898 and *Trzaji* (Spasms) in 1902. He died in 1908 before the publication of his last book *Pjesme* (Poems). His poetry and also some of his prose works testified to his visions of freedom from foreign oppression, and a new awareness for social justice. He abstained from hollow rhetorical patriotism and expressed his innermost feelings with warmth and poetic eloquence.[17]

In addition, Kranjčević had served as a teacher and supervisor of the Croatian schools in Sarajevo for 18 years. Nevertheless, Constantine Hörmann, Kranjčević's immediate chief, rebuked Kranjčević and demanded his compliance with the existing regulations.

Nonetheless, the chief of the Austrian government in Sarajevo, Johann Appel, felt obliged to supply another report about Kranjčević's transgression for the Viennese office. He sternly cautioned that in the future Kranjčević "must abide by this warning."[18]

---

16 Besarović, *Kultura i Umjetnost u Bosni i Hercegovini,* p. 297.

17 Antun Barac, *A History of Yugoslav Literature,* Ann Arbor, University of Michigan, Michigan Slavic Publications, 1973, pp. 180-182.

18 Besarović, *Kultura i Umjetnost u Bosni i Hercegovini,* p. 298. Appel's report was dated 15 November, 1902.

Musical Life and the Role of Choral Societies in Bosnia-Hercegovina

During the Austro-Hungarian occupation, the choral societies had almost exclusively provided various musical programs enhancing the appreciation of musical art. Moreover, the Serbian churches had always supported choral singing during liturgical services and special religious holidays. The idea of an organized Serbian Church Singers Society was at first brought up in Tuzla. It was after a very successful Saint Sava celebration in January of 1879, with the participation of a fine group of local singers, that the formation of a choral society was suggested:

> During the St. Sava *besjeda,* the necessity of the foundation of a Serbian Church Singers Society was broached for the first time. The mentioned Society would be asked to perform at the *besjeda* recitals in addition to providing mellifluous singing during the holy liturgy. The Society should cultivate vocal - and if possible instrumental music. [19]

It took some six years of diligent work to receive the formal permission for the foundation of the Society. Finally, in 1885 the Serbian Church Singers Society was formally founded in Tuzla as the first officially organized choral society in Bosnia-Hercegovina. Over the years, the Society was able to hire accomplished choral conductors who succeeded in presenting an admirable choral repertoire. Thus, the Society promoted commendable entertainment as well as musical education for its members and public at large.[20]

In 1888, the Choral Society *Sloga* was founded in Sarajevo. The Society was fortunate that the composer Jovan Paču provided invaluable guidance in the initial organization and repertoire policies. Paču was an accomplished concert pianist and composer.

---

[19] Roksanda Pejović, *Pevačka društva, Srpsko muzičko izvodjaštvo 1831-1941*, Belgrade, Pro Musica. 1986, p. 19.

[20] Pejović, *Pevačka društva, Srpsko muzičko* izvodjaštvo *1831-1941*, p. 19.

Although trained as a physician and active in the medical field and in the Serbian Red Cross, Pač̆u produced instrumental and vocal compositions highly acclaimed by his contemporaries. His compositions testified to his Slavophil orientation pointing to the solidarity of Slavic peoples. During his musical tour of Russia in 1885, he performed in Kiev. His concert program consisted exclusively of works of Slav composers which found favorable reception of the critics and public at large.[21]

During the first decades of the 20th century, guest performances of choral societies had continued to enjoy great popularity among the Serbian and Croatian population alike. The Choral Society *Gusle* from Mostar gave frequent performances while on concert tours throughout Bosnia and Hercegovina. *Gusle* was formally founded in !888, even though most of its core members took part in various celebrations during the early 1880s. Choral concerts by the Choral Society *Gusle* had been greatly appreciated by its devoted public. The famed poet Aleksa Šantić was its founding member, and served as the president of the Society at one time. Šantić was an accomplished singer and had occasionally conducted some special choral performances of the Society. Moreover, Šantić wrote the poetic verses for the hymn of the *Gusle* Society. These verses were set to music by the composer F. Maćejovski.

Choral groups from Serbia had toured occasionally in Bosnia-Hercegovina. The well known *Belgrade Choral Society* was invited to tour the provinces in 1910 with their esteemed conductor and composer Stevan Stojanović Mokranjac.[22] The Academic Singers Society *Obilić* was also invited to perform at appropriate times. The young members of this famous choir were enrolled as students at the Belgrade University. The Singers Society *Obilić* gave a memorable concert in Sarajevo in 1911. The daily *Srpska Riječ* reported that the

---

21 Stana Djurić-Klajn, *A Survey of Serbian Music Through the Ages*, Belgrade, 1972, Association of Composers of Serbia, p. 99.

22 Djurić-Klajn, *A Survey of Serbian Music through the Ages*, pp. 88-89.

concert hall was filled to the capacity. After the concert, the enthralled public escorted the young singers to the railway station.[23]

The Croatian Singers' Society *Trebević* had a similar successful role in the cultural life in Sarajevo. The daily *Hrvatski Dnevnik* published an article in 1907 marking the 15th anniversary of the Society from its inception. The article noted that *Trebević* had provided the first manifestation of Croatian thought in Sarajevo "coming to its own concrete expression." [24]

> The first sign of Croatian consciousness in Bosnia-Hercegovina found its expression in singers societies and *tambura* orchestras ... everywhere in Bosnia and Hercegovina next to the singers - and *tambura* societies the reading and entertaining societies have been formed. The Croatian heart rejoiced listening to the mellifluous songs. The young ones danced *kolo* in the round and the old people thanked God that the suffering had ceased and that the merry Croatian song is resounding again. [25]

An article in *Hrvatski Dnevnik* discussed the role of cultural societies striving to perform a multifaceted role:

> Today our cultural societies should be the centers and meeting points were the representatives of the people meet in order to follow all events and obtain orientation central to the Croatian ideology. This is important more than ever. The songs and *tamburica* provide the entertainment but the main goal should be the political organization.

---

[23] *Srpska Riječ* 3 June 1911, No 98, p. 2. Quoted after Besarovic, "Specifičnosti kulturnog razvitka u Bosni i Hercegovini 1878-1918," *Iz kulturne i političke istorije Bosne i Hercegovine,* p. 21.

[24] Quoted after Besarović, "Specifičnosti kulturnog razvitka u Bosni i Hercegovini 1878-1918," *Iz kulturne i političke istorije Bosne i Hercegovine,* pp. 19-20.

[25] *Hrvatski Dnevnik,* Sarajevo, January, 4, 1906, No. 3 p. 1. Quoted after Besarović , *Iz kulturne i političke istorije Bosne i Hercegovine,* p. 31.

Surely that the tenor of this article differed very much from previous discussions about the role of cultural societies in Bosnia-Hercegovina. In contrast to previous reporting in local daily papers, the anonymous reviewer proposed openly that these societies must assume a political profile strengthening Croatian ideology.[26]

The musical life was enlivened by occasional guest performances of German artists. Thus, the Viennese Music Society *Schubertbund* had presented several concerts of German music in Mostar and Sarajevo. The Society was pleased with the favorable reception of their musical programs by the native public. The musicians declared their guest appearance as specially successful since it helped to promote the German music and German songs *(Lieder)* in foreign countries whose population did not speak German: "In den fremdspächigen Ländern gelang es dem Schubertbunde, der deutschen Kunst die allgemeine Bewunderung zu erringen."[27]

Around the turn of the new century, Franjo Maćejovski started his long and distinguished career in the musical life of Bosnia. Maćejovski, a graduate of the Prague Conservatory, came to Bosnia in 1900. He was a trained conductor, composer and folk song collector. At first, Maćejovski accepted a position in Banja Luka as the conductor of the Croatian choir *Nada*. In 1905, Maćejovski moved to Sarajevo where he remained till the end of his life in 1938. Maćejovski became the founder and director of the first music school in Sarajevo that opened in September of 1908.[28]

An article in the journal *Hrvatski Dnevnik* described the courses offered by Maćejovski in his newly founded school. The curriculum was designed to prepare students for the teaching positions in middle schools. A special program was planned to prepare

---

[26] *Hrvatski Dnevnik*, Sarajevo, 3 November 1907, No 199, p. 1. Quoted after Besarović, Kultura i Umjetnost, *Iz kulturne i političke istorije Bosne i Hercegovine*, p. 56.

[27] *Jahres Bericht des Schubertbundes*, Vienna,1904-1905. Quoted after Risto Besarović, p. 21.

[28] Zija Kučukalić, *The Development of Musical Culture in Bosnia-Hercegovina*, Sarajevo, Association of Composers of Bosnia and Hercegovina, 1967, p. 33.

candidates for the state examinations or for entrance examinations at the Conservatories in Vienna and Prague.

The music school had a good start and continued to offer music classes gaining professional recognition. In 1913 a reviewer praised Maćejovski's efforts and of his colleagues teaching at the school. The school had achieved professional competence to the extent that it was compared with the well known *Glazbeni zavod* (Musical institute) in Zagreb. The same reviewer mentioned that the school had submitted a petition to the *Landesministerium*. The petition requested the approval of the rules and regulations governing schools' policies. Subsequently, the supporters of the school decided to elect a board that took over the responsibility of running the school.[29]

The guest appearances of numerous operetta companies were questioned in the journal *Hrvatski Dnevnik*. The anonymous reviewer stated that many operetta companies visited Sarajevo and it seemed that the public was guilty of giving to much encouragement to such seemingly dubious performances.[30]

A similar opinion was voiced two years later: it appeared that Sarajevo had became "a true El Dorado for the more or less obscure German theater groups." The unknown writer concluded that the public did not wish such "artistic trash" on the stage of the *Društveni dom* (Social club).[31]

Several operetta companies performed in 1912 and among these *Gastspiel Richter* gave performances in German language.

---

29 *Srpska riječ*, Sarajevo, 9. May, 1913, No. 100, p. 3. quoted after Besarović "Specifičnosti kulturnog razvitka u Bosni i Hercegovini 1878-1918," *Iz kulturne i političke* ... p. 15.

30 *Hrvatski Dnevnik*, "Bečko operetno društvo," Sarajevo, 19 October 1910, br. 241, p. 3. Quoted after Besarović, "Specifičnosti kulturnog razvitka u Bosni i Hercegovini 1878-1918," *Iz kulturne i politička istorije Bosne i Hercegovine*, Sarajevo, Svjetlost, 1966, pp. 12-13.

31 *Hrvatski Dnevnik*, "Nemački glumci u Sarajevu, Sarajevo, 1 April 1912, br. 74." Quoted after Besarović, "Specifičnosti kulturnog razvitka u Bosni i Hercegovini 1878-1918," *Iz kulturne i politička istorije Bosne i Hercegovine*, p. 12.

Gastspiel Gartner performed also in German language. Moreover, a Serbian operetta company appeared in 1913 and was well received by the public.

The frequent guest appearances of German theater companies in Bosnia-Hercegovina had not been motivated only by the wish to capture new audiences or to provide entertainment to the German speaking bureaucrats. These guest appearances became a way out for solving financial difficulties that the Austrian theaters apparently faced in the first decade of this century. The rising popularity of the first moving pictures presented a great competition for the music theater.

The number of movie theaters was constantly increasing. According to the statistical survey in 1909 there were 76 movie theaters *(Kinematographentheatern)* with a total seating capacity of some twenty thousand people. The annual number of visitors was more than nine and a half million of people.[32] The newspapers in Vienna commented frequently about the "cinematic danger" *(Kinogefahr)*, or about the "obsession with the movies" *(Kinomanie)*.[33] Facing the shrinking pool of theater public, the guest appearances in Bosnia-Hercegovina presented a possible solution for a number of theatrical groups and operetta companies.

Even in Bosnia proper, a couple of years before the First World War, the movies and movie theaters became popular but not as much as in Vienna. Most often, Austrian businessmen and entrepreneurs asked for a concession for presentations of the moving pictures. In Sarajevo such performances took place during the summer months and in the open air.[34]

In the winter of 1911, the initiative for forming a music association, *Musikverein,* had been announced patterned after

---

32 *Reichspost*, Vienna 15 June 1908, No.162, p. 6. Quoted after Besarović, "Specifičnosti kulturnog razvitka u Bosni i Hercegovini 1878-1918," *Iz kulturne i političke istorije ...* p. 13.

33 *Reichspost*, Vienna 11 January 1912, No 15, p. 7. Besarović, "Specifičnosti kulturnog razvitka u Bosni i Hercegovini 1878-1918," *Iz kulturne i političke istorije ...* p. 13.

34 Besarović, "Specifičnosti kulturnog razvitka u Bosni i Hercegovini 1878-1918," *Iz kulturne i političke istorije Bosne i Hercegovine*, p. 14.

similar associations in the Dual Monarchy. It was also announced that the government would finance the society's needs. The daily paper *Narod* criticized these plans by stating:

> We have had many musical societies previously with a similar profile comparable to the newly founded society. But we never asked or received subvention from the government. The subsidy conferred to this society would suggest helping a society only because it has a foreign character and spirit. This would show again that there are two sets of rules one for us and one for them.

Moreover, the organizers of the *Musikverein* were portrayed as "unpleasant foreign individuals who distort our language and our folk music." [35] It seemed that the question of the *Musikverein* did not subside and was still discussed two years later in November of 1913. The daily *Srpska Riječ* saw some potential merits from such an association. The article did not discuss the subvention but stated that the association "could awaken the appreciation of good music by presenting concerts, and also by providing an affordable music education for the youth." [36]

In spite of the great love and support for music that the Austrian intellectual elite seemed to impart, the Austro-Hungarian authorities in Sarajevo did not make it any easier for the performing artists to present recitals for the public. In July of 1914, the authorities proposed a new ordinance demanding additional taxation for musical performances. The ordinance explained the necessary procedures in granting permits for music performances *(Musik- und Gesangs- sowie Artisten- Lizenzen)* and asked for a tax of 2 crowns for the petition and 2 crowns for the permit[37].

---

35 *Narod,* Sarajevo, 31 December 1911, No. 156, p. 3.

36 *Srspka Riječ*, Sarajevo, 2 November 1913, No. 188, p. 3, quoted after Besarović,"Specifičnosti kulturnog razvitka u Bosni i Hercegovini 1878-1918, *Iz kulturne i političke* ... p. 18.

37 Besarović, *Kultura i Umjetnost u Bosni i Hercegovini pod Austrougarskom Upravom,* p. 563-564. These taxes (Stempelpflichtigkeit)

Moreover, this document specified that the leader of a music society applying for such a permit should be at least 30 years old. The members should not be younger than twenty with exception of female members who could be eighteen years old. The permit should be given for the duration of one year, and only to the citizens of Bosnia-Hercegovina, Austria and Hungary.[38]

In June of 1914, another effort was made to establish an association of music lovers *(Musikverein)* in Sarajevo. An ardent supporter of this association, Olga Zurnić, wrote several letters trying to raise necessary funds. In her letter Zurnić stated that the Association would foster cultural goals by cultivating "good music" *(Gute Musik zu pflegen)*. The activities of the Society would eventually lead to the foundation of a music school in Sarajevo. She addressed her plea to Dr. Leon Ritter von Bilinski, who was the Joint Minister of Finance in Vienna. Another letter was addressed to Dr. Paul Robert von Khun-Chorbak, a prominent official *(Sektionschef)* of the Provincial Government in Sarajevo. Zurnić was asking for a contribution of 100 crowns. Zurnić stated that the donors would be acknowledged as the founders of this new music association. The plea for help was honored, and the newly formed *Verein* thanked Khun-Chorbak and the Minister Bilinski expressing their gratitude in letters dated 18 June 1914 and signed by Dr. Vladimir Ćorović, secretary of the Society and its President Dr. Franges.[39]

A Belated Preamble for the Foundation of a Theater in Sarajevo

In January of 1912, Radivoje A. Dinulović had written a detailed proposal about the necessity of establishing a theater titled

---

were not applicable for the theater, variety shows and cinematography. The ordinance was dated 11 July 1914.

38 Besarović, *Kultura i Umjetnost u Bosni i Hercegovini pod Austrougarskom Upravom,* pp. 563-4 The ordinance was signed by Dr. N. Mandić and was dated 11 July, 1914.

39 Besarović, *Kultura i Umjetnost u Bosni i Hercegovini,* pp. 560-562

Bosansko-Hercegovačko Zemaljsko Pozorište (Bosnian-Hercegovinian Provincial Theater). Dinulović postulated that the role of the theater through history was always to act as a mirror for the culture of a people. The productions of a theatrical play united invariably exceptional minds of poets, writers, painters, sculptors, musicians, actors, journalists, and critics. Moreover, a cultured people could not exist without the theater. The theater had its role during the Antiquity, Middle Ages and before the printed word of Gutenberg. The actors had endeavored to depict the past and the future, the good and the bad. In Germany and Austria almost every larger city had a theater. *Zemaljsko Pozorište* (Provincial Theater) should not only operate in Sarajevo, but arrange guest performances in other larger cities, such as Mostar, Tuzla and Banja Luka. In each of the mentioned cities, the Provincial Theater should stay about 6 weeks, in addition of 3 months of residency in Sarajevo. During the rest of the year, the Theater could visit other regions such as Ilidža, Travnik, Bijeljina, Brčko and Bihać and give performances during the remaining three and a half months.

Dinulović thought that the financing should come from state subventions and subsidies of the cities, ticket subscriptions, and regular evening performances. Most of all, the finance matters should be guided by a competent and wise management.[40] Dinulović did not disclose who had asked for such a proposal or the reason for writing this proposition.

Shortly after, on 26 February 1912, the *Serbian Dilettante Theater* in Sarajevo requested the approval of the submitted statute proposal *(Statutenentwurf)*. The statute presented an extensive and detailed document encompassing 58 paragraphs. It defined the duties of the members of the board as the governing body, their supervising authority, and the nature of board meetings. It also defined the roles of officers, regular members and the annual meetings of the membership at large*(skupština)*. The statute specified that the minutes of all the meetings as well as of the annual assembly should be safeguarded for evidence. In the case of this theater's cessation, the Singers Society *Sloga* should receive and preserve the property

---

40 Besarović, *Kultura i Umjetnost u Bosni i Hercegovini*, pp. 731-732. The proposal (Nacrt) was dated January 1912 and signed by Radivoje A. Dinulović.

until a similar group could be formed again. The statute was submitted to the authorities by the president of the Singers' Society *Sloga*, Svetozar T. Zrnić, and its secretary Dušan Djokić. The statute was dated 26 February 1912.[41] Finally, the *Serbian Dilettante Theater* was founded in 1912 which presented a significant attempt in providing an organized theatrical life.

In 1913, the Counsel to the Government in Sarajevo, Franjo Brodnik, approached the young drama director Mihajlo Marković with a suggestion to evaluate the feasibility of a permanent theater in Sarajevo. Marković agreed to write the proposal assessing the cultural advantages and the financial requirements for such an enterprise.[42]

In his proposal, Marković posited that the future theater in Sarajevo should aim to serve the cultural and educational goals of the citizens. The future theater should cultivate drama and operetta, and to a lesser extent the grand opera. The theater should perform from October to April in Sarajevo. During the rest of the year, the theater should give guest performances throughout the country.

The drama repertory should concentrate on the works of native writers. The performances of their works would very likely stimulate the writing of new plays. Classical works should be also staged and, finally, selected works of the contemporary dramatic literature of prominent foreign writers should be also included. In regard to the operetta and opera repertory, the selection should depend on the taste of the public having in mind that "one should pay attention to the decency and moral content of these works."

---

41 The Statute was writen in Serbian and titled: Nacrt Pravila Srpskog Diletantskog Pozorišta za Bosnu i Hercegovinu. Quoted after Besarović, *Kultura i Umjetnost u Bosni i Hercegovini pod Austrougarskom Upravom*, pp. 732-740.

42 Marković's proposal was titled: Bosansko-Hercegovačko Narodno Pozorište, Elaborat Mihajla Markovića o Stvaranju Stalnog Pozorišta u Sarajevu, Bosansko-hercegovačko zemaljsko narodno pozorišta. Kratki pregled i proračun istog (Bosnian-Hercegovian National Theater, A short Survey and Cost Estimate). Quoted after Besarović, *Kultura i Umjetnost u Bosni i Hercegovini pod Austrougarskom Upravom*, pp. 741-745. Marković's proposal was written in the Serbian language.

The acting roles should be given to the native sons and daghters if appropriate. Concerning the singers, the direction should strive to send to Vienna or Prague two or three singers every year for specialized studies. These policies should bring propitious results by producing a domestic cast of singers. These efforts would enhance, to a great extent, the cultural and artistic development in Bosnia-Hercegovina.

At first, the performances could take place in *Društveni dom* (Community Hall). Marković thought that twenty performances should be scheduled each month: ten dramatic works, and ten musical productions from the operatic repertory. Once a month the direction should offer popular performances, with a lower price of tickets, and three performances with reduced prices for students.

Marković also proposed a tentative budget of the theater including the projected support of governmental subvention, the support from the city of Sarajevo, and several other larger cities in Bosnia-Hercegovina.

Marković concluded that by establishing a serious national cultural institution the proliferation of smaller theatrical groups would be prevented. He argued that these improvised groups, formed ad hoc, could not properly serve the cultural and educational needs of the country and its people. [43]

Subsequently, Franjo Brodnik, Counsel to the Government, wrote a lengthy proposal in reference to the foundation of a permanent National Theater in Sarajevo. Very likely that he relied to a great extent on Marković's proposal. Brodnik's recommendation was titled *Studie* (Study) and was dated 1 July 1913. [44]

Brodnik stressed that the founding of a theater in Sarajevo would have considerable political advantages. There existed already a Serbian theater group, *Srpsko diletantsko pozorišno društvo*, that was founded not long ago. This theater and its repertory presented no immediate threat, but it should be watched since it may evolve

---

43 Ibid., p. 745.

44 Both Brodnik's and Marković's proposals had the same signature: No. 980, Reg. ex 1913. Quoted after Besarović, *Kultura i Umjetnost u Bosni i Hercegovini pod Austrougarskom Upravom*, pp. 745-751.

into a stronghold of Serbian national aspirations. He thought that the Croats were less likely to be involved in the propagation of national goals. However, Brodnik felt that the political situation was volatile and filled with explosive notions. Brodnik mentioned several successful guest performances in two last seasons, 1912 and 1913. The operetta performances were also successful and brought a total of 1300 Crowns. [45]

Moreover, guest performances were given by the Croatian *Pokrajinsko Kazalište* in 1911. In 1912 two companies, such as the *Bauerntheater* and the *Direktion Huble,* performed plays in German language. [46]

Most importantly, Brodnik wrote that the Austrian government in Bosnia should not allow that the education and development of national consciousness be controlled by the Serbs or Croats. The Austrian government should take education into its own hands, in order to help specific goals set by the government. Therefore, the theater and its repertory should also be under the aegis of the governmental agencies.[47]

Brodnik disclosed that a very suitable theater director was found in the person of Mihailo Marković. Although Marković was born in Serbia and was a Serb, practicing the Christian Orthodox religion, he was proven to be correct and loyal to the Austrian government. Marković had lived in Zagreb and was a former member of the Croatian Provincial Theater *(Landestheater)* in Zagreb. He enjoyed sympathies and support equally from Serbs and Croats. Therefore, Brodnik thought that Marković would be a very suitable Director of the future *Landestheater* in Sarajevo.

Brodnik thought that the Provincial Theater should be ready to open in the season 1913-1914. The Theater should have a Drama and Operetta sections. The operatic repertory should be limited to less demanding works. He suggested a yearly subvention by the

---

45 Besarović, *Kultura i Umjetnost u Bosni i Hercegovini pod Austrougarskom Upravom,* p. 747.

46 Besarović, *Kultura i Umjetnost u Bosni i Hercegovini pod Austrougarskom Upravom,* p. 749.

47 Besarović, *Kultura i Umjetnost u Bosni i Hercegovini pod Austrougarskom Upravom,* p. 751.

state in the amount of 85 000 crowns. The eventual deficit, if it should occur, could be covered with a five percent taxation generated from the gross income of the movie theaters in Sarajevo.

As the situation in Bosnia-Hercegovina and in the neighboring Serbia became increasingly precarious, Brodnik realized that the opening of the Theater in Sarajevo had to be postponed. Marković had planned the opening for the end of September 1914. The contracts had been signed and the actors were supposed to start their new employment on September 1, 1914. The government in Sarajevo had decided that the opening of the Theater would not be opportune due to the political situation. Moreover, Brodnik had disclosed that Marković, as a Serb and due to current circumstances, had asked to be relieved of his appointed duty. Therefore, Brodnik suggested that all other contracts should be voided. He asked that the decision for closure should be validated from Vienna with a swift official communication, preferably with a telegram.

Interestingly enough, Brodnik as the head of the government in Sarajevo, had expressed hope to proceed with the foundation of the Provincial Theater sometime in the future. [48] Brodnik, as many other high ranking government officials, was confident that Austria-Hungary would be victorious and would continue to rule Bosnia-Hercegovina.

---

48 Besarović, *Kultura i Umjetnost u Bosni i Hercegovini pod Austrougarskom Upravom,* pp. 776-777.

CONCLUSION

Observed as a whole, the Austro-Hungarian occupation did encourage a broader economic and cultural development compared to the previous period of Turkish reign. The opening of Bosnia-Hercegovina to Europe through new railroad connections facilitated an exchange of favorable economic and cultural incentives. Moreover, the urbanization of Sarajevo, and a number of townships throughout the provinces, marked a noteworthy progress. The process of industrialization was enhanced, and the middle class of merchants and entrepreneurs profited from the growing trade with Central Europe.[1]

The Austro-Hungarian Provincial Government took great precaution defining its long term goals. The *Landesregierung* counted on the support of rich Muslim landowners declared as an influential state building entity. In order to ensure the support of the Muslims, the administration decided to postpone the much needed agrarian reforms and maintain the feudal bondage of the rural population. This decision was detrimental for the prospect of any substantial economic as well as cultural growth of both provinces.

The investment of foreign capital was encouraged in order to harness the natural resources of the land pursuing the principles of a colonial capitalistic economy. The improvements of the road system and narrow track railroads enabled easier access to markets, encouraging economic development. These improvements were financed by the local revenues and executed mainly by the mandatory

---

[1] Dimitrije Djordjević, "The Berlin Congress of 1878 and the Origins of World War I, " *Serbian Studies*, Vol. 12, No.1, 1998, p.7.

labor of the mostly rural common folk.[2] During the 1890s, the indistrial production reached fifteen percent per year, and a number of state sponsored industrial enterprises were founded, Nonetheless, these enterprises demanded higher tax revenues aggravating mostly the Serbian and Croatian tenents. In the ensuing period, the industrial production declined due, in part, to the backwardness of an obsolescent agrarian economy. Gradually, the industrial production dropped off to barely three percent for the period 1906-1913.[3]

The Austro-Hungarian occupation proved to be a take-over of all the domains of public life. The Provincial Government introduced new obligations gaining strict control over the population, natural resources and revenues of the land. Moreover, the old taxation system instituted previously by the Porte was continued.

The presence of military personnel and police, in addition to numerous newly erected fortifications along the borders caused the Dual Monarchy to be dubbed as a "prison of nations" *(Völkerkerker)*.[4] An English politician noted that he was surprised to observe such a strong military presence in a territory counting a sparse population of million and a half. He stated that England had only slightly more soldiers in India where the indigenous population comprised some 300 million.[5]

The intellectual subjugation of Bosnia-Hercegovina was perpetuated with the hiring of foreign bureaucrats, judges, and legal clerks appointed to newly created administrative posts. Such policies of the Monarchy were contested over the years by the native intellectual elite demanding greater autonomy in cultural and educational affairs, as well as an increased participation in the

---

2 Milorad Ekmečić, *Stvaranje Jugoslavije 1790-1918*, Belgrade, p. 83 and p. 95. All males aged form 16 to 60 were required to provide free labor in the duration of one week every three years.

3 Lampe , Yugoslavia as a History, pp.66-67, p.80.

4 Andreas Moritsch, Ed., *Der Austroslavismus*, Vienna, Böhlau Verlag, 1996, p. 8.

5 Jovan Cvijić, *Aneksija Bosne i Hercegovine i srpski problem*, Belgrade, Državna Štamparija 1908, p. 29. Cvijić recorded his conversation with the unnamed English politician some three years prior to the Annexation of Bosnia-Hercegovina.

economic development and in the governing process at large. These concerted efforts did not fulfill the projected expectations. The local professionals had a very slim chance in gaining access to governmental jobs: preceding the Annexation of 1908, only 11 percent of all employed civil servants in the Provincial Government were from Bosnia-Hercegovina. [6]

The beginning of the new century brought the foundation of several influential educational societies into the cultural life of Bosnia-Hercegovina. These societies were conceived and sponsored by the local intellectual - and professional elite with the aim to help students requiring financial assistance. The importance of education became of paramount concern to many citizens. The societies offered scholarships to the young students pursuing their education in high schools and universities.

The Provincial Government endeavored also to provide financial help for outstanding students needing assistance for their higher education at the universities in Austria. These students were openly recruited to study at these universities with good chances of securing well paid positions upon completion of their studies. The Government was aiming to produce loyal employees counting on the valuable services, constancy and devotion of former students.

The benefits of higher education at the universities in Austria were soon recognized by the public at large. Similar privileges were not granted to those who chose to study at the universities of Zagreb or Belgrade. The young graduates of these universities needed additional examinations in order to obtain a comparable job, if any.

Although aware of the implicit motivation that fueled the generosity of the governmental purse, many educators and scholars in Austria provided good education to foreign students from neighboring Slavic lands. On the other hand, the formative years spent while studying in Vienna or Graz must have instilled appreciation for all the cultural refinement that an old and glorious Empire had to offer at the fin de siécle. The high art of the Burgtheater, the incomparable concerts of the Vienna Philharmonics, and the artistic allure of the Viennese Opera presented another fascinating aspect of the cultural life in Austria. Not to be forgotten were the sights and sounds of the popular culture, such as the liveliness of operettas, valses and polkas by Johann Strauss and

---

6 Vasiljević, *O Bosni i Hercegovini*, p. 25.

members of his equally gifted family members. All these experiences remained to be appreciated by the citizens of the Habsburg Empire, as well as by young students from neighboring states pursuing their education at Austrian universities.

During the Austro-Hungarian occupation and the subsequent annexation, numerous traveling theaters, classical and popular music ensembles, and operetta companies toured the cities and townships of Bosnia-Hercegovina. These guest appearances were well received by the general public and, in turn, provided needed revenues for the artists. These often ad-hoc arranged performances, although not always of the desired artistic quality, were instrumental in building a cultural fund bestowed to all who were willing to accept it with no apparent strings attached.

This shared cultural repository coupled with greater consideration for the occupied population and respect for their civil rights could have helped to establish a harmonious union of the peoples within the multiethnic Empire.

The hopes and aspirations of the venerable Czech historian Frantisek Palacky, who saw the future of the Slavs in Austrian Monarchy, could have been fulfilled. Palacky argued repeatedly that all nationalities assembled under the Austrian scepter should enjoy complete equality of rights and respect under the law. If a union of various nations was to be firm and lasting, no nation must have cause to fear repressive measures. Palacky ascertained that Austria should proclaim the fundamental rule of justice concerning the long-standing ethnic, religious, and linguistic boundaries.[7]

Palacky's farsighted pronouncement was not considered by those in power. The Austro-Hungarian regime continued to rely most of all on power *(Macht)* as it was recognized, albeit to late, by the ruling class. Count Gustav Kalnoky, Foreign Minister to Francis Joseph, realized with regrets that Austria's glory depended most of all on military power of the Habsburg Monarchy.[8]

Consequently, the Austro-Hungarian occupation did not fulfill the mandate proposed by the Berlin Congress but aspired most of all to

---

7 Alfred J. Bannan and Achilles Edelenyi, *Documentary History of Eastern Europe*, New York, Twayne Publishers Inc., 1970, p. 147.

8 Quoted after Salomon Wank: "The Habsburg Empire," *After Empire*, Eds. K. Barkey and M. v. Hagen, Boulder, Westview Press, 1997, p. 48.

preserve its colonial dominance of Bosnia-Hercegovina as a stronghold for further expansion into the Balkans.[9] The ensuing policies of the Provincial Government exacerbated the economic, ethnic and confessional divisiveness .of the population. This ill-fated legacy foreshadowed to a great extent the recent disintegration of Bosnia and Hercegovina as a constituent republic of former Yugoslavia.

9 Valeria Heuberger/ Heinz Ilming, *Bosnien-Herzegovina 1878-1918, Althe Ansichten vom gelungenen Zusammenleben,* Vienna 1994, p.22

Index

1.Prince Mihailo Obrenovic, who ruled Serbia from 1839-1842 and 1869-1868.

2. Ilija Garasanin, Prime Minister and statesman, served with distinction both the Karadjordjevic and Obrenovic dynasties.

3. Metropolitan Mihail Jovanovic, distinguished theologian, historian. and educator. He was a staunch supporter of Panslavic thought with close ties to the Slavic Benevolent Society and its President I. S. Aksakov. Metropolitan Mihail was elected President of the International Relief Committee in Paris to help the refugees from Bosnia-Hercegovina during the 1875-1878 uprising.

4. Jovan Ristic, leading politician and historian, served as a Regent after Prince Mihailo's demise.

5. Benjamin Kállay, Austro-Hungarian Consul in Belgrade 1868-1875; Joint Minister of Finance and Governor of Bosnia 1882-1903. Kállay was an accomplished historian who he wrote two books on the history of Serbian people.

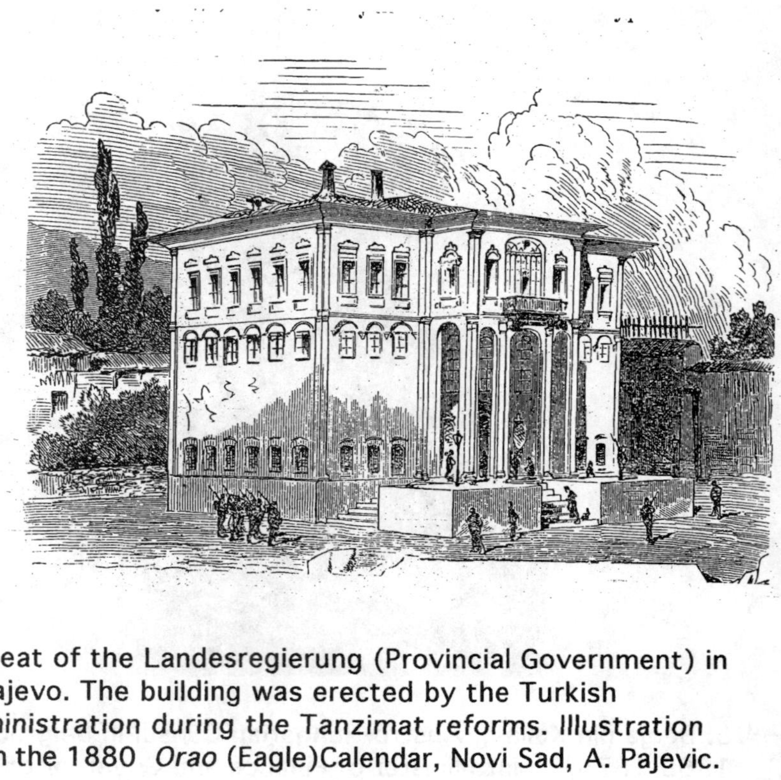

6. Seat of the Landesregierung (Provincial Government) in Sarajevo. The building was erected by the Turkish administration during the Tanzimat reforms. Illustration from the 1880 *Orao* (Eagle)Calendar, Novi Sad, A. Pajevic.

7. Serbian Orthodox Church in Sarajevo. Illustration from the 1880 *Orao* (Eagle)Calendar, Novi Sad, A. Pajevic.

8. Mostar, the capital of Hercegovina. Illustration from the 1880 *Orao* (Eagle)Calendar, Novi Sad, A. Pajevic.

9. The Old Building of the University of Belgrade was given to the Serbian people by Captain Misa Atanasijevic in 1863. The architect was Jan Nevole who moved from Prague to Belgrade in 1845 on the urging of the venerable panslavist Frantisek Palacky.

10. Church of the Holly Trinity in Gornji Adrovac commemorating the death of the Russian Colonel N.N. Raevskii who fought in the Serbian-Turkish war in 1876. Raevskii served under General M.G. Chernaev who commanded the joint Serbian and Russian forces.

11 The Serbian Church of Saint George in Pest, XVII century. Photo courtesy of Dinko Davidov.

12 .Iconostas of the Serbian Archeangel Church in Saint André was painted in 1771. Photo courtesy of Dinko Davidov.

13. Belfry of the Church of Ascension in Saint André in classical style erected in the second half of the XVIII century. Photo courtesy of Dinko Davidov.

14. Hercegovinians returning to their shattered homes. Painted by Jaroslav Charmak in 1877. From the 1880 *Orao* (Eagle)Calendar, Novi Sad, A. Pajevic.

15. The Market in the Muslim part of Sarajevo. Illustration from the 1880 Orao (Eagle) Calendar, Novi Sad, A. Pajevic.